Division of Professional Growth & Development
2671 Carver Road
Gambrills, MD 21054

Why Didn't I Learn This in College?

A. I knew it for the test, but then I forgot it.
B. I didn't take that course.
C. I think I did, but that was a long time ago.
D. I wasn't listening that day.
E. At the time, I didn't think it was all that important.
F. They forgot to mention it.

Paula Rutherford

Just ASK Publications, a division of Attitudes, Skills & Knowledge (ASK), Inc.
2214 King Street, Alexandria, VA 22301 800-940-5434, fax 703-535-8502, www.askeducation.com

About the author

Paula Rutherford is president of **Attitudes, Skills, and Knowledge (ASK), Inc.**
Just ASK Publications and **ASK Group** are divisions of ASK, Inc.

She is an **educational consultant** specializing in instruction, educational leadership, induction, and supervision and evaluation. Much of her time is spent in multifaceted work with school districts where leadership and staff are committed to educating all students and are willing to engage in the hard work necessary to make educational excellence a reality for all. In addition to her extensive work as a consultant and trainer, her experience base includes work in regular education K-12 as a teacher of high school history and social sciences, physical education, Spanish, and kindergarten, and as a special education teacher, coordinator of special education programs, school administration at the middle school and high school levels, and as a central office staff development specialist.

In addition to this book, Paula is the author of *Instruction for All Students* and *Leading the Learning.* See the last pages of this book for publications ordering information. Paula may be contacted directly at paula@askeducation.com for training, consulting, or facilitating services.

Contact ASK, Inc. at info@askeducation.com for information about **ASK Group** consulting services. Visit **www.askeducation.com** for an overview of the Group's consulting services.

Why Didn't I Learn This in College?

Published by Just ASK Publications

A division of Attitudes, Skills, and Knowledge, (ASK), Inc.
2214 King Street
Alexandria, Virginia 22301
TOLL FREE 800-940-5434
VOICE 703-535-5434
FAX 703-535-8502
email: info@askeducation.com
www.askeducation.com

Printed in the United States of America
ISBN 0-9663336-1-6
Library of Congress Control Number 2002092073

Table of Contents
Why Didn't I Learn This in College?

I.	**Introduction**	**1-6**
II.	**A Good Place to Learn**	**7-44**
	Points to Ponder:	
	The First Day & Every Day!	9
	Creating a Learning-Centered Environment	10-11
	The Myth that Some Students Can't Learn	12
	Oh Yes, They Can Learn!	13-14
	Communicating Expectations	15-17
	Attribution Theory	18
	Student Reflections	19
	Communication Skills	20-21
	Praise, Encouragement & Feedback	22
	Miss Manners in the Classroom	23-24
	Getting to Know You	25-28
	OUR Classroom: Establishing Rules Together	29-30
	A Good Place to Learn...	31
	Dealing with Unmet Expectations	32-33
	Engaging Students in Problem Solving	34-35
	Plan B	36-38
	Students with Special Needs	39-42
	Where Do I Begin?	43
III.	**Framing the Learning & Questioning**	**45-62**
	Points to Ponder:	
	Some Things Never Change	47
	Framing the Learning	48-51
	Now Hear This!	52
	Discussion Partners	53
	When & Why We Ask Questions	54-55
	Getting Started with Important Questions	56
	Designing Questions	57-60
	Where Do I Begin?	61

IV. Learning is NOT a Spectator Sport

IV. Learning is NOT a Spectator Sport — **63-108**

Points to Ponder:	
Beyond Who Can Tell Me?	65
If You Want...	66-67
Anticipation Reaction Guides	68-69
Biopoems	70-71
Connection Collections	72-74
Consensogram	75
Consensus Conclusions	76
Corners	77
Frame of Reference	78
Graffiti	79-80
Journals	81-82
Interactive Notebooks	83-84
It's All in The Cards	85-86
I Have the Question. Who Has the Answer?	85
Tic-Tac-Toe	86
Inside-Outside Circles	87
Learning Links	88
Line-Ups	89
Numbered Heads Together	90
Scavenger Hunt	91-92
Sort Cards	93-95
Stir the Class	96
Teammates Consult	97
Think-Pair-Share	98
Three-Two-One	99
Three Column Charts	100
Through The Eyes & Voice Of...	101-103
Ticket to Leave	104
Walking Tour	105
ABC to XYZ	106
Where Do I Begin?	107

V. Surprise! You're a Reading Teacher! 109-136

Points to Ponder:
    We All Teach Reading 111-112
Balanced Literacy 113-114
Reading to Learn 115-125
    Using Prior Knowledge 116
    Making Inferences 116-117
    Text Structure 118-119
    Graphic Organizers 118-122
    Vocabulary Development 123-124
Reading and Writing Across the Curriculum 126
Unsuccessful Readers 127-131
English Language Learners 132
Reciprocal Teaching 133
Think Alouds 134
Where Do I Begin? 135

VI. Assessment 101 137-168

Points to Ponder:
    IT Hasn't Been Taught, If IT Hasn't Been Caught! 139
An Assessment Continuum 140
Preassessment Strategies 141
Checking for Understanding 142-146
Homework 147-149
Self Assessment 150-158
Assessing with Balance 159
Classroom Test Design 160-16?
Award Winning Performance Assessment 1'
Assessment Criteria 165
Where Do I Begin?

VII. Beginning with the "Ends" in Mind: The Year, The Unit, & The Lesson — 169-192

Points to Ponder:
Positive Planning Practices & Potential Pitfalls 171
Planning in a Standards-Based Environment 172-174
SBE Planning Process 175
Planning Instruction for the Year 176
Essential Understandings 177-180
Planning Units of Instruction 181-183
Planning Lessons 184
Task Analysis 185
Getting Started with Differentiation 186
Planning the First Week of School 187-188
Summer Planning Advice 189-190
Where Do I Begin? 191

VIII. Organizational Systems for You, the Learners, & the Classroom — 193-252

Points to Ponder:
Systems Design 195
In the Beginning 196-198
Starting the Year Right 199-203
Meet & Greet 204
Take a Tour 205
Culture, Collaboration & Communication 206
Dealing with the Paper Work 207-216
Generally Speaking 207-208
To & From the School & School System 209
Your Instructional Materials 210-212
To & From Your Students 213-216
Using Technology as an Organizational Tool 217-219
Substitute Essentials 220-221

VIII. Organizational Systems continued

Avoid Mayhem!	222-223
First, You Have to Get Their Attention	224-226
Giving Directions	227
Time Templates	228-229
Transition Tidbits	230-231
Procedure Potpourri	232-235
Sponges, Fillers, & Anchoring Activities	236
Classroom Interior Design 101	237-241
Did You Do Anything While I Was Gone?	242
Putting Students Into Groups	243-244
Structuring Small Group Work	245-250
Where Do I Begin?	251

IX. Parents as Partners — 253-266

Points to Ponder:	
Parents are People, People with Children	255
Communication Systems	256-258
Parent Conferences	259-260
Back to School/Open House	261-262
When There is a Problem	263-264
Where Do I Begin?	265

X. Tools — 267-316

Learner Tools	269-282
Instructional Design Tools	283-304
Organizational Tools	305-314
Where Do I Begin?	315

XI. Resources & References — 317-328

1

Introduction

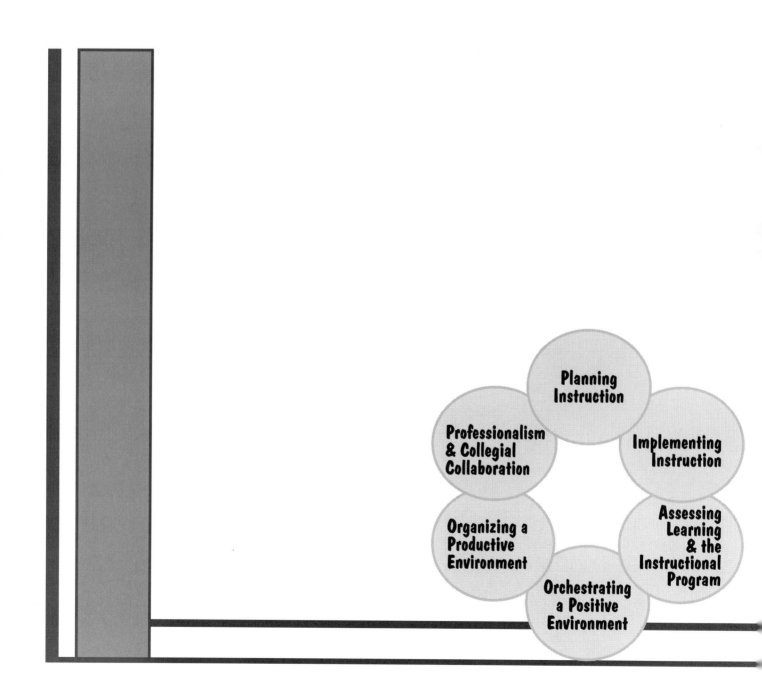

Planning
Instruction

Professionalism
& Collegial
Collaboration

Implementing
Instruction

Organizing a
Productive
Environment

Assessing
Learning
& the
Instructional
Program

Orchestrating
a Positive
Environment

The Study of Teaching & Learning
What New Teachers Need to Know

As a result of over thirty years of teaching, leading, and learning from children and adults, it is clear to me that while beginning teachers may say they need classroom management skills, what they really mean is that they need to know how to set up classroom conditions where high level engagement and learning can occur. It is easier to say that new teachers need classroom management skills than it is to say that they need to develop strong instructional programs. **The dilemma with focusing on management is that the end we have in mind for our learners is not that they be well-managed, but that they be well-educated.** This book is based on the tenet that the best management system is a strong instructional program.

When we focus on well-educated as opposed to well-managed, we must communicate from the first day that we not only believe in the capacity of our students to achieve at high levels but that we also have a sense of self-efficacy. We can do this many ways. The most basic level we need to let students know that we know (or want to know) who they are; that we know what we are talking about; and that we are well prepared. To do that, we need **knowledge of content & content standards,** as well as **skills for designing learning experiences** in ways that make learning accessible to all learners, and, last but not least, we need **incredible organizational skills** for setting up and leading a micro-society.

The term **leadership** is preferable to the term **management** because "to manage" means to "maintain the status quo." "To lead" means "to take to a new place and, therefore, implies that change is expected." Entries defining **manage** in *Webster's Ninth New Collegiate Dictionary* include "to handle or direct with a degree of skill," "to make and keep submissive," "to alter by manipulation." Entries describing **lead** in the same dictionary include "to guide on a way especially by going in advance," "to tend toward or have a result," "to direct on a course or in a direction." The desired outcome in our classrooms is clearly the latter.

The essential questions on the next page are based on the belief that leading the learning is preferable to managing the learning. To retain our best and brightest teachers, we have to cast them as leaders and agents of change capable of not only leading students in their content learning but in learning how to learn and in developing a sense of self-efficacy. This is true not only for teachers new to the profession but also for all those who see themselves as life-long learners.

Framework for The Study of Teaching & Learning

The essential questions that must be addressed by 21st century teachers are:
- What is a learning-centered classroom and what do I need to do to create and lead in such a learning environment?
- How do I translate "beginning with the end in mind" into planning and pacing for the year, the unit, and the lesson?
- What are systems for organizing me, the learners, and the learning environment?

What follows is an incredibly complex and perhaps even overwhelming list of skills and knowledge needed to address those questions. They are organized in the six arenas frequently identified as areas of professional practice for educators. While no educator ever completely masters all of them, it is important for all educators, even novices, to have a complete picture of the complexity of the job so that they can target potential areas for professional development throughout their career. Supervisors, mentors, and coaches must help novice teachers identify which skill sets can have the greatest impact on student and teacher success in any given situation.

Those listings marked with an ** or an * are explicit areas of focus in this book. Those marked with ** are significant areas of focus. They have been identified based on the essential questions listed above. Many of the areas not presented in this book are presented in *Instruction for All Students.* Some points are so essential that they appear in both books.

The last page of each chapter is entitled **"Where Do I Begin"** and is provided as a space to record reflections and to make a **"To Do List"** of what you want to do to establish a learning-centered classroom. The last page of this chapter provides a model **"To Do List."**

Planning Instruction

Implementing Instruction

Assessing Learning & the Instructional Program

Orchestrating a Positive Environment

Organizing a Productive Environment

Professionalism & Collegial Collaboration

ASK Framework for The Study of Teaching & Learning

Planning Instruction

** Standards-Based Teaching, Learning and Assessment
** Lesson, Unit and Course Design
   Content Specific Pedagogy
   Learning Styles, Multiple Intelligences and Brain Research
   Diversity of Students
** Active Learning
 * Connections to the World Beyond The Classroom
   Integration of the Curriculum

Implementing Instruction

 * Framing the Learning
 * Dealing with Naive Understandings and Misconceptions
** Communicating Purposes, Expectations, and Directions
 * Using a Repertoire of Strategies, Materials and Resources
** Designing Rigorous Questions and Assignments Aligned with Desired Outcomes
   Promoting Connections and Meaning Making
   Incorporating Literacy Instruction
   Differentiating Instruction
 * Accommodating and Adapting for Special Needs Students

Assessing Learning & the Instructional Program

 * The Assessment Continuum
 * Checking for Understanding
 * Designing, Selecting, and Assessing Paper and Pencil Assessments
   Designing, Selecting, Implementing, and Assessing Performance Tasks
   Designing and Using Rubrics and Performance Assessment Task Lists
   Using Assessment Results to Inform Teaching Decisions

Planning Instruction

Professionalism & Collegial Collaboration

Implementing Instruction

Organizing a Productive Environment

Assessing Learning & the Instructional Program

Orchestrating a Positive Environment

Framework continued...

Orchestrating a Positive Learning Environment

** Building a Community of Learners
** Having and Communicating High Expectations to All Students
   Using Attribution Theory to Reframe Belief Systems
 * Building Capacity Through Learning How to Learn Strategies
   Using Errors and/or Lack of Background Knowledge and Skills as Learning Opportunities
 * Building in Reflection and Metacognition
   Developing Thinking Skills for the 21st Century
 * Building Appropriate and Positive Personal Relationships with Students

Organizing & Leading a Productive Learning-Centered Environment

** Creating and Using Organizational Systems for Professional and Instructional Materials
 * Developing and Implementing Organizational Systems for Learners and the Classroom
   Planning Proactively to Work with Reluctant and Resistant Learners

Professionalism & Collegial Collaboration

   The Ways We Collaborate: Consultant, Collaborator, and Coach
   Formats for Collaboration and Job-Embedded Learning
   Peer Observation
   Mentoring
   Co-Teaching
   Professional Responsibilities
 * Parents as Partners

Where Do I Begin?

Top 10 Teaching Tips

1. Begin with the end in mind...the end of the year, the end of the unit of study, the end of the lesson. How do I want my learners to be different as a result of the time they spend with me?

2. Make the use of **10:2 Theory & Wait Time** as much a part of my professional practice as brushing my teeth is of my personal life!

3. Help students **access & use prior knowledge** at the beginning of each new unit of study! Don't ever skip this step!

4. Use a wide range of strategies to allow students to **process & summarize** their learning both inside and outside of class; facilitate their analysis of what works best for their own learning.

5. Help students develop strong **self-assessment habits** that include analysis of effort and errors followed by **self-adjustment**.

6. Use the research on **differences in learners** (learning styles, multiple intelligences, modality preferences, etc.) as a check and balance system on your instructional decisions.

7. Make learning active! Be sure that the students are the workers, not the spectators watching me work!

8. Be thoughtful about the **levels/kinds of thinking** required in standards and assessment and use questions and assignments which mirror those levels.

9. Make the **classroom environment** as much like life beyond the classroom as possible. Double check my perceptions about that world.

10. Always remember: Kids are people and deserve to be treated accordingly. **Focus on learning** rather than on compliance and control.

II

Orchestrating
a Positive Learning Environment
A Good Place to Learn

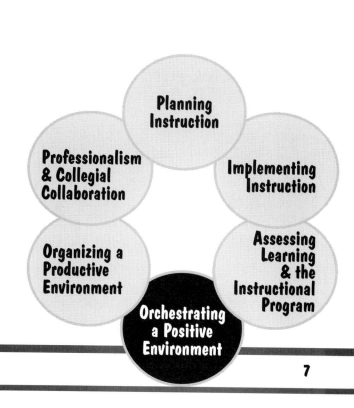

Recommended Site for Creating a Learning-Centered Classroom

surfaquarium.com/MI/MIinvent.htm   This site has a reproducible Multiple Intelligences inventory for students. Permission is given to reproduce it for classroom use.

Points to Ponder...
The First Day... & Every Day!

The career you have selected is quite different from the jobs your friends have chosen who are going into the corporate world. From the first day, you will be responsible for the work of others. Your friends, on the other hand, will work for months, if not years, before they are given that responsibility. It is essential then that you begin your work realizing that you need extraordinarily sophisticated people skills from the opening bell.

When twenty to thirty people of any age spend 180 plus days together in a relatively small space, careful attention must be paid to how property, space, time, and human interactions are handled. Think first of the issues facing any group of people spending that much time together, and consider what instructional pieces you might use once you've clarified in your mind how this society might function. You can work on this aspect of your preparation even if you do not know exactly where or what you will be teaching.

When considering how to set up the learning environment use all you have ever learned about etiquette, group process, conflict resolution, problem solving, personality types, safety, time management, etc. Even if those curriculum documents and district standards are not available for you to study yet, there is plenty for you to do. Go to the library or book store and read up on communication, social, leadership and organizational skills. You are going to need every single one of them. The good news is that these are all skills, and by definition that means you can learn to do whichever ones you choose to master.

If you have not spent your life around children of the age you will be teaching, spend some time at a park, at the neighborhood swimming pool, at the theater, and at the shopping mall watching the children. Capture the enthusiasm, curiosity, joy, and wonder they exude, and contemplate how you can bring that into the classroom rather than creating an environment where they are expected to leave all of that outside.

The classroom should be as much like life beyond the classroom as possible. The students are real people, who just happen to be a little younger than the teacher, and who have been ordered to report to your care. If you are inclined to set up a dictatorship, be prepared to deal with stealth attacks and/or revolutions; if, however, you are interested in establishing a more democratic type setting, be clear what the parameters are. Not only must you be clear, you must clearly communicate those boundaries to the students as all of you collaborate to create an effective and efficient learning environment.

Recommendations for Creating a
Learning-Centered Environment
Instead of a Environment Based on Compliance & Control

- At the beginning of the school year, work with the students to develop positive statements about how all of you will work together in the classroom. Ensure that these guidelines are consistent with the guidelines published in the school's handbook and that they are in the interest of student learning. (See pages 29-31.)

- Be specific and clear in directions. When directions are multi-step, present them both orally and in writing. Check for understanding of directions. (See page 227.)

- Use a range of consequences matched to the frequency, intensity and cause of any misbehavior. Be sure that consequences are designed to move students back into a learning mode rather than to remove them from the learning environment. (See pages 29-34.)

- Employ active learning strategies in which students are interacting with the information, the materials, and each other. Decrease time spent in whole group instruction and individual seat work. (See pages 63-107.)

- Give frequent positive recognition for effective effort and for gains in achievement and improvement of learning and/or social behavior. (See pages 18-19 and 22.)

- Provide nonevaluative feedback to students that gives them a clear sense of their progress in school. There is no need to grade all work; rather, allow significant portions of class work to be works-in-progress for which you provide clear but nonevaluative feedback. (See page 22.)

- Display student work.

- Engage students who are misbehaving in problem-solving activities. Avoid win-lose situations and threats, and offer choices. (See pages 32-35.)

- Avoid labeling students or using authoritarian tones and language.

- Treat students with respect and dignity. Kids are people too!

- Do not confuse "motivation" and "compliance." (Kohn)

- Remember that faster is not smarter. Be careful to communicate the value of craftsmanship, self-assessment, and self-adjustment.

Creating a
Learning-Centered Environment
Continued...

- Have students evaluate their learning, the effectiveness of their effort, the classroom learning environment, and instructional program on a regular basis. Have them support opinions with data.

- Ensure that students are not only consumers of information, but also producers of information.

- Use "I" or assertive messages to discuss problem behaviors. Teach students to do the same with each other. (See pages 20-21.)

- Use every opportunity to communicate an acceptance of, and an appreciation for, diversity.

- Clearly communicate that being unable to read well or to speak English proficiently is not the same as being unable to think well.

- Avoid periods of delay at the beginning of classes, between activities, and at the closing of classes. Create systems that minimize the amount of class time spent on record keeping and paper flow. (See Chapter VIII.)

- Teach students explicitly, within the context of their academic learning experiences, the interpersonal and communication skills they need to work and learn collaboratively. This includes skills such as speaking clearly, listening, clarifying, asking for help, and disagreeing agreeably. (See pages 20-21.)

Based on *Structuring Schools for Student Success: A Focus on Discipline & Attendance*, the Massachusetts Board of Education, 1991.

"But...Some Students Can't Learn!"

The Myth

Some special or remedial students can't learn difficult concepts because they don't have the capacity to learn something that hard. This has led to tracking and "watering down" the curriculum.

The Problem

Most learning experiences require students to have prior knowledge or skills in order to be successful. Learning difficulties often occur because students lack the background information or prerequisite skills.

The Reality

We all have different prior knowledge and skill proficiency when we begin a task. These variables determine how easily we understand a concept and how successfully we can complete an activity. Many second language learners, special needs and remedial students who are often treated as if they are unable to learn, in reality, have not had, or have not yet taken advantage of, the opportunities to acquire prerequisite knowledge or to practice expected skills.

A primary predictor of success in learning is what the student knows and can do before the learning experience begins. When a student has trouble learning new material, we need to find out **WHY** the task is difficult and **WHAT** the student needs to know to master the concept.

Tasks are more difficult when students lack the mental hooks on which to hang new learning, or hold misconceptions or naive understandings, or when we give unclear directions, fail to establish and communicate criteria and provide models, and/or do not provide formative feedback during the learning experiences.

Students are certain to struggle with (and perhaps resist) learning when they do not have the necessary prior knowledge and skills. It is our job to identify and fill in the gaps. This chapter addresses creating an environment where all students feel welcome and a part of the learning community. The next chapter addresses specific instructional strategies that work well in a learning-centered environment.

"Oh Yes, They Can Learn!"
I not only Believe in THEM, I Believe in ME!

Much has been written about the necessity for all educators to believe in the capacity of all children to learn. This is an extremely important belief system that all educators need to examine. Equally important, however, is our belief in our capacity to teach these children so that they achieve at a high level.

Do You Believe...

- In the capacity of all students to learn?
- In the capacity of all students to achieve at a high level?
- In your capacity to teach all of these children?
- In your capacity to teach all of these children at a high level?
- That all includes non-English speaking students, struggling readers, as well as the learning disabled?
- That it is your job to teach children who do not learn at the same speed or in the same ways as other children?
- That it is part of your job to collaborate with other educators to help all students achieve at a high level?
- That regular educators and special educators should work as equal partners in the interest of all children?
- That all of the students in this school belong to all of us?
- That all the adults in this school system are part of a preK-12 team and that we should not only be committed to the success of all students but to the success of each other?
- That parents should be treated as partners in the education of their children?
- That we should look at data and make informed decisions about how we and our learners are doing?
- That there is a knowledge base about best practice, that it is constantly evolving and that it is part of your job to seek it out and use it in your practice?

Yes, of course, you do or you would not be in this profession.

Now the question becomes how do you teach in such a way that students believe in themselves. Even when we have these belief systems in place, we do not always have the knowledge and skills to get the job done. Even when we believe, we can get discouraged when we work so hard and do not achieve the results we want. That is why learning how to teach is a lifelong journey. We have to constantly examine not only our belief systems, but our knowledge base about the content we are tasked with teaching, the learners with whom we work, and our repertoire for chunking the content in developmentally appropriate ways, while concentrating on the essential understandings.

"Oh Yes, They Can Learn!"

I not only Believe in THEM, I Believe in ME!
Now... How Do I Get Them to Believe in Themselves?

Knowing what to do in a theoretical sense is quite different from knowing how to do it on a day to day basis. I may, for example, know about autism, gifted education and second language learners, as well as be an extraordinary mathematician. Being able to translate what I know about math in ways that members of this particular group of students can learn it at a deep and enduring level is a completely different ball game. An additional challenge is, of course, convincing students that they can learn this math, and that it is worth the effort.

In order to help all students achieve at a high level and to help students believe in themselves, teachers need to develop a level of competency that allows them to focus on the needs of the learners. Given the complexities of the learning process and the diversity of our students this is an ongoing career-long endeavor. The work of both researchers and practitioners as presented on the following pages provides insight into how to promote and support a sense of self-efficacy in students.

Expectations Messages

Anne Wescott Dodd writes in an article in *Educational Leadership*, "To motivate and engage students, teachers must create a classroom environment in which every student comes to believe,

I Count, I Care, I Can."

Jon Saphier writes in *The Skillful Teacher* that the three messages of expectations are:

"This is Important!"
"You Can Do It!"
"I Won't Give Up on You!"

Linda Albert writes in *Cooperative Discipline* that students need to feel,

connected, capable, and" contributing."

Ways to Let Students Know You Believe
They are Capable of
Achieving at a High Level

1. **Communicate clear expectations.** Include criteria for success, such as rubrics, task performance lists, and exemplars of good performance.

2. **Model enthusiasm for what is to be learned, the work to be done, and for student effective efforts and successes.**

3. **Organize the learning environment for thinking.** Carefully plan questions, craft examples, stories, and activities which promote transfer and retention.

4. **Monitor student attributions and use attribution retraining** with those who make external attributions.

5. **Provide feedback from multiple sources** so that learners are able to learn from the feedback and make adjustments in their future work.

6. **Design a brain-compatible classroom through the regular use of active learning, feedback, and varied sources of input in a safe environment.**

7. **Coach students in setting challenging yet attainable goals and in designing and implementing action plans for attaining those goals.**

8. **Include opportunities for all categories of thinking** in discussions with and assignments for low-performing students. Teach students to think **about their thinking** and to learn what kind of thinking is required in various situations.

9. **Promote and teach effective effort strategies:**
   - task and error analysis
   - choice of sources, processes, and products
   - focus groups for skill development
   - graphing of progress
   - interactive notebooks

10. Once unit and lesson objectives are clear, plan how you will **differentiate instruction** so that all students can successfully process learning and demonstrate mastery of the objectives.

4th Grade
Elements of Performance Preparation

Orchestra Performance Goals

Instrument Hold - Left Hand
- Elbow under
- Thumb place
- Over on shoulder
- Fingers over "dot's"
- Don't "squish" therapy

Bow Grip
- Bent thumb
- Fingers over frog
- "Lazy Sailor" on the ship

Enjoy the Music
- Pretty melody
- Our video is a "celebration"
- We're proud of what we can do

Practice
- 20 Minutes
- 5 Days a week

Learn the Notes
- Sections
- "Do, De's"
- Play it a lot
- Play for a parent

Big Tone
- Use more bow
- Use more bow warmups
- Tug on string
- Straight bow

Mary Louise Veremeychik, West Irondequoit Central Schools, Rochester, NY

Through the Voice of...Expectations Messages
A Good Reader Can...

I wanted to help my second graders examine what they could do to be good readers. I had taught each one of the skills individually, but the students didn't have a concrete representation of each thing they could do to help themselves. I devised this **A Good Reader** Sheet.

A	A good reader can look at the picture for clues.
	A good reader can guess a word that makes sense.
G	A good reader can say/check the beginning letters of a new word.
O	A good reader can try fixing it.
O	A good reader can read the sentence again and try something else.
D	A good reader can look for "chunks" in tricky words.
	A good reader can skip the tricky part, read on, and then go back and fix it.
R	A good reader practices EVERYDAY.
E	A good reader talks about books with family and friends.
A	A good reader can ask does that make sense?
D	A good reader can ask does that sound right?
E	
R	A good reader can ask does it look right?

This sheet is posted on the inside front cover of their Poetry Notebook. Before we do anything in class, the students take out their notebooks and they recite what **A Good Reader CAN** do.

I found this strategy to be very successful. Although the children had been taught the items on the list, they weren't always able to follow through. Since they now have the sheet right in front of their notebooks they are almost forced to concentrate on their abilities. This has now become an essential part of my everyday teaching. I am laminating a smaller copy of the **A Good Reader** statements so that the students can use them when they return to their homerooms.

I learned that the more we see something the more likely it may actually sink in. The students were excited at the idea of all the things they had actually learned. I was thrilled that a simple list of their reading skills and strategies would enable the class to become better, more accomplished readers.

I adapted this strategy for my first graders. Each student has a flower and they place the **A Good Reader** statements on the petals. As soon as they accomplish a skill, they put another petal on their flower.

Marita O'Brien, Grades 1-5 Reading Improvement, Calumet School, District 132 Oaklawn, IL

Development of the intrapersonal intelligence causes one to examine the effectiveness of one's effort. Teaching students to assess what works and what doesn't work for them in the learning process may be the most important thing we teach them. Younger children believe ability and hard work combine to promote success. As students get closer to adolescence, they tend to believe that those who succeed are smart or are just plain lucky. One thing they "know for sure" is they do not want to be caught trying, because if they fail, everyone will know they are dumb! This perception is a reality for them that greatly impacts their willingness to expend effort. **Attribution retraining** can make a huge difference in the lives of our students.

Attribution Theory

	internal	external
stable	ability	task difficulty
unstable	effective effort	luck

- Weiner, 1970

Attribution Retraining

A learning environment where students learn how to learn includes opportunities for students to reflect on their efforts and to learn from their errors. Successful adults know that it is the effectiveness and efficiency of effort that determines how well we reach the goals we set for ourselves. Our tendency is to tell students this "fact of life" rather than systematically teaching them through our modeling and by insisting that they analyze their own work.

The single most effective way to respond to students who say the task was too hard, or they were unlucky, or that they are just too dumb is to say, "Given that you believe/think/feel that....., what might you do about it?" The least effective response is to try to confuse them with logic by pointing out how unclearly they are thinking; they will not buy it. Allow them to see the world as they see it AND create conditions that cause them to consider how they might do something to improve the results in the future. For example, catch them being right and point out that effort must have played a part, mention that you work hard to prepare interesting and challenging lessons, and include recognition of effective effort in your verbal and written praise.

Through the Voice of...

Reflections on My Week

Name: _____ **Week of:** _____

What I Learned This Week:

How I Can Use It:

Areas in Which I am Making Progress:

What I Learned About How I Learn:

My Goal for Next Week:

What I Enjoyed Most This Week:

Stacy Holahan & Margie Cawley, 4th Grade Blended, Sherman School, Rush-Henrietta School District, NY

Communication Skills
Reading, Writing, Listening & Speaking

I'm a Great Listener! What's Your Problem?

There are four main categories of communication skills: reading, writing, speaking, and listening. It is amazing to learn that the ones in which we have had the least instruction and training are the two that we use the most. While we teach and study reading and writing, it is speaking and listening that we engage in most of the time. Think for a moment about your life in the past week. Upon reflection you will find that you have spent more time using listening skills than you have any of the other three skills. In the classroom you will find that well developed listening and speaking skills are absolutely essential to creating and leading a positive and productive learning-centered environment.

The fact is that there are very few really **skilled listeners.** The good news is that listening is a set of skills just like riding a bicycle is a set of skills and can be learned and refined with practice.

The guidelines for listening skills are the same for the classroom as they are for any other situation. The basics to concentrate on using and modeling for students are:

- Make **eye contact** and hold it. Do not try to look through a pile of papers while a student is talking with you. Put the papers down and listen. If you have to look for papers, ask the student to wait until you are ready to fully attend.
- **Smile.**
- Call people **by name**.
- **Don't interrupt.**
- Listen to the **entire statement** or question. If you find yourself thinking about your response, stop, and **refocus.**
- **Pause** before responding. **Wait time** is essential in instruction and in communication.
- **Paraphrase**. We almost always repeat a phone number to see if we heard it correctly. Certainly we should do that when we are engaged in conversation. This would be called **checking for understanding.**
- **Probe.** Ask the person with whom you are talking for a couple of examples or to tell you a little more before you say, "Oh, sure, I understand!" Do not do this for "nosiness" but for clarity.

These are the basic skills. Check your skill levels, and when you are a pro at these read *People Skills* **by Robert Bolton; it is an excellent resource on communication skills. He writes with clarity and humor and uses great examples to make his points.**

Communication Skills continued...

"Could You Speak in Sentence Form, Please?"

Kay Toliver in the wonderful PBS videotape, "Good Morning, Miss Toliver" expects her students to speak in complete sentences at all times. The result is amazing. Not only do they sound incredibly articulate, you can hear the cognitive connections they are making because of the expression of a complete thought. An important side effect of both teacher and students speaking in complete sentences is that students hear correct language models. This might eliminate our hearing them say, "Me and him are going to the movies" and "Kelly gave it to myself."

"I Messages"

Thomas Gordon gave us a great gift when he wrote about **"I Messages."** Outside of education, **"I messages"** are called assertiveness training. Whatever the name, it means politely but firmly explaining how the behavior of another impacts you and how you feel.

An **"I Message"** has three parts. They are:
- **Name the behavior that is bothering you in nonjudgmental terms**
- **Describe its impact on you**
- **Explain how it makes you feel**

An example of what that would sound like in the classroom is, "When you leave your backpacks in the aisle, I have difficulty concentrating on your questions because I am afraid I'm going to trip on them." Consider how different that sounds from, "If I have told you once to move those back packs, I have told you at least five times. Move them now!"

Before we can engage in problem solving, consensus building, and conflict resolution, we have to build skills as listeners, speakers, and send assertive messages rather than roadblocks to communication. The first step is to listen to yourself and others in informal settings. Monitor both the speaking and listening habits of all parties and identify one skill to work on improving. You may need to do some reading on the topic to further clarify productive and unproductive habits.

Written Comments on Student Work

Susie Boyle, 7th grade English teacher at Lake Braddock Secondary School, Burke, Virginia, is so thoughtful of the work students put into big projects that she writes her comments on their autobiography project on a separate piece of paper and attaches it to the project. The student work is therefore intact as a valued school memento.

Praise, Encouragement, & Feedback

On Praise

Jere Brophy writes, **"Effective praise can be informative as well as reinforcing, can provide encouragement and support, and can help teachers establish friendly relationships with students."** He further suggests that praise should be specific; that is, it should expressly mention what the person did to deserve the praise, and should attribute success to effort and ability. An important finding of his extensive research on effective praise is that it should not be controlling, as in, "I really like what you did", but rather designed to build internal or intrinsic motivation as in, "You must be really proud of yourself to have been so resourceful in finding the necessary materials to finish the task." An interesting variable of his findings was that most praise is best given privately.

On Descriptive Praise & Encouragement

Adele Faber and Elaine Mazlish write about describing what a child did well and summing it up in a word. **"You picked up all the sticks and leaves that fell during the storm, now that is what I call..."** Select from the list below; you might chose responsible, considerate, thoughtful or showing initiative to complete this particular descriptive praise. Descriptive praise helps students know the meaning of these abstract terms when we link them to their own behaviors.

alert	courageous	enthusiastic	honest	positive
award	creative	flexible	Integrity	problem solving
candid	curious	focused	initiative	prompt
caring	determined	friendly	organized	punctual
considerate	efficient	generous	patience	purposeful
consistent	effective effort	gracious	perseverance	responsible
cooperative	emphatic	helpful	persistent	trustworthy

Create **Now That's What I Call... cards** and have a stack of them in the classroom. Encourage students to complete them and give them to one another.

On Feedback

Grant Wiggins writes, **"Feedback is not about praise or blame, approval or disappointment. Feedback is value-neutral. It describes what you did and did not do. ...Praise is necessary but praise only keeps you in the game. It doesn't get you better."** Many rubrics use judgmental language, such as excellent or good, very clear or somewhat clear, etc. This is evaluation rather than feedback. We want to give as much objective and nonjudgmental feedback as we can by using either carefully constructed rubrics or other means so that students can begin to both self-assess and self-adjust.

Miss Manners in the Classroom Says... Your Mother Was Right!

My Mother Said:

Meet all guests at the door and welcome them into our home. Make them feel comfortable and introduce them to someone if they do not immediately see someone they know.

Miss Classroom Manners Says:

Meet the students at the door, make eye contact and welcome them to class not only on the first day of school but on every single day you can possible do so. Give them a signal as to where to go and what to do. If the directions or bell work are written on the board or on an overhead transparency, direct their attention there. Pre-established homework check groups can maximize learning time.

My Mother Said:

Work the crowd. Be sure that you chat with all the guests. Do not spend all of your time with only those who seek you out. Learn something about each guest so that you can include that information when you introduce them to someone else.

Miss Classroom Manners Says:

Work the crowd. Be sure that you are not constantly surrounded by groupies. That's right! Rock stars are not the only ones with groupies. Informally track whom you interact with before, during and after class.

My Mother Said:

Escort all guests to the door when they are leaving, let them know you remember their names and that you are glad that they came.

Miss Classroom Manners Says:

Stand at the door as they leave, make eye contact, let them know you were glad that they were there. Use as many names as possible in the process.

Miss Classroom Manners Says continued...

My Mother Said:

Never embarrass our guests. Should it be necessary to let them know that they just sat on another guest's dessert plate or that they have spilled something down the front of their shirt, do so quietly and privately. Additionally, do not overdo public praise without the permission of the guest.

> **Miss Classroom Manners Says:**
> Never embarrass each other... student to student, student to teacher, teacher to student. Corrections, difficult discussions, attitude adjustment chats, and even praise are best handled privately.

My Mother Said:

Do not interrupt when someone else is talking. In fact, make eye contact and listen carefully. When you are really good, you will paraphrase what has just been said as you add to the discussion.

> **Miss Classroom Manners Says:**
> Do not interrupt when someone else is talking. In fact, be sure students do not wave their hands in the air to add their thoughts because that is a clear signal that they have stopped listening. There must be a better way to help students listen to one another and not interrupt. Paraphrasing and/or checking for understanding always moves the discussion forward.

My Mother Said:

There is a time and place for... and this is neither the time nor the place.

> **Miss Classroom Manners Says:**
> There is a time and place for... and this is neither the time nor the place. You get to fill in the blanks with the appropriate behavior just like "My Mother." It might be throwing a ball, running, rough-housing, yelling, etc. Just be sure that your expectations are appropriate for the age of the students, and, you guessed it, the time and place.

Getting to Know You

"I wish someone had told me then that knowing my students was as important as knowing my subject."

The quote above is from an ***Educational Leadership*** article written by Anne Wescott Dodd entitled "Engaging Students: What I Learned Along the Way." As a former secondary school teacher, she reflects on how she could have avoided power struggles if she had gotten to know her students as people and understood their perspectives rather than trying to control them. She suggests that one way to accomplish this is to have students complete a questionnaire or survey or write their teachers a letter or paper about themselves on the first day of school so that they know them more personally. It might be entitled **"My Math Autobiography"** or **"Carter, the Student"** or **"The Top Ten Things You Should Know About Me."**

Ann Muse writes in ***Executive Skills,*** a training manual for the Department of Defense Education Activity (DoDEA), that key questions students come to school wanting to have answered include, **"Who are the kids in my class?"** and **"Who are my teachers/is my teacher?"** We have a responsibility for orchestrating experiences where these questions can be answered. Yes, we want to spend as much time as possible guiding our students to mastery of high standards. But, they will be better able to take academic risks and to cooperate with one another if they feel comfortable and safe. We do not have to sacrifice one for the other.

Be sure to let them get to know you. Go to the band or orchestra room and play with them, go to art class or to physical education with them. Share family pictures and stories, especially when they support the kinds of behaviors, interactions and learnings you want for them. Share the books you are reading and the things you are interested in learning more about.

On the following pages you will find a menu of activities and questions from which you can select to design exercises which will promote students getting to know you and each other.

Take Pictures

Artifact Bags

Learn Names ASAP

Tent Cards or Nametags

That's True About Me!

Interest Surveys

Create Bulletin Boards

Biopoems

Menu of Questions, Stems & Activities for
Getting to Know You

Dreams

Table discussions or journal entries that could turn into a class book or newsletter.

Famous person you would like to meet
Country you would like to visit
If you were the mayor, governor, president
If you could have dinner with any one in history
If you could have dinner with any character from a book you have read

Dream vacation
My dream car
If you were the teacher
If you were the principal
If you could change one thing
If you had a million dollars
When I am an adult I want to be

Favorites

Favorite holiday
Favorite ice cream flavor
Favorite time of day
Favorite season of the year
Favorite sport
Favorite books
Favorite music groups

Favorite television shows
Favorite video games
Favorite foods
Favorite school subjects
Favorite color
Favorite piece of classical music
Favorite song

Interesting Tidbits About Me

- Can be a **"That's True About Me!"** activity in which the teacher calls out characteristics and those it represents stand and shout, **"That's True About Me!"**
- Have students interview each other in new work groups to find five characteristics the entire group has in common. Students could, of course, add their own.
- Use one of the **Awesome Activities** listed on page 28.

...is a pet owner
...has no cavities
...has had a manicure
...has/had braces
...has never traveled by plane
...always wears a watch

...has never had a speeding ticket
...has more than 5 pairs of shoes
...likes camping
...pulls Oreos apart to lick out the filling
...knows his/her mother's/father's birthday
...likes chocolate

Menu of Questions, Stems & Activities for
Getting to Know You continued...

Interesting Tidbits About Me continued...

...has not had chicken pox
...has changed the oil in a car
...always places your napkin in your lap
   when eating
...keeps his or her elbows off the table
   during meals
...always passes the salt and pepper together
...is wearing red/blue/orange/ _____
...plays computer games every day
...helps with the housework
...helps with the yard work
...speaks a language other than English
...can count to ten in Japanese/Chinese/German or _____
...can name the four components of photosynthesis
...can recite the Preamble to the US Constitution
...can count by five from 5 to 100
...can name the colors of the rainbow
...can name ten countries in Europe
...has not missed a day of school all year
...can sing "Happy Birthday" in a language other than English

...has visited another country
...has lived in another country
...has lived in another state
...has lived in another town
...has to clean his or her own
   room
...has _____ hair
...has _____ eyes

People Connections

...has nieces or nephews
...has at least two cousins
...has a sibling in this school
...has a relative who is a teacher
...has a relative who is a firefighter
...has a relative who is a _____
...knows someone famous
...remembers kindergarten teacher's name

Menu of Questions, Stems & Activities for
Getting to Know You continued...

Lets Get Active

...plays a musical instrument
...likes to sing
...likes to dance
...likes to ride a bike
...knows how to snowboard
...knows how to water ski
...knows how to snorkel
...knows how to sail
...knows how to figure skate
...can ride a unicycle
...has been swimming in the
   Atlantic or Pacific Ocean

...likes to rollerblade
...likes to skateboard
...likes to play soccer
...likes to jump rope
...likes to shoot baskets
...likes to play "Kick the Can"
...likes to play "Hide and Seek"
...likes to play hopscotch
...likes to swing
...likes to play tag
...likes to play outside
...likes street skating

Awesome Activities

- Conduct interest surveys.
- Organize scavenger hunts: Find someone who _____ .
- Artifact Bags: Have students bring 5 to 10 objects from home that represent who they are, what they enjoy most, what they are experts at, and what they are most interested in learning about.
- BioBags: Erin McCurry of Skyline High School, St. Vrain Valley School District, Longmont, Colorado, has students bring articles that represent their goals, their family heritage, significant events, people in their lives, and their interests in a bag that also represents who they are. An athlete might use a gym bag while someone who works at The Gap might bring their artifacts in a Gap bag.
- Prepare a bulletin board (or even handouts) with digital or Polaroid camera pictures of students.
- Create biopoems. See pages 72-73.
- Have students prepare collages about themselves using photos and magazine pictures.
- Have students prepare a Top Ten List of _____ .
- Have students interview each other to find similar interests and characteristics and then create mind maps or Venn diagrams.
- Conduct the getting to know you exercises in the target language.

Establishing Rules Together

Laws, policies, rules, and procedures are necessary. The lack thereof is anarchy. In classrooms, the "rules" situation ranges from close to anarchy with nonexistent and/or unclear rules to so many rules and regulations that the teacher spends far more time and energy on rules enforcement than on teaching. The ends of these continuums are like edges of cliffs. Do not go to either end unless you are well prepared to go over the edge.

Research shows that approximately 85% of students are willing and able to live within reasonable and clearly defined rules, yet we insist on making possibly unreasonable and unenforceable rules for 100% of the students in order to "control" the 15% who are more persistent in testing the limits. Nearly all of the 15% will "fall in line" with clearly established and reasonable limits, while three to five percent will challenge not only classroom rules but the rules and norms of society as well. **Curwin and Mendler** wrote of this distribution in *Discipline with Dignity* in 1988. The research for this information is grounded in the Pareto Principle which was established by Vilfredo Pareto, a turn-of-the-century Italian economist, and was later translated into management practice by Dr. Joseph Juran with the 85\15 Rule.

William Glasser wrote in *Control Theory in the Classroom* that beyond the need to survive and reproduce we have four basic needs. These needs are **to belong and love, to gain power, to be free, and to have fun.** Involving students in setting up the norms of the classroom, within the laws of the land and the policies established by the school and the school district, makes all the sense in the world. Students can then have a sense of belonging and a sense of power. When the parameters or principles are clearly articulated by the teacher and the rules are generated by all parties, students and teacher can engage in discussions not only about desired working conditions, but also about why these rules are necessary. See page 31 for one example of principles on which rules could be based.

Thomas Gordon in his landmark book *T.E.T.: Teacher Effectiveness Training,* published in 1974, said that his "Method III" used in a Rule-Setting Class Meeting was based on the earlier work of John Dewey.

Given this history, we can safely assume that this idea of working together to establish rules and norms is not a new one. In adult settings, we call the way we do business "norms" rather than "rules." In either setting, what we are describing is how we will interact with each other and the work conditions that need to be present for us to accomplish our goals.

Establishing Rules Together continued...

Rule-Setting Class Meeting
Using the Six Step Problem Solving Process

Gordon (1974) offers his "Method III", which is often called Six Step Problem Solving, as an approach for working with a class to set up class rules. The process is described below.

- **Define the problem**: Identify the situations and working conditions where rules are needed so that the group can learn well and work productively together. The teacher can contribute to the list.

- **Generate possible solutions**: Brainstorm a list of rules that might work in those situations. The teacher can contribute to the list.

- **Evaluate the solutions**: Ask if anyone objects to that rule. The teacher can eliminate any that would violate school policies and procedures.

- **Decide which solution is best**: Identify the set of rules to use.

At this point, the **Rule-Making Class Meeting** is over. The teacher can either post the rules around the room or print out a copy for each student.

Determining how to implement the decisions and assessing how well the solutions solved the problem are the last two steps in the process. They are ongoing components of classroom life and will be used and revisited when the rules are not followed or do not seem to be appropriate. See page 31 for suggestions on how to engage students in problem solving of classroom problems.

Curwin & Mendler's Social Contract

Curwin and Mendler write that the most successful social contracts:

- Are based on clearly articulated principles such as "be respectful," "be courteous," and "try your best at all times." See page 31 for an example of principles that could be used.

- Have rules based on the principles.

- Have a range of consequences based on intensity and frequency of problem behavior.

- Have checks for agreement and understanding by students and parents.

- Have a system of evaluating the contract and for changing it as necessary.

For details on how to create and implement a social contract, see Chapter 4 "The Social Contract" in *Discipline with Dignity.*

A Good Place to Learn is...

- A classroom where students' basic emotional and academic needs are met.

- A classroom where students are taught at the level at which they can learn, where they receive encouragement and recognition for the progress they are making.

- A place where people are courteous and where laughter springs from joy brought about by involvement with caring people involved in learning.

- One where communication is practiced and not preached, where teachers and students talk with, not at, each other.

- One that has reasonable rules that everyone agrees to because they are beneficial to individuals and to the group - rules that both teachers and students have a democratic stake in because everyone has a say in making and changing the rules as the need arises.

- A place where students feel accepted as persons with dignity who are asked to evaluate their own behavior and to take the responsibility for better behavior or suffer the natural consequences for their actions.

- A place where every effort is made to let each learner know that the expectations are that they will meet high standards of learning and every effort is made to ensure that each learner has a reasonable chance of success - that is, a place that lets all students know that they "belong," that they have a stake in what goes on here and that we expect them to succeed and to be responsible.

- A place where all learners know what excellence looks and sounds like and all are engaged in the pursuit of that excellence.

adapted from an unknown source

Dealing with Unmet Expectations
in a productive & positive learning-centered environment

- Focus on finding fault. Instead, catch students being right!
- Use rewards for good behavior. Students begin to work for the reward rather than because the work is interesting or the behavior is the right thing to do.
- Ask students to make promises. They often promise anything to get us off their backs.
- Nag, scold, and threaten. These may lead to immediate compliance, but there is high potential for resentment and frustration.
- Chastise in public. Names on the board is not acceptable practice!
- Blame the parents. We do not teach the parents. We have the next generation of parents in our classes today. If we miss the chance to influence difficult students, they may become even greater problems in our society later, as parents and citizens.
- Be overly concerned about your own authority base. Real authority comes from knowing what you are talking about and modeling respectful behavior.
- Use double standards. The same standards should apply for students and teachers.

- Identify causes of inattentive or disruptive behavior and match your response to the perceived cause.
- Clearly communicate your expectations for work and behavior.
- Focus on future behavior rather than on past behavior.
- Establish a relationship based on trust and mutual respect with each child.
- Wait to hold discussions about inattentive or disruptive behavior, or unmet expectations, until both of you are calm.
- Use logical consequences directly related to the behavior. Logical consequences are designed to get students back to work.

Beyond survival our
Basic Needs:
To Belong
To Gain Power
To Be Free
To Have Fun

William Glasser, 1986
Control Theory in the Classroom

Dealing with Unmet Expectations
in a productive & positive learning-centered environment

Do

- Teach that fairness has to do with equity rather than equality. That is, you get what you need when you need it rather than everyone getting the same thing at the same time.
- Distinguish between the behavior and the person exhibiting the behavior. Build self-efficacy by focusing on what effort is needed.
- Admit your own mistakes.
- Work for responsibility, motivation, and respect...not obedience, compliance, and fear.
- Remember that responsibility is taught by giving responsibility. Include students in developing procedures for handling inappropriate behavior or unmet expectations.

Responsibility, motivation, and respect are not the same as obedience, compliance and fear.

Kohn, 1996

WHEN THE GOING GETS ROUGH...

- Stay calm, move slowly, get close, be quiet, and relax.
- Make eye contact.
- If you must talk, lower your voice rather than raising it.
- Try to keep situation in perspective. Don't overreact and escalate minor incidents into major confrontations.
- Avoid public confrontation. An audience for a confrontation escalates any differences.
- Avoid threats you can't or don't want to carry out.
- Keep both feet on the ground emotionally! It is easy to get knocked over if you try to balance on one foot!

Engaging Students in
Problem-Solving

"Some teachers tend to focus on what is happening rather than on what is being learned. They may wish simply to stop the incident rather than consider which of many possible interventions is most likely to stimulate long-term development and learning."

Lilian Katz

The Six Step Problem Solving (Gordon, 1974) is the logical process to use when there is a problem, especially if you used it to establish class rules and/or if you have used the scientific process as part of your curriculum. It is an excellent thinking skills exercise because the students practice convergent and divergent thinking in alternating steps of the process. The Total Quality Management movement in business and industry caused millions of adults to learn or relearn this problem solving process.

One of the biggest problems we face in problem solving is that we try to solve the wrong problem. As Lilian Katz says in the quote at the top of the page, we may stop the behavior in the moment, but if we have not identified the cause and identified alternative ways of dealing with the issues, the problem will reoccur. The third grade problem solving session described on the next page demonstrates that the process does not have to be complex; in fact, it is pretty straight forward. As you read the scenario, identify the steps in the problem solving process.

Six Step Problem Solving

- Define the problem
- Generate possible solutions
- Evaluate the solutions
- Decide on a solution
- Determine an action plan
- Assess how well the solution/plan is working

Through the Voice of... Student Problem Solving

Dear Abby:

We had been having trouble "getting organized" in the morning. The children come into the classroom at 8:20; the bell rings at 8:30. A couple of mornings a week we have a special class at 8:35 or 8:45. We weren't ready to go. I was feeling "frazzled." The kids weren't responding by moving more quickly. The end of the day had some similarities. They got very chatty as we began preparing for departure. Kids were missing things I wanted them to take home or to bring back, etc.

When the children came back from art (the 8:35 class for which we were late), I said "I have a problem that I'm trying to work out in my head. I'm just not enjoying the beginning of the day and the end of the day. It's like having a great sandwich and the bread keeps falling off. The pieces of bread that hold our day together are the beginning and the end." Then I talked through the possibilities that maybe I was expecting them to do too much before art, maybe we need to do some of these things after art, maybe we should have no talking until everybody's settled in, maybe at the end of the day I need to allow more time...

I asked them if they had ever heard of Dear Abby. Most had. I said I thought I needed to write a Dear Abby letter. I wrote "Dear Abby" on chart paper, stated my problem and signed it "Frustrated Teacher." Then I asked them if they'd please be Abby and write back. Every child did. Then I had them meet in groups of four to share their solutions and make a list of what the group thought were the best choices. One person recorded for the group. We then came back together, shared the ideas and wrote them on chart paper with no comment until all were recorded. After all the solutions were shared, we discussed them. Eventually we agreed on the ones we would try.

Both the group sharing process and the solutions were impressive! They suggested that we should have the people with "Morning Jobs" to do come in five minutes early to get their back packs and other materials put away, to get their desks organized and to get set up for their jobs. It's made all the difference in the world and I didn't think of it!

Kay Nelson, Third Grade Teacher, Listwood School, West Irondequoit Central School District, Rochester, NY

Plan B...
What to Do When Plan A Doesn't Work

Thinking about potential problem situations in advance helps keep you from being surprised when all your enthusiasm and excitement about teaching and learning doesn't transfer to one or more of your students! Rather than being reactive, you can be proactive because you have already thought about what your options are before you encounter one of these challenges...with an audience, no less! Some probable situations you will encounter include:

- Students who do not do their homework
- Students who are off task during class
- Students who do not participate or answer
- Students who do not contribute to group work
- Students who do not like to work with others
- Students who do not get along with others
- Students who constantly seek attention
- Students who have learning challenges
- Students with emotional problems
- Students with language challenges
- Students who give up
- Students who are disorganized
- Students who do not seem motivated
- Students who can't or won't read
- Students who are frequently absent

Kay Burke's book *What to Do With the Kid Who...* is an excellent resource for expanding your repertoire of "Plan B" strategies. While there is no one response or action that will work all the time, special educators and reading specialists in your school are walking talking experts on helping struggling, reluctant, and resistant learners. Do not hesitate to drop them a note or an email asking for help.

The next six pages contain actions that practitioners have found productive in working with students who are not learning at the desired rate or level.

Passing Notes

Because many of the students in our co-taught English class are receiving special education services, there is a wide variety of learning differences. We are finding that even with two teachers in the room, we are sometimes outnumbered by the growing demands of student needs. I sometimes leave class feeling unsatisfied because we were not able to get through the planned lesson. I found myself being interrupted by the need for constant verbal or physical cueing to the many students who consistently fall off task.

I came up with a strategy that has turned into a very successful tool. Instead of interrupting the speaker or myself to cue a student, I have started "passing notes." I often walk around the room as I am teaching anyway, but now I walk around the room discreetly putting post-it notes on kids' desks. I was able to find a stack of gray colored post-it notes that are not very obvious so as not to embarrass a student. As I am teaching, or talking , or walking, I can write "Please take your book out" or "We're on page 15" and the point is well taken. I have also been making an effort to put some positive comments down as well.

I have noticed that the students respond to this type of cueing much better. They do not have to be singled out or reprimanded verbally, but can still recognize the urgency or tone through the note. Also, for kids with ADD, the note is a constant reminder on their desks to keep focused. Some kids do not want to be singled out even when they are doing something positive. By discreetly showing them that you are noticing their behavior, kids seem to respond more positively. I am very pleased with the way this has been working out so far and wish to continue and share this with other teachers who feel their lessons are constantly being disrupted.

Suzanne Kisielica, New Trier High School, Winnetka, IL

What to Try with
Students Who Do Not Participate

It is unacceptable for students not to participate, so we need a multitude of strategies for helping them become active members of the learning community. The better we can identify the cause for the lack of participation, the better we can select our intervention. No one of these options is guaranteed to work all the time, but teacher commitment to having all students participate is the first step.

- Use wait time. That is three to five seconds, not three minutes!
- Give choices. "Is it A or B?"
- Ask opinion questions. "If you had to decide which action to take, what would you do/recommend?"
- Repeat question using simpler language.
- Use positive non-verbal encouragement such as nods, smiles, eye contact.
- Have students call on another student by naming that student and repeating the question for that student.
- Use limited number of "I Pass On This One" cards.
- Use slates or signal cards as a means of non-verbal responses.
- Have students work in pairs and report their partner's answer.
- Listen in during small group discussions/work to see if the student is responding/participating in that setting. If so, either you or a student in the group can paraphrase what the student said.
- Interact with the student during small group discussions.
- Conventional wisdom is that questions should be "beamed" to the entire class. With students who tend not to participate, call the name before asking the question as in, "Jose, how did...?" To hold the rest of the class accountable, you can call on another student with a follow-up question such as, "Maria, what variable did he have to analyze to...?"
- Hold private conferences for building relationships, identifying causes of lack of participation, and pinpointing areas of interest or concern of student.
- Following private personal interaction, meet the student at the door and privately say one of the following as appropriate to the situation:
  a. "Here is the answer to #10. I'll call on you to answer it."
  b. "We're going to review Exercise 2B and I am going to ask you to answer #5. Be ready."
  c. "We're going to be doing exercise 2B. Look through it and signal me which one you'll be ready to answer."

What to Try with
Students Who Have Special Needs

All learners have unique learning profiles, but some learners have greater needs than others. Our goal is always to have as many students as possible participate in regular classroom instruction. In fact, it is usually the practice of committees or task forces considering requests for special education placement to ask classroom teachers what strategies have been used to help that learner succeed in the learning process.

If we are committed to educating all students in the least restrictive environment, we need to first identify the ways in which the learning problem is manifesting itself and then have a variety of strategies to consider in planning our interactions and teaching approach with that student. **Many of the reading and writing strategies are extremely useful in working with English Language Learners.**

The strategies listed below are, in fact, strategies that are good for all learners, but they can be absolute lifesavers for students who are struggling. As you read through the lists, you will find that some strategies appear on several lists. Those are the ones that you will want to consider incorporating into your daily practice first.

If Reading is an Issue:
- Use paired reading or Think-Pair-Share to allow students who have difficulty decoding words the opportunity to work with a partner. (See page 98.)
- Provide a variety of books at different reading levels for students to select and read independently.
- Use books on tape, when available, or engage parent volunteers to read with students.
- Provide books at the student's instructional level with pictures and/or diagrams to aid in comprehension of the text.
- Use peer tutoring.
- Ask students to quietly read aloud.
- Teach self-questioning.
- Paraphrase key points and have students paraphrase.
- Summarize key points and have students summarize.
- Use and teach students to use graphic organizers.
- Sequence key points as a reading guide for students.
- Identify main ideas, especially if they are not stated in first sentence of the paragraph.
- Identify 5 W's - who, what, when, where, why.
- Allow highlighting of text passages, key words, or concepts. Use inexpensive transparencies to lay over the page so text is not permanently marked up.

What to Try with
Students Who Have Special Needs

Reading continued...

- Use removable sticker dots to highlight main ideas, key vocabulary words, or other points of interest.
- Preview lessons, chapters, and units with students.
- Teach students to code text.
- Use visual imagery.
- Place wide "whiteout" tape in the margin for students' notes "in the text."
- Use prereading and post reading activities to preteach or reinforce main ideas such as Anticipation Guides and KWL's. (See Chapter IV.)
- Explain idioms that appear in reading passages.
- Provide students with read aloud situations with the class, a partner, a parent, or books on tape.
- Teach text structure.
- Use reciprocal teaching.
- Build in discussion.

If Writing is an Issue:

- Provide computers or Alpha Smart word processors for students who have difficulty with paper and pencil tasks.
- Provide a tape recorder so students can first dictate and record information, then listen to the recorded information and write it down at their own pace.
- Supply students with models and checklists for revisions and editing when given a writing assignment.
- Engage parent volunteers to act as scribes for youngsters with fine motor problems that significantly affect writing output.
- Use oral quizzes or tests in place of written examination.
- Have students dictate ideas to peers.
- Require lists instead of sentences.
- Use Post-It notes for organization.
- Provide note takers.
- Provide students with frequent writing conferences and assistance opportunities with teachers, peers, and parents.
- Provide students computer lab time for composing and/or assistance by scripting their writing.

What to Try with
Students Who Have Special Needs

If Attention is an Issue:

- Set up a space that restricts visual distraction and noises so students can concentrate on their work.
- Break up the task to be completed, and give the student a time frame in which to complete each part of the task.
- Set up an incentive program where the student can gain points toward a reward by accumulating points for tasks completed.
- Pair the student with another student who is task oriented to help the student stay on task.
- Create novel assignments and activities that will grab the student's interest so that he/she will be motivated to complete the task.
- Use proximity to reinforce on task behavior.
- Build in movement within a lesson.
- Teach self-monitoring strategies.
- Help the student set and monitor personal goals.
- Provide opportunities to change tasks or activities more frequently.
- Provide reminder cues or prompts.
- Use private signals to cue appropriate behavior.
- Prepare the learner for changes in routine.
- Use graphic organizers.
- Connect previous learning to new information.
- Use flow charts.
- Use active learning.
- Use cooperative learning.
- Allow students to work with a favorite partner if effort and productivity remain at an increased level.
- Give students some choice of working contexts: individual, whole class, small group, partners, etc.
- Provide frequent feedback.
- Give forced choices such as, "Do A or B."
- Recognize effective effort.

What to Try with
Students Who Have Special Needs

If Organization is an Issue:
- Provide organizers such as color coded pocket folders for each assignment to help the student keep track of the paper work.
- Offer students an organization system, for example a folder with several pockets used only for this task/assessment and help them develop a strategy for using it.
- Pair students with organized peers who will encourage them to keep their work orderly.
- Provide a materials check list of the things necessary to complete a task. Assign a check list buddy to make sure the student has all the items on the list before beginning the task.
- Teach time management skills so the student knows how much time should be allotted to each task.
- Break up the task to be completed and give the student a time frame in which to complete each part of the task.
- Use a calendar for long term assignments. List all the assignments to be completed, then schedule the time needed to accomplish each task in order to meet the deadline.

If Self-Confidence is an Issue:
- Have students give oral reports to you after school and then move to small group presentations.
- Provide frequent reassurance and encouragement.
- Provide advance notice that you are going to call on them.
- Do attribution retraining.

If Social Skills are an Issue:
- Supervise closely during transitions.
- Give guidance and rehearsals.
- Identify "essential" skills and focus on teaching and reinforcing those skills.
- Recognize small steps forward.
- Do mini-lessons in small groups as needed.

Ellen Erekson, G.W. Brown School, Newburyport, MA and Elizabeth Coene, Rogers Middle School, West Irondequoit Central Schools, Rochester, NY suggested many of these strategies.

Where Do I Begin?

Use this page to jot down your reflections and to make a "To Do List" of the actions you want to take to create a learning-centered environment.

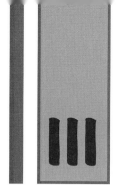

Implementing Instruction
Framing the Learning & Questioning

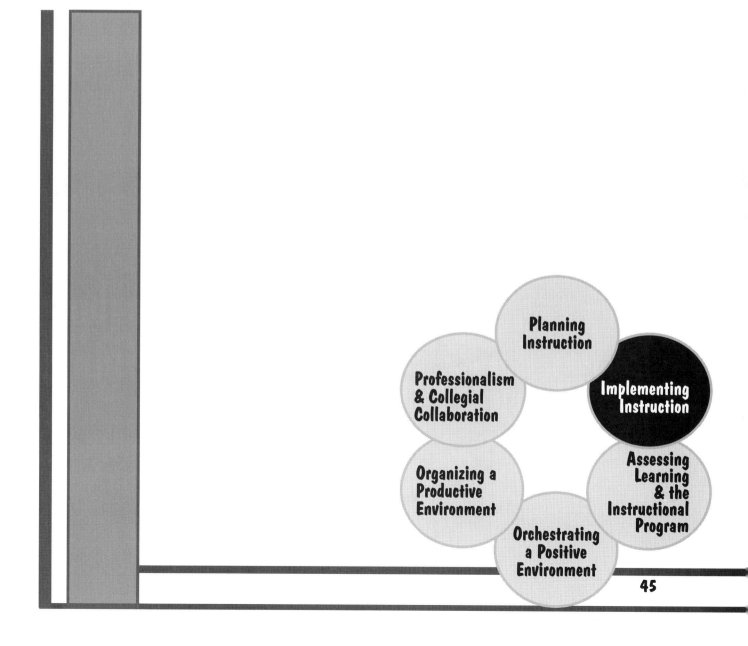

Planning
Instruction

Professionalism
& Collegial
Collaboration

Implementing
Instruction

Organizing a
Productive
Environment

Assessing
Learning
& the
Instructional
Program

Orchestrating
a Positive
Environment

The Best in Print

Instruction for All Students by Paula Rutherford

   The 2002 edition of this book has chapters on presentation modes, including lecture, demonstration, and discussion formats, the use of multiple intelligence theory to design assignments, active learning, thinking skills, and differentiation.

Classroom Instruction that Works by Robert Marzano, Debra Pickering, and Jane Pollock.

   This 2001 book reviews the research on nine instructional strategies that affect student achievement. It also provides brief descriptions of what the strategy looks like in the classroom. The nine strategies are identifying similarities and differences, summarizing and note taking, reinforcing effort and providing recognition, homework and practice, nonlinguistic representations, cooperative learning, setting objectives and providing feedback, generating and text hypotheses, questions, cues and advance organizers.

The Skillful Teacher by Robert Gower and Jon Saphier

   This 1997 book examines the knowledge base on teaching and provides information on instruction in chapters on clarity, learning experiences, models of teaching, and principles of learning.

Points to Ponder...
Some Things Never Change!

A look at research over time reveals that good teaching and learning has been defined the same way for many years! According to a 1988 report, The Institute for Research on Teaching states that:

Good Teachers...

☑ are clear about their instructional goals.

☑ are knowledgeable about their content and the strategies for teaching it.

☑ communicate to their students what is expected of them...and why

☐ make expert use of existing instructional materials in order to devote more time to practices that enrich and clarify the content.

☐ are knowledgeable about their students, able to adapt instruction to their needs and anticipate misconceptions in their existing knowledge.

☑ teach students metacognitive strategies and give them opportunities to master them.

☑ address higher, as well as lower, level cognitive objectives.

☐ monitor students' understanding by offering regular appropriate feedback.

☐ Integrate their instruction with that in other subject areas.

☐ accept responsibility for student outcomes and are thoughtful and reflective about their practice.

These ten points are presented in **"Synthesis of Research on Good Teaching: Insights from the Work of the Institute for Research on Teaching"** in the May 1988 edition of *Educational Leadership.* The five points marked with checks are the focus of this chapter. While all points are addressed throughout this book, in this chapter you will find explicit guidelines for helping students build mental bridges by "**Framing the Learning**" and for **developing questions** that promote student thinking and engagement in the learning process.

Framing the Learning

We seldom start out for an automobile trip without having in mind a destination and a plan for getting there. If only the driver knows the destination and the plan, the passengers are limited in their ability to make the trip alone or to explain it to someone else. The same is true for learners in the classroom. Information is power, so put students in the driver's seat by letting them know where the learning is headed.

Communicate Standards, the Learning Process, & Assessment by
- Explaining what students need to know & be able to do.
- Clarifying why students need to know & be able to do what the standard targets.
- Delineating the activities & assessments students will experience in order to process their learning.
- Articulating how students will demonstrate learning & the criteria to be used for assessment.
- Providing models for processes & products.

We need to clearly articulate these variables at the beginning of the learning experience and provide opportunities for students to translate them into their own words.

Letting students know the desired outcomes in **age appropriate language** is an important part of **Framing the Learning**. Telling students that they will be working on "telling time" or on "solving problems with irrational numbers" is NOT communicating what they are supposed to know and be able to do. It is simply telling them the topic. Instead, we want to say something to the effect of, **"By the time we finish this lesson (or unit) you will know and/or be able to..."**. "We will know that you know that and/or able to do that because you will be assessed by ... ." Many learners also need a rationale for "learning this stuff" and unfortunately, "Because I said so!" is not sufficient reason. In fact, for some students the fact that it is "going to be on the test" is not the least bit motivational. We have to be clear in our own minds about the essential understandings we are asking students to learn. In order to "market and sell" the knowledge and skills we want them to acquire, we also need to be clear how what we are asking them to learn is used in the world beyond academics.

LET STUDENTS KNOW:

WHAT THEY ARE
LEARNING

WHY THEY ARE
LEARNING IT

HOW THEY WILL
LEARN IT

HOW THEY WILL
KNOW THEY KNOW IT

Framing the Learning continued...

Provide the Agenda/Outline for the Day, Unit & Year

Depending on the age of the students the agenda may be written daily on the board or be included in a unit overview packet. An important consideration is explicitly linking whatever appears on the agenda to the learning outcomes as the students engage in the agenda items.

Identify Student Naive Understandings & Misconceptions & Help Students Reframe Their Thinking as Appropriate

Our students are not the only ones with naive understandings and misconceptions about the world around us and how it works. We all have them. Ours may be about how the stock market and the Dow Jones Average are related, how a fax machine works, what a well-to-do neighborhood in New Delhi looks like, or whether it is better to lease or buy a car. When those discussions are going on around us, we often pretend that we know what people are talking about, or we may tune out. If we are reading about something for which we do not have the prior knowledge to fully understand (we may not even know we do not know enough) we may force connections or just skip that part. That is exactly what students do in classrooms. It is essential that we surface those naive understandings and misconceptions or they will hook new learning to inadequate or incorrect knowledge, perhaps without even knowing that they are doing it.

Help Students Access Prior Knowledge & Make Connections
- To past experiences both inside & outside of school
- Between concepts/activities at transitions
- To future areas of study & to life beyond the classroom

Have Students Process, Summarize & Use Learning in Meaningful Ways Which Promote Retention & Transfer

The remaining pages of this chapter and the following chapter entitled "Learning is NOT a Spectator Sport" offer many ways for you to help students surface misconceptions, build on or fine-tune naive understandings, access prior knowledge, and make connections. There are also strategies for having them process, summarize, and use learning in ways that promote retention and transfer.

See Chapter IV "LEARNING IS NOT A SPECTATOR SPORT" for ways to help students make connections!

Framing the Learning continued...

Whether you use demonstrations, discussions, field trips, guest speakers, lectures, multimedia presentations, printed text or any other mode...
This One is NOT Multiple Choice!

In speech-making, the rules of the road are to tell the audience what you are going to say, say it and then tell them what you said. The rules of the road for teaching are to **Frame the Learning** by asking them what they already know, presenting new information, and asking them to make connections as you go and, at the end of the lesson, having them tell you what they have learned and the connections they have made or questions they are pondering.

Marzano, Pickering and Pollock, in their book *Classroom Instruction that Works*, identify nine categories of instructional strategies that have proven to promote student achievement. Several of those categories can be used in the context of **Framing the Learning** at the beginning, during, and at the end of lessons or units. Generating and testing hypotheses, questions, cues and advanced organizers, nonlinguistic representations, summarizing, and note taking are some specific variables to consider when planning how you will **Frame the Learning** for your students.

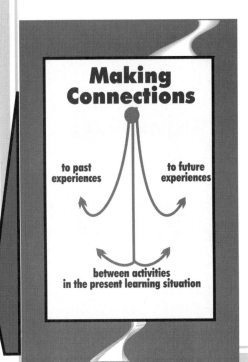

In the Beginning: Making Connections
- Help students recall what they know about the topic to be studied and/or where they have used or learned related information.
- Have students make predictions about the content and give rationales for their predictions.
- Through accessing prior knowledge and preassessments, identify misconceptions and naive understandings and use those as starting points for the learning.
- Work with students to set purposes for study and to generate questions to be answered during the lesson.
- "Beginnings" occur frequently. Each learning session is a new beginning for students even if the topic or area of study is a continuation from the day before.

Framing the Learning continued...

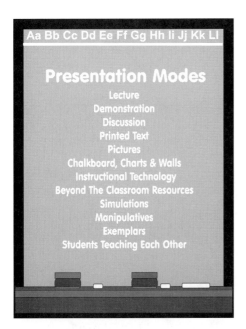

Presentation Modes

Lecture
Demonstration
Discussion
Printed Text
Pictures
Chalkboard, Charts & Walls
Instructional Technology
Beyond The Classroom Resources
Simulations
Manipulatives
Exemplars
Students Teaching Each Other

Presentation of New Information

... via text, videotape, field trip or guest speaker

- Process/summarize at meaningful points. **(Practice 10:2 Theory.)**
- Assess old predictions, make new predictions and/or identify significant information at the processing points.
- Relate new information to prior knowledge.
- Collaboratively generate more questions throughout the lesson.

Wrapping Up: Connection Making and Locking It In

- Process/summarize the whole lesson.
- Evaluate predictions.
- Return to the purposes set for study to see if they were accomplished.
- Identify additional information that would be interesting or helpful.

Implementation Tips:

- These **"making connections"** components are important at the beginning of new units of study, throughout units to build bridges between fragmented learning segments, and at the close of lessons and units. **Do not rush to cover material without having students pause for processing!**

- Use **active learning structures** to help students make connections. See pages 66-106 for descriptions and directions more than three dozen active learning structures.

- See the following pages for suggestions on how to build in processing time in **upper elementary and secondary classrooms.**

PAUSE for PROCESSING: PRACTICE 10:2 & WAIT TIME

51

Now Hear This!

Any time we ask students to **listen to us** when we explain a concept or give directions, we are lecturing. It may last only five minutes, but it is still a **lecturette**. In all teaching and learning experiences it is important to break the learning into **chewable chunks**. In extended instructional periods, often referred to as **block scheduling**, it is absolutely essential to break up the input of new information and provide opportunities for students to make meaning of presented material.

To ensure that learners do the intellectual work of **making meaning** or organizing, summarizing, and integrating the new information with prior knowledge and experiences, include one or more of the following during the learning process.

- **Think-Pair-Share**   Page 98
- **Discussion Partners**   Page 53
- **Processing Time**   Page 222
- **Graphic Organizers**   Pages 119-122
- **Journals**   Pages 81-82
- **Interactive Notebooks**   Pages 83-84
- **Signal Cards**   Pages 184-185
- **Checking for Understanding**   Pages 142-146

We Learn...

10% of what we read
20% of what we hear
30% of what we see
50% of what we both see and hear
70% of what we discuss with others
80% of what we experience personally
90% of what we teach to someone else

William Glasser

When there is lots & lots of information, use
Discussion Partners

One of the easiest ways to ensure that students are attentive and making meaning of the material being presented is to pause for processing. Since 75% of our learners are extroverted thinkers and learn by talking, partner discussions throughout the lecture make a great deal of sense. This process works equally well with lectures, videotapes, and in-class reading sessions.

1. Write a **focus question**, stem or provocative quote on the board or on the overhead. If you work with primary students, an oral question will work. This discussion technique can focus learning, surface prior information and/or promote predictions. You may or may not choose to process in large group or to have students write a summary of their discussions in their journals or interactive notebooks. While you may want to have students share with the large group on occasion to ensure accountability, you would not want to use the time to do it after each small group discussion or you would never have time to present the new material.

2. Present the **first chunk of information.** For secondary students this might run 10 minutes, whereas for elementary students 3 to 5 minutes would probably work best.

3. Give the discussion groups the **first processing/discussion topic** to discuss for 3 to 4 minutes. Possible areas of focus might be for students to summarize, react to, elaborate upon, predict, resolve differences, or hypothesize answers to a question. A fourth grade teacher reading a book to her class might have students fill in a KWL chart during each processing pause.

4. Present the **second chunk of material** or information.

5. Give the small groups a **second processing/discussion topic.**

6. Continue **presentation chunks and discussions** until finished.

7. Give the students a **final processing focus.** The purpose of this closure discussion is for students to process and make connections between the bits of information presented in the lecture and hook them all onto their own mental hooks.

To ensure that students are discussing what you want them to discuss, you may need to model, to circulate and listen in. Additionally, you may want to call on one or two pairs occasionally to share with the class what they have been discussing.

adapted from *Leading the Cooperative School*, Johnson and Johnson.

Using Questioning to Promote Meaning Making...
Don't leave it to chance or textbook publishers!
Words of Wisdom on Questioning

A Japanese teacher when asked what she and her colleagues talked about when they discussed improving their teaching practices said,

"A great deal of time is spent talking about questions we can pose to the class...which wordings work best to get students involved in thinking and discussing the material. One good question can keep a whole class going for a long time; a bad one producing little more than a simple answer."

Stevenson and Steigler go on to say, "In the United States curriculum planners, textbook publishers, and teachers themselves seem to believe that students learn more effectively if they solve a large number of problems rather than if they concentrate their attention on only a few. The emphasis is on doing rather than on thinking. American teachers place a high premium on their ability to cover a large number of problems, and may regard that as the mark of an expert teacher. In a study comparing expert versus novice elementary school teachers in the United States, expert teachers were found to cover many more mathematics problems in a single lesson than novice teachers did, suggesting that with experience teachers grow more adept at getting students to cover a large amount of material. Contrast this with Japan and Taiwan, where teachers concentrate so intently on only a few problems.

Covering only a few problems does not mean that a lesson turns out to be short on content. In fact, this does not appear to be the case. When many problems are covered, the same mathematical content tends to be repeated with each new problem; when fewer problems are presented, *there is time for the kind of discussion that transforms the solution of problems from something that must be memorized to something that is understood."*

The Learning Gap, Stevenson and Steigler

An essential skill of teaching is the skill of planning and using purposeful questions. On the following pages there is a brief overview of when and why we ask questions as well as thought provoking stems and tools used by the elementary teachers in West Irondequoit Central School District, Rochester, New York, and some examples of Bloom's Taxonomy in action. The use of Bloom's Taxonomy to plan questions and learning experiences has taken on new importance as we design learning experiences to be rehearsals for the level of understanding required by the standards of the state and district.

When & Why We Ask Questions

The obvious reason we ask questions is to assess comprehension/check for understanding...or at least knowledge about the topic, concept, or information under study. It is, however, considerably more complicated than that. While we want to be masters at checking for understanding, the results of carefully planned questions actually provide direction to the flow of learning and promote a productive classroom learning environment, which actually facilitates comprehension, transfer, and retention. The list below provides an extensive array of purposes of questions. Until we have a mental script in our heads, we need to write out the questions which will facilitate the learning process.

We Use Questions At the Beginning of Learning Experiences:

- To initiate a discussion
- To pique student curiosity
- To focus students on a new concept or a different aspect of a concept
- To access prior knowledge and experience
- To consolidate previous learning
- To surface misconceptions

We Use Questions During and Following Learning Experiences:

- To break down complex tasks and issues
- To promote transfer and retention
- To control shifts in discussions
- To keep discussions on track
- To invite student questions
- To elicit student opinions
- To promote student interaction
- To facilitate flexible thinking
- To challenge the obvious
- To check for understanding
- To help student confront their misconceptions and reframe their thinking
- To focus on process
- To promote student evaluation of credibility of sources and strength of evidence
- To cause students to consider alternative viewpoints
- To help students make connections

Getting Started
with Important Questions
which promote student thinking

- What do you need to do next?
- Based on what you know, what can you predict about ...?
- Does what ... said make you think differently about ...?
- Tell me how you did that?
- How does ... tie in with what we have learned before?
- Suppose ... what then?
- How does this match what you thought you knew?
- What might happen if ...?
- When have you done something like this before?
- What might ... think about this?
- How would you feel if...?
- How did you come to that conclusion?
- How about...?
- What if ...?
- What do you think causes ...?
- Yes, that's right, but how did you know it was right?
- When is another time you need to...?
- What do you think the problem is?
- Can you think of another way we could do this?
- Why is this one better than that one?
- How can you find out?
- How is ... different (like) ...?
- What have you heard about..?
- Can you tell me more?
- What else do you see?
- How does that compare with...?
- What do we know so far?

West Irondequoit's
Extended Thinking Program

West Irondequoit Central School District, Rochester, NY, has developed an Extended Thinking Skills program for use in the elementary grades. The program is based on Bloom's Taxonomy and on the beliefs that:

- **Thinking abilities can be developed.**
- **Efforts to improve thinking should involve all students.**
- **Because of the developmental nature of thinking abilities, the improvement of thinking should be addressed throughout the grades and should begin in primary classrooms.**
- **Thinking is fundamental to all students and should be addressed with each content area.**
- **Teaching thinking within content areas improves the quality of student thinking and promotes deeper understanding of content materials.**

A district task force designed developmentally appropriate Thinking Wheels for use by teachers and students in grades K-6. The wheels are a consistent tool that provides a comprehensive overview of levels of thinking. An enlarged version is posted in each classroom and the students use a blank wheel to analyze their thinking at the end of lessons. As the students move through the grades, the descriptors at each level of thinking becomes more extensive, building on the work in previous years.

The task force translated the levels of Bloom's Taxonomy to "Kid Language."		
Knowledge	Find!	Recall specific ideas and information
Comprehension	Understand!	Understand ideas, meanings, and information
Application	Use!	Apply information, ideas, and principles in new situations
Analysis	Break down!	Break down information into its parts
Synthesis	Create!	Put together parts to make a whole and do something new with the information
Evaluation	Judge!	Judge the value or ideas, purposes, and methods

Students in Grades K-6 list on the Thinking Wheel several times a week the ways they have engaged in the various levels of thinking during their learning experiences.

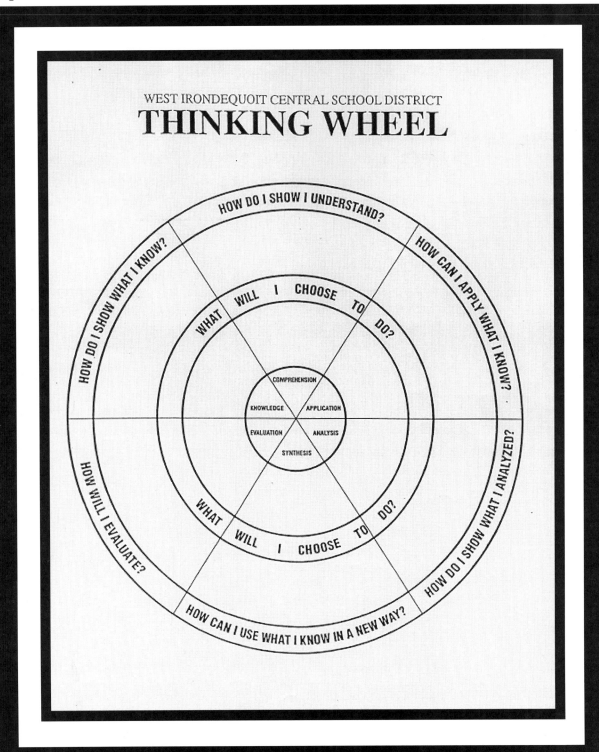

Reprinted with permission of West Irondequoit Central School District, Rochester, NY

Through the Voice of...Extending Thinking/Rigor
Five Brave Explorers: Chapter One

Second Grade

Knowledge/Comprehension	Application/Analysis	Synthesis/Evaluation
Create either a linear or pictorial time line.	Create a Venn diagram to compare life now to life then or to compare Esteban and Columbus.	Write to the Governor of Mexico requesting Esteban's freedom and give reasons he should be freed.
Use a map to trace the events. List three facts about each place.	Read page five. Then write three to four predictions. Read the rest of the chapter. Note when you were right or wrong. Give events and page numbers.	Imagine an escape plan. How is it managed? Where would he go? How would he survive?
Make a coloring book with at least seven pages. Use a sentence on each page to describe the event.	Do a mock interview of Esteban. Write his remarks. or Pretend you are Esteban and keep a diary. Include facts and feelings.	Act out someone requesting Esteban's freedom. Justify your response by using puppets or by acting it out.

Carolyn Vanderberg, Mary Kalinowski, Cathi Kwit, and Carol Kress, West Irondequoit Central Schools, Rochester, NY

Bloom's Taxonomy
Question & Task Design Wheel

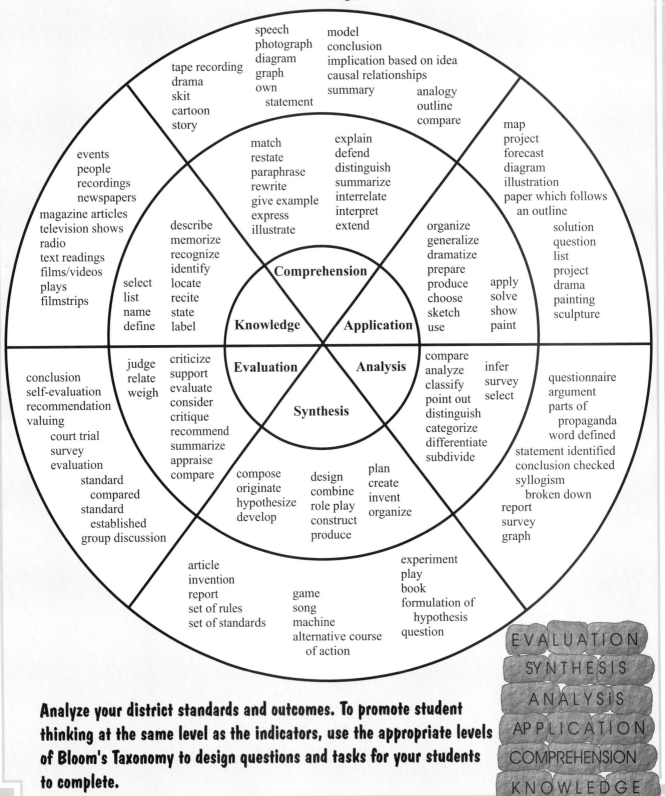

Analyze your district standards and outcomes. To promote student thinking at the same level as the indicators, use the appropriate levels of Bloom's Taxonomy to design questions and tasks for your students to complete.

EVALUATION
SYNTHESIS
ANALYSIS
APPLICATION
COMPREHENSION
KNOWLEDGE

Where Do I Begin?

Use this page to jot down your reflections and to make a "To Do List" of the actions you want to take to ensure that you frame the learning for learners and develop questions at levels of thinking matched to the district standards.

IV

Implementing Instruction
Learning is **NOT** a Spectator Sport!

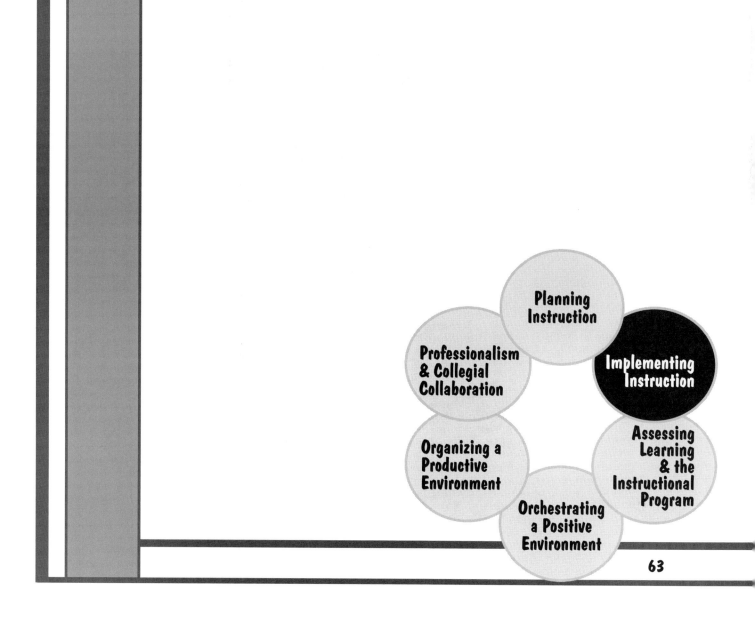

Planning Instruction

Professionalism & Collegial Collaboration

Implementing Instruction

Organizing a Productive Environment

Assessing Learning & the Instructional Program

Orchestrating a Positive Environment

The Best in Print

Instruction for All Students by Paula Rutherford
> The 2002 edition of this book has information on active learning, an extensive listing of products, roles, and audiences students can address, the use of multiple intelligence theory to design lessons, thinking skills for the 21st century, and building in student choice.

Inspiring Active Learning by Merrill Harmin
> This ASCD book is a handbook of active learning strategies, tips for setting up the classroom, and for communicating high expectations.

Activators and ***Summarizers*** by Jon Saphier and Mary Ann Haley
> These two books from RBT are written in a teacher-friendly way with reproducibles provided for many of the active learning structures.

Points to Ponder...
"Beyond Who Can Tell Me?"

"No matter how well planned, how interesting, stimulating, colorful, or relevant the lesson, if the teacher does all the interacting with the material, the teacher's... not the student's brain will grow."

Pat Wolfe

One of the most frequently used teaching strategies is the **Whole Class Question-Answer** strategy. The steps are as follows:

1. The teacher asks a question.
2. Students who wish to respond raise their hands.
3. The teacher calls on one student.
4. The student attempts to state the correct answer.

Recognize it? It often starts with "Who can tell me...?" Since this strategy, also known as a **recitation,** is used so frequently, it is important that we ask ourselves just how effective it is. The bad news about this strategy is that the teacher is really the only one in the classroom actively engaged with all the questions and answers; many students may be simply putting in seat time while a few students answer the questions. For those students who are not auditory learners, the recitation may serve as background noise while they visualize who knows what. **When we use it, we really are making learning a spectator sport.**

Fortunately there are many alternatives to **Whole Class Question-Answer a.k.a. "Who can tell me...?"** If we really want to engage learners, create a brain compatible classroom, communicate high expectations, and check for understanding, there are literally hundreds of ways to engage all learners in the process. The next 40 pages explain the rationale for several of these strategies and provide directions for their use, as well as examples of how they have been implemented in the classroom.

Aa Bb Cc Dd Ee Ff Gg Hh Ii Jj

Active Learning Strategies to Use
If You Want...

Students to work in pairs
Think-Pair-Share - 98
Learning Links - 88
Learning Buddies - 246
Reciprocal Teaching - 133
Discussion Partners - 53

Students to work in small groups
Teammates Consult (Kagan, 1994) - 97
Reciprocal Teaching - 133
Graffiti - 79
Numbered Heads Together (Kagan, 1994)- 90
Sort Cards - 93-95
Consensus Conclusions - 76

To gather preassessment data
Anticipation Reaction Guide - 68
Signal Cards - 144-145
Sort Cards - 93-95
Frame of Reference - 78
Line-Ups (Kagan, 1994) - 89
Think-Pair-Share - 98

Stir the Class - 96
Journals - 81-82
Three Column Charts - 100
Graffiti - 79

Students to access prior knowledge
Anticipation Reaction Guide - 68
Corners (Kagan, 1994) - 77
Stir the Class - 96
Frame of Reference - 78
Line-Ups (Kagan, 1994) - 89
Think-Pair-Share - 98

Three Column Charts - 100
Journals - 81-82
Word Splash - 123, 125
Graffiti - 79
Learning Links - 88

To surface misconceptions and naive understandings
Anticipation Reaction Guide - 68
Journals - 81-82
Three Column Charts - 100
Frame of Reference - 78
Line-Ups (Kagan, 1994) - 89
Think-Pair-Share - 98

Active Learning Strategies to Use
If You Want...

Students to set purpose for reading, listening or viewing

Learning Links - 88
Walking Tour - 105
Three Column Charts - 100
Corners (Kagan, 1994) - 77
Line-Ups (Kagan, 1994) - 89
Word Splash - 123, 125

Journals - 81-82
Anticipation Reaction Guide - 68

Students summarize their learning

3-2-1 - 99
Ticket to Leave - 104
Journals - 81-82
Interactive Notebooks - 83
Reciprocal Teaching - 133
ABC to XYZ - 106

Discussions over Time and Place - 101
Biopoems - 71
Learning Links - 88
Scavenger Hunt - 91
Consensus Conclusions - 76
Collection Connection - 72-74

To check for understanding

Signal Cards - 144-145
Ticket to Leave - 104
Journals - 81-82
Sort Cards - 93-95
Scavenger Hunt - 91
Line-Ups (Kagan, 1994) - 89

3-2-1 - 99
It's All in the Cards - 85-86
Slates - 146
Numbered Heads Together(Kagan, 1994) - 90

To have students "handle" their learning

It's All in the Cards - 85-86
    Tic-Tac-Toe
    I Have the Question, Who Has the Answer?
Connection Collection 72-74
Sort Cards - 93-95
Inside-Outside Circles (Kagan, 1994) - 87

To build in movement

Scavenger Hunt - 91
Stir the Class - 96
Graffiti - 79
Consensogram - 75
Line-Ups (Kagan, 1994) - 89
Simulations - 101

Walking Tour - 105
Learning Buddies - 246
Corners (Kagan, 1994) - 77
Inside-Outside Circles (Kagan, 1994) - 87

Anticipation Reaction Guide

Anticipation Reaction Guide, developed by Bean and Peterson, can be completed in its usual written form or students who cannot yet read can signal with hand signs or signal cards which of the statements they think is true or false.

Purpose:
- To establish a purpose for reading
- To access prior knowledge
- To help students reframe their thinking as necessary

Process:
- Prepare a series of statements related to the reading or other input source.
- Have students, before reading, indicate whether they think the statement is true or false.
- Have students read the selection or watch the video or demonstration.
- Have students, after reading, answer the same questions again.
- Have students discuss where they found the information that changed their thinking.

Earthquakes
Anticipation Reaction Guide

Before Reading		After Reading
_____ 1.	Earthquake experts are called meteorologists.	1._____
_____ 2.	Most earthquakes happen along a fault.	2._____
_____ 3.	California has 5-10 earthquakes each year.	3._____
_____ 4.	Most earthquakes are felt by humans.	4._____
_____ 5.	The San Andreas Fault stretches 600 miles and is located in California.	5._____
_____ 6.	Scientist estimate that a huge earthquake will occur in California within the next 25 years.	6._____
_____ 7.	Earthquake drills occur in southern California schools.	7._____
_____ 8.	Missouri has suffered more major earthquakes than California.	8._____

Chemistry
Anticipation Reaction Guide

Directions:

1. Respond to each statement before you read.　T=true　F=false

2. Read section B.9, page 11.5.

3. Respond to each statement after you read.　T=true　F=false

4. Rewrite the statements that are false so that they are true.

Before Reading　　　　　　　　　　　　　　　　　**After Reading**

_____1.　Many properties of elements are determined largely by the number of protons in their atoms and how these protons are arranged.　_____

_____2.　Metal atoms lose their outer electrons more easily than do nonmetal atoms.　_____

_____3.　Active metals can give up one or more of their electrons to ions of less-active metals.　_____

_____4.　Stronger attractions among atoms of a metal result in higher boiling points.　_____

_____5.　Understanding the properties of atoms does not help to predict and correlate the behavior of materials.　_____

Cholesterol

Lynn Hiller, New Trier High School, Winnetka, IL

69

Biopoems

Biopoems provide students an opportunity to make personal connections with any character or concept studied. Provide K-12 students with the following guidelines so that they can create a personal representation of the material studied. See examples on the following page.

Line one   First Name

Line Two   Three or four adjectives that describe the person/object

Line Three   Important relationship (daughter of..., mother of..., etc.)

Line Four   Two or three things, people, or ideas that the person/object loved/was attracted to

Line Five   Three feelings the person experienced

Line Six   Three fears the person experienced

Line Seven   Accomplishments (who composed..., who discovered..., etc.)

Line Eight   Two or three things the person wanted to see happen or wanted to experience

Line Nine   His or her residence

Line Ten   Last name

B.S. Abaromitis. "Bringing Lives to Life: Biographies in Reading and the Content Areas" *Reading Today*. June/July 1994

Biopoems

Para

Opposite sides & angles equal, no line of symmetry
Relative of square, rectangle & rhombus
Love to rotate
Feel slanted left & right most of the time, need kite by my side
Fear being stretched out of shape
Give square & rectangle all my properties
Would like to see rhombus, my child
Resident of Quadrilateral

Llelogram

Chua Guat Kheng, Raffles Girls' Secondary School, Singapore

Harry

Magic, Young, Friendly
Friend of Hermione
Quidditch, Hedwig the Owl
Happy, Sad, Scared
Slytherin, Malfoy, Lord Voldemort
Winning the House Cup for Gryffindor
Win at Quidditch, Not get Hagrid in trouble
Hogwarts

Potter

Written by Mike Rutherford, representing all nine year olds around the world

Connection Collections

Purposes
- to help students make personal meaning
- to connect learning to life beyond the classroom
- to promote creative thinking

Process
- Either the teacher or the students collect objects that represent literal or metaphorical connections to the content under study and place them in a bag, baggie, or box.
- Students identify the connections between the items and the content under study or make predictions about an upcoming study.
- The objects can be pictures or actual artifacts.
- Optional: Prepare five bags of five objects and call it "Facts in Five."

Examples

• THE RENAISSANCE
Joanne Fusare White, Rush-Henrietta School District, Henrietta, New York, introduced the idea to her middle school students by preparing bags of artifacts connected to important people from the Renaissance. She used these bags combined with short readings about each person to provide information on figures such as Michelangelo, the Medicis, and Leonardo de Vinci. Students were given a purpose for reading and were able to speculate about the meaning of the objects as they learned new material.

• BOOKS IN A BAG
Linda Denslow, second grade teacher, Rush-Henrietta, New York used **Connection Collections** as a culminating activity for the books and stories she and her students had read during the year. She created a model connections bag for one of the stories, then asked students to choose a favorite story for which to create a bag. She wrote the directions so she could keep the bags to use the next year when she introduced each story.

• PHOETRY (photo poetry)
A third grade teacher in Chapel Hill, North Carolina, had her students create connections or artifacts bags as a prewriting assignment at the conclusion of a unit on poetry. They were given small brown bags and were asked to return the next day with a picture and two other items in the bag that related to the picture but were not actually in the picture. The students then wrote their poems about the item and the picture.

Biography in a Bag

You are a member of a team of anthropologists studying the leaders of the Renaissance/Reformation. You and your team are to collect artifacts representing significant information about your leader to place in a Biography Bag. All data will be documented in your individual journals. Each team on the expedition is responsible for gathering the data on one leader. The leader for which your team is responsible will be identified by the Expedition Leader. The leaders to be studied are as follows:

- Leonardo da Vinci
- Martin Luther
- Queen Elizabeth I
- John Calvin
- Raphael
- Michelangelo Buonarroti
- William Shakespeare
- Henry VIII
- Niccolo Machiavelli

Research findings are to include:
- Information about your leader as a person.
- Information about your leader as a leader.
- Information about your leader as a person influenced by the time in which he or she lived.
- Information about how your leader not only influenced his or her own country, but how he or she had an impact on another region of the world.

In your teams, you are to conduct a basic study that should yield at least six important facts about your leader. Use readily available resources, such as your library available here in our home office (a.k.a. your classroom). After you identify the important facts, document them in your journals and then locate an artifact that describes/relates to each of the facts you have identified. The artifacts might be a painting, drawing, a piece of jewelry, etc. Once again, document the artifacts and their relationship to the important information about your leader in your journals and place the artifacts in your Biography Bag.

It is now time to do research beyond the confines of the home office. You may choose to visit other establishments that contain printed material about your

Through the Voice of...
Biography in a **Bag** continued...

leader, or you may decide to sail along the World Wide Web. In any case, you are to identify ten more significant bits of information about your Renaissance or Reformation leader, and then locate an artifact to support each of these new tidbits. Once again, place the information you identified in your individual journals and the artifacts in your team bag.

When you have gathered all sixteen of the artifacts and placed them in your Biography Bag, as well as recorded the information about the leader and the artifacts in your journals, it is time for each team member to write a brief report. This typed report should be one page long. It, and each of your journals, will be submitted to the Expedition Leader.

As the final step in preparation for your presentation, please decorate the Biography Bag to represent your leader.

After all the written reports are submitted, the teams will come together and present information about their leaders using only the artifacts in the Biography Bags to guide the presentations. These presentations will be made to the Expedition Leader and the other teams.

This Collection Connection in a RAFT format was designed by Tami Loftus, Global History teacher, Rush-Henrietta High School, Rush-Henrietta Central School District, Henrietta, NY. See page 102 for information on RAFT.

Consensogram

Have learners place a Post-it note next to the percentage that represents how much they think they currently know about the subject under consideration. An alternative use is to ask how much they like something or what percentage of the class they predict knows, thinks, likes, etc. Young children could use 8" x 11" pieces of paper to make a bar graph on the floor or they could simply line up in columns to create a human bar graph.

100%

90%

80% ☐

70%

60%

50% ☐ ☐ ☐

40%

30%

20% ☐ ☐ ☐ ☐ ☐

10% ☐ ☐

0% ☐

Consensus Conclusions

Facts in Five

- Have students individually generate a personal list of the five most important concepts or facts they have learned about the topic being studied.

- Have students move into groups of five.

- Have the group reach consensus on the five most important facts or concepts and clarify their rationale for selecting each.

- Have each group present their selections and the rationale for each selection to the larger group.

- Lead a discussion about the content identified, the similarities and differences and about the process.

- If time is short, post the choices on the bulletin board for later examination.

1-3-6

- Have students follow the same sequence as in Facts in Five but after they work individually, have them move to groups of three and then to groups of six.

- This format takes longer, but may be most effective if students have little experience with building consensus. In fact, you could start with 1-2-4 to help students learn how to talk with each other about the rationale for including certain concepts.

- Students could complete the "1" component as homework in preparation for the discussions the next day.

Formative Assessment Note: This is a great way to gather formative assessment data about the connections students are making, about the levels of thinking they are doing, and about the clues they are picking up from you about what is important.

1 Corners

Process

- Pose a question that has multiple answers or asks students to rank order several options.

- Give students time to consider their own thinking about the topic; then have them move to the corner of the room that has been designated as the meeting place of all those holding the same opinion or view.

- In the corner meeting places, have students discuss why they think or believe the way they do. If the groups are large, have students divide into pairs or triads so that all can voice their opinions and their rationales.

- As appropriate, have selected students or volunteers report for their corner. Large group sharing can be oral or the corner groups can generate and share charts listing their rationales for choosing that particular answer/viewpoint.

- This exercise can be followed by presentation of new material, by journal entries, or research exercises.

Sample Topics

- CEOs of major corporations salaries should be... Post alternative amounts, ratios, and rationales for setting salaries

- Which character in the book would you most like to meet?

- What volleyball skill would you most like to develop?

- If you were the leader of your country/state, which issue would be your top priority...A, B, C, or D?

- Favorite season

- Most interesting/important biome

- How strongly do you agree or disagree with the statement, "All forms of violence should be censored on television"?

- Post the names of four inventions. Have students decide which is most significant?

- Post the names of four historical figures. Have students decide who changed the world the most?

Corners 2

4 Corners

Corners 3

Frame of Reference

Purpose
These initial notations help students surface prior knowledge or related experiences. They are also helpful to the teacher in understanding where students are coming from as they start studying new material.

Process
- The **topic or issue** to be discussed is placed in the center of the matted frame where a picture would be placed in a picture frame.

- Students are given several minutes to individually jot down **words or phrases** that come to mind when they hear or see the term "pictured." These words go in the "mat" area of their frame of reference.

- Students are then asked to jot down how they came to know what they know or think...that is the sources, people, events that have **influenced their thinking.** These reactions go in the "frame" area of the graphic.

- Following the individual reflection and writing, students are asked to share their "frames of reference" with a partner or a small group.

Variations
A variation of **Frame of Reference** can be used to process learning by having students place the name of a historical character in the center. The students then jot down how this person would describe his or her own life and times, and then the events and people who influenced his or her thinking. Assigning different students different persons/perspectives can lead to powerful "in the voice of " discussions when the historical frames of references are completed.

Frame of Reference can also be used as an introductory and community building exercise. Students put their own names in the center, describe themselves, and then cite those people and events that have shaped their thinking and lives.

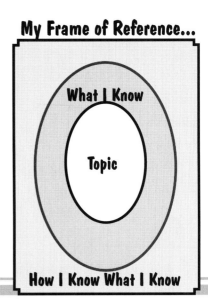

My Frame of Reference...

What I Know

Topic

How I Know What I Know

Graffiti

Process

- Write problems, formulas, sentences to be translated, ideas to brainstorm on pieces of large chart paper, and post them around the room. Students move in small groups from chart to chart.

   or

- Give each piece of chart paper to a group of three or four. Students work at their tables and the charts move from table to table. Kathy Anderson of New Trier High School, Winnetka, Illinois, calls this version **Ready...Rotate.**

   In either case,

- each group works on a different question, topic, issue, or statement related to the concept being studied and writes responses or "graffiti" which can be short words, phrases, or graphics on their chart paper.

- After the allotted time period, have the students or the charts move.

- Repeat the process until all groups have reacted to all charts.

- Post the charts and have students react to the statements or topics, identify patterns, and/or make predictions based on what is written/drawn on the charts.

Variations

- This strategy can be used any time during a lesson or unit. At the beginning, you and your students can find out what they already know and can do; in the middle of a lesson, it is a useful way for you and them to check on their learning. At the end of study, it can serve as a great review for an exam or even for predicting what might be on the exam.

- Individuals or groups can use different color markers to track contributions.

Chemical Graffiti

- Divide students into groups of 3 or 4.
- Place 5 or 6 multi-process chemical problems on separate sheets of paper. Post the charts around the room or spread problems around the table. Each group will eventually work each of the problems.
- Have each group work on a problem for 90 seconds and then rotate clockwise to the next problem on the cue.
- When a group comes to a new problem, the students check the work of the previous group, make any needed changes, and continue with the problem.
- Have students initial all work and final answers they believe to be correct.
- Students may cycle through problems 2 or 3 times as appropriate.
- As appropriate, use the completed problems to review the concepts under study.

Tim Taylor, Jennings County High School, North Vernon, IN

Amazing Adjectives Graffiti

Students essentially created their own Word Wall with this exercise.
- Post five pieces of chart paper with one of the following five words in the center of each: **Water, Apple, House, Dog and Alien.**
- Have students then move around the room in small groups and write adjectives that might be used to describe each noun.

Results included:
- **For water:** cool, clear, icy, cold, hot, bubbling, dirty, cloudy, fast, meandering, blue, shimmering, beautiful, muddy, deep.
- **For dog:** big, small brown, black, friendly, gruff, aggressive, scary, loud, quiet, happy, sad, grumpy, wild, sleek, funny, gross, hungry.

Shared by a teacher from the International School of Beijing, Beijing, China

Journals

There is a strong emphasis in 21st century for integrating literacy across the curriculum. The use of journals supports that initiative. Journals may be kept in hard copy or on computers.

Possible uses of journals in any classroom are:

🖊 To record daily thinking and learning...aha's and questions, implications, general musings

🖊 To prepare for discussions...questions, key ideas, etc.

🖊 To summarize lessons and ideas...such as 3-2-1 or "As a result of today, I..."

🖊 As an alternative to homework assignments when unclear as how to proceed

🖊 To make predictions about next steps, rationales, effects of actions

🖊 To identify and solve problems

🖊 To make connections to prior learning and/or life beyond the classroom

🖊 To respond to discussions, printed text, videos, demonstrations or lectures

🖊 To generate possible topics for research

🖊 To let off steam

🖊 To set priorities and schedules

🖊 To record and evaluate study habits, efforts, and academic progress

🖊 Alternatives to "journal writing," such as creating graphic organizers, pictures, poems, charts, etc.

🖊 As an interactive notebook

The use of journals appeals to the verbal/linguistic and intrapersonal learners. It may be that journaling may open learning avenues in content areas which are usually presented in a more logical/sequential manner. See pages 82-83 for further information on how to integrate writing into all content areas. See *Instruction for All Students* pages 129 and pages 224-226 for more ideas.

Journals continued...

📖 **First Thoughts!** Write down thoughts that come to mind when you examine the cover of a book, the illustrations in a article, the name of a video, or the announced topic of a speaker. Jotting down initial thoughts helps you set purpose for learning and make predictions about what you will find in the information source.

📖 **Practice 10:2 Theory!** Pause every ten minutes or so at logical stopping points and write down your reactions. Write for two or three minutes before continuing so that you capture your thinking as you learn rather than waiting until you have completed the practice set, book, or article. This pause for processing helps you remember more than you would if you waited until the end to analyze and reflect.

📖 **Make Connections!** What are the connections you make as you study this information? The connections you make can be to your own life, to other texts or problems you have solved, or to the world beyond the classroom.

📖 **Question!** What surprises you? What makes you want to consult other sources? How is what you are learning not aligned with what you thought you knew? Such questions can frame your learning as you continue. What is puzzling in the moment may become an "aha" a few minutes later. When you are unable to continue with homework because you do not know how to proceed, write down the questions and possibilities you are considering.

📖 **Take a Stand!** Interact with the text or other source by creating a dialogue journal. Write about the points with which you agree and disagree; support those positions with evidence from the source and from your own life experiences. You might choose to pretend that you are someone else taking a stand on the issues or ideas under consideration and write your comments "through the voice of ..." that person.

📖 **Perspective!** Identify the speaker's or author's point of view. Write about how this perspective influences the development of the plot or the way in which information is presented. In what ways are the belief systems or attitudes of the writer or speaker influencing the points selected for emphasis as well as the use of language? How might the same information or same story be different if told from a another point of view?

Interactive Notebooks

One of the most exciting innovations to promote student processing of new learning is the **Interactive Notebook**, described in Addison Wesley's *History Alive!* and widely used by teachers of history and other social sciences. The uses of the **Interactive Notebook** extend to all areas of study and to all ages because the structure and potential contents capture the essence of active participation, multiple intelligences, and the variables of the brain-compatible classroom.

To get started with the **Interactive Notebook** process, ask students fourth grade or older to purchase and bring to class each day an 8-1/2" by 11" inch spiral notebook with at least one hundred pages, as well as a container holding a pen, a pencil with an eraser, at least two felt tip pens of different colors, and at least two highlighters of different colors. Other desirable equipment includes a small pair of scissors and a glue stick. If the cost is prohibitive for some students, create classroom supply kits. For younger students, the pages can be collected in a portfolio and later bound into a book.

Teach students productive methods of note taking during lectures, readings, or other presentations, and have them record their notes on the **RIGHT** side of their notebooks. Encourage them to vary size of letters, boldness of letters, the use of upper and lower case letters, indentations, underlining, and bullets. If a well-designed worksheet is necessary, simply have the students use a glue stick to attach it to the right side of their notebook.

The **LEFT** side of the notebook is reserved for student processing of the information recorded on the **RIGHT** side. Students can be asked to review and preview, draw maps, think of a time when..., summarize in a sentence, create graphic organizers, create a metaphor, respond to what if questions, take a stand, etc. Additionally, encourage them to add newspaper clippings or political cartoons, drawings and illustrations, or other such personal touches. The use of color and visual effects is highly encouraged! The **LEFT,** or processing side, can be completed in class or as **homework.**

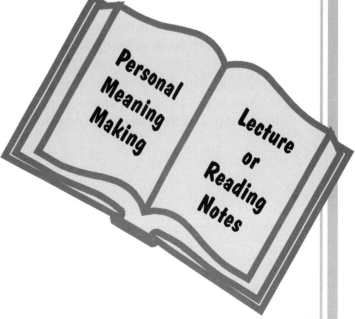

Interactive Notebooks continued...

It is difficult for teachers to collect exemplars of interactive notebooks because students become so attached to them. They are no longer simply a set of class or reading notes but a scrapbook of personal meaning. They are the makings of the "memory drawers" that parents keep for their children.

Interactive Notebooks in Action

Interactive notebooks provide a wonderful transition from one grade to another. In Virginia where the Standards of Learning assessments at the **middle school** level cover multiple years in social studies and science, teachers collect the interactive notebooks from seventh grade and pass them on to the eighth grade science and social studies teachers. The materials for a cumulative review are already prepared...by the students.

Stephanie Bice, who teaches **English 10** in Greece Central School District, Greece, New York, assigned her students an interactive notebook for their reading of **Animal Farm.** Students were directed to reflect, clarify, predict and pose questions at approximately twenty page intervals during their reading. Additionally they kept a character log, selected ten quotes of significance to them and did a book reflection. The essential question given to focus the reading was, "How and when are the same kind of things happening every day around me?" Students interacted with their notes by connecting the character log, the quotes and the book reflections to poems, songs, people or events of their lifetime and by drawing pictures or symbols and making collages to represent the connections.

The **second grade students** of Michelle Korn, Mary Jo Fichtner, and Shannon Zimmerman at Autumn Lane Elementary School in Greece Central School District, New York, study poetry throughout the school year. For each poem they read or write, they illustrate their interpretation of it. The teachers collect the student work and hold it for the end of the year when they put together a poetry notebook. This process is a combination portfolio/interactive notebook because they not only have their poetry collection, they have interacted with each poem.

It's All in the Cards

Once you or the students have prepared cards with vocabulary words or problems with matching definitions, solutions, examples or translations, you can use them in a multiple of ways. You can use pictures with primary-age learners.

I Have the Question, Who Has the Answer?

Purposes
- Review concepts through active participation.
- Heighten attention and engagement of all students.

Materials
- Prepare two sets of index cards or slips of paper approximately 3" x 5". One set contains questions related to the unit of study. The second set contains the answer to the questions.
- To keep students engaged, prepare more answer cards than question cards.
- To promote cumulative review and connections between units of study, on occasion, mix in key concepts, events, or terms from previous units.

Process
- Distribute answer cards to students.
- Place a stack of question cards face down in the middle of each of the student tables.
- Designate a student to start the process of turning over a question card. The students says, "The question is...Who has the answer?"
- All students check their answer cards to see if they have the correct answer or a possible one. If the student thinks he/she has an answer, she reads the answer. If it is a match, the student with the answer turns over the next card, reads the question aloud, and the process continues.

See pages 93-94 on "Sort Cards" for more ways to have students "handle" their learning and make connections through the use of index cards.

It's All in the Cards continued...

Tic-Tac-Toe

Tic-Tac-Toe

Tic-Tac-Toe

Free Market System	Gross National Product	International Monetary Fund
Zaibatsu	Democratic Socialism	Good Neighbor Policy
Five Year Plans	Cartels	Capitalism

Purpose

To have students go beyond memorizing definitions and to look for patterns and **connections** embedded in the vocabulary words and concepts being studied.

Process

- Place, or have students place, vocabulary words or important concepts on **index cards.**
- Give each student or group a set of cards.
- Have students shuffle their cards and deal out nine cards in a **3x3 format.**
- Ask students to form eight sentences each, including the three words straight across in a **row**, straight down in a **column**, or on the **diagonals.**
- Have the students or groups share the sentences that capture important **connections**, or "misconnections," between words and concepts being studied.

Inside-Outside Circles

Process
- On index cards, write vocabulary words, math or science problems, or questions about important points in the unit. Give a card to each student. Have students turn the cards over and write the answer to their question on the back of the card.
- Have the students number/letter off as "1s" and "2s" or "As" and "Bs". Ask one subset to stand and form a circle. When the circle is formed, have them face the outside of the circle. The remaining students then go and stand facing a student in the "inside" circle.
- Have students ask each other their questions. Advise them that if their partner does not know the answer, to immediately show them the question and the answer.
  - **As ask their questions of the Bs.**
  - **Bs then ask their questions of the As.**
  - **At the signal, students switch cards. Now the As have the Bs cards and vice versa.**
- Have the outside circle move to the left or the right until they reach the second or third person in the inside circle.
- These new partners quiz each other as before. Continue this sequence for as long as is appropriate.
- It is important to **have the students exchange cards** after each questioning session or they will get bored asking the same question over and over and won't learn nearly as much.

Variation on a theme...
Cake Walk
- Questions are written on the board or on an overhead transparency.
- Students form concentric circles.
- The teacher or a student plays music. While the music plays, the circles move in opposite directions. When the music stops, students in the outer circle turn to face students in the inner circle.
- Students discuss the question to which their attention is directed.
- Repeat the process for as long as it is appropriate.

Learning Links

Purposes
- To focus students on the key concepts, big ideas and essential understandings
- To help students access prior knowledge
- To establish purpose for reading or listening
- To help students make meaning
- To help students see patterns and connections

Process
Key Concepts Identified
- Teacher provides students with a list of key concepts from the material to be discussed. Students do not write on the original list. Notes are taken on another sheet of paper keeping original list intact.

Key Concepts Explored
- Students take notes from their textbooks, class lectures, and discussions to organize details around the major concepts, as listed by the teacher, until they have clusters of information around each of the concepts.
- Students choose how to graphically display the "details" to the key concepts. For instance, they might create a web or mind map about the concepts. These graphics would be great journal or interactive notebook entries.

Key Concepts Understood
- Working independently, students review their lists of the key concepts (with no notes by them) to mentally review the information they have gathered until they can readily associate newly learned information with each listed key concept.
- Following the individual review, students work in pairs to discuss the concepts in their own words. Students are encouraged to add personal meaning and background knowledge to the discussion to help each other learn.

adapted from Associational Dialogue, Judy Wood, 1987

Line-Ups

Purposes
- To get students to take and defend a position on a topic
- To evoke curiosity and heighten attention/focus during instruction
- To help students fine tune their estimation skills
- To help students develop their ability to articulate their rationale

Process
- Have students take a stand, make a prediction, or make an estimation pertaining to the topic of instruction. Have them write their predictions on a small piece of paper or a Post-it note.
- Designate one end of the room as the low end/beginning and the other as the high end/ending. Have students line up in the order of their predictions or estimates. Have students hold their written estimate where it can be seen and line up without talking.
- Have students report their estimates so that all students can see the wide range of responses.
- Fold the line on itself so the person with the highest estimate or the end is facing the person with the lowest response. Or, find the center of the line and have the students move so that the person holding the highest estimate is facing someone with a mid-level response.
- The partners share their estimates, as well as the rationales and strategies they used to determine their responses. Students can be asked to report on their partner's answers and rationale or on their own.
- If there is a correct answer, you may want to have them determine it or do research to find out the answer or the opinions of experts in the field.

Examples
- Sequence the steps in changing a tire. Place one step on each slip of paper and distribute randomly.
- Distribute cards with numbers represented as square roots, fractions, decimals, exponents, etc. Have students line up from smallest to largest.
- Distribute steps in a process or events in history. Have students line up in what they think is the correct sequence.
- Estimate the percentage of Americans (French) who exercise the right to vote.

Numbered Heads Together

Process
- Have students form teams of 4 or 5.
- Have students within each team count off from 1-4 or 5 (depending on the number of group members). If teams are uneven, when #5 is called to answer, the #4 person on 4 member teams answers with the #5 people from 5 member teams.
- The teacher asks a question.
- Students put their heads together and collaboratively generate an answer.
- Members of the team make sure each member can answer the question.
- The teacher calls a number at random. All students assigned that number stand or raise their hands; one of these students is selected to answer the question.

Variations
- Using a spinning wheel, dice, or playing cards to identify the spokesperson makes this structure even more engaging.
- If the answer has several parts, #1 from one table can answer the first part, than another #1 adds the second part, etc.
- When a student gives a partially correct answer, another person with that number can be called upon to add to the response. Another variation is to have all teams put their heads together again to check understanding and supply the missing information.
- When divergent answers are the goal, use Numbered Head Ambassadors to have the identified group member move to the next table to tell that group what the ambassador's "home" group thinks.

Scavenger Hunt

Purposes

- To review, preview, and expand a topic
- To demonstrate to students that collectively they know a great deal
- To build in movement

Process

- Prepare a set of questions on a topic.

- If students are not already in table groups or teams, they will need to be in groups to discuss their work after the scavenger hunt.

- Have students individually read through the questions, select one for which they will be the expert, and answer only that question on their sheets. As an alternative, you may assign a specific question to each student or have them draw the question number out of a hat.

- You may wish to initial the answers before they start the hunt to ensure that a "virus" does not spread around the room, or you may wish to let students discover and deal with any errors.

- Students can use all the people and materials in the room as resources to obtain the rest of the answers. Students may only obtain one answer from each person they ask.

- Answers can "flow through" one person to another, but the "third party" and middle person should be prepared to fully explain the answer. The name the student lists as a resource is the person from whom they actually obtain the answer.

- When time is called, students return to their table groups or teams, verify answers, and complete any unfinished answers.

- Only unresolved issues need be discussed with the entire class.

Math Scavenger Hunt

The formula for finding volume is:

Sign. ____

Define:
Mean =
Median =
Mode =
Range =

Sign. ____

Show an example of an obtuse angle:

Sign. ____

Define a least common denominator (LCD):

Sign. ____

What is the reciprocal of:
13/6 =
4/7 =

Sign. ____

Give the decimal values for:
1/4 =
1/2 =
3/4 =

Sign. ____

Math Scavenger Hunt

What are the next 3 place values after a decimal?

____ ____ ____

Sign. ____

When you're dividing fractions do you need to find a LCD? and why?

Sign. ____

1mm = ____ cm
1cm = ____ m
1m = ____ km

Sign. ____

Show 3 formulas for finding perimeter:
P =
P =
P =

Sign. ____

Math Scavenger Hunt

PEMDAS stands for what:

Sign. ____

Show an example of an acute angle:

Sign. ____

Show 2 different formulas for finding area:
a =
a =

Sign. ____

The product is the ____ in a ____ problem.

Sign. ____

Show the formula for finding the circumference of a circle.

Sign. ____

Define a greatest common factor (GCF):

Sign. ____

C. Regelsberger/ A. Lightholder, West Irondequoit Schools, Rochester, NY

Sort Cards

Kinesthetic learners need to "handle the information." Index cards, Post-it notes, or the backs of old handouts cut into 4" x 6" segments will work equally well.

Process at the Beginning of Learning

- Students, working individually, generate words and short phrases that come to mind when they think of a designated topic. They record each idea on a separate index card.
- Working in small groups, students:
  - share ideas
  - clarify similar ideas
  - eliminate duplicates
- Students sort the ideas generated by the group into categories. The categories can be created by the students, or the teacher can identify categories for student use.
- When the sorting and labeling is completed, the students take a tour around the room to observe and analyze the work of other groups. One student stays behind at the base table to answer questions.
- Groups return to tables to discuss what they observed and to revise or add new ideas/categories.
- Groups use the generated ideas and categories as a basis of future study or discussion.
- Ask students to do meta-cognitive processing; that is, have them process how they went about their thinking as they generated, sorted, categorized, labeled, and analyzed the work of others.
- Once these cards are generated, they can be used for a multitude of other instructional purposes. Students could sort them again later in the lesson or unit based on new learning or they could see which important words of phrases were missing. They could identify twenty or so to use when writing about the topic.

During the Learning Process or When Checking for Understanding

Give each student a set of index cards with the key ideas, vocabulary terms, events, etc., recorded on them or have the students create their own cards. They could use the cards they generated at the beginning of the lesson. They could sort them again based on new learning and/or identify which important words are

Sort Cards continued...

missing. They could identify twenty or so words of phrases to include in a journal entry about the topic or they could use them for **Tic-Tac-Toe**.

This pack of index cards can work miracles in helping you and your students know who knows what! Students use the cards to "sort" their learning. Some possibilities include:

- **vocabulary terms and definition matching**
- **sequencing historical events or scientific processes.** See Joe O'Shea's example on the next page.
- **categorizing**
- **"I know," "I sort of know," and "I haven't a clue" piles**

The World of Plants
Sort Cards Assessment

Julie Wenzloff gave her students these words on 2" x 4" slips of paper:

cold	needles	wind
harsh	alternate leaves	animals
permafrost	deciduous	opposite leaves
destruction	whorled leaves	succulents
extinction	water	birds
tundra	nonseed plant	mosses
frozen	ferns	conifers
deforestation	simple leaves	seed plant
peril	liverworts	horsetails
pollution	monocots	compound leaves

The students were asked to sort the cards into two categories. The assessment on **"The World of Plants"** was to label the two lists of words and then to write a rationale for why the words were placed as they were placed. This approach matches the "list-group-label" steps that are the first phase of Hilda Taba's model. The teacher's addition of having students give the rationale for the grouping causes students to think about their thinking and communicate it in writing.

Julie Wnezloff, Farmington Elementary School, Kewaskum, WI

Photosynthesis: The Light Reactions

H_2O	Photosystem I	Electron Carrier
Photosystem II	NADP+	NADP+
H+	$NADPH_2$	ADP+P
H+	H_2O	ATP
e-	Electron Transport System	ATP Synthetase

O_2

 Joe O'Shea, Evanston Township High School, Evanston, IL

Stir the Class

Process

Provide each student with a data collection sheet with ten to twenty lines or have them number their own sheets.

Have each student write, as directed, three reasons, three causes, three points of interest, etc. about the topic/concept to be studied. Ask them to make the third one on their list unique.

At a signal, students move around the room collecting/giving one idea from/to each student. Ideas received from one student can be passed "through" to another student.

After an appropriate amount of time, students return to their seats. At this point, you can have students compare lists, prioritize, categorize, identify cause and effect, sequence, design research projects, etc.

Now students can continue with a lesson format appropriate to the level of thinking you want them to do. They have had time to focus on the subject and to hear ideas from classmates.

Possible Topics

- Ways we use **AVERAGES** in daily life...
- Potential problems with a **FLAT INCOME TAX**...
- Significant pieces of **LITERATURE** you've read...
- Animals that live in **AFRICA**...
- Causes of **PREJUDICE**...
- Places you see or use **METRIC MEASUREMENT**...
- Primary causes of **EROSION**...
- Facts about **INUITS**...
- Effects of human behavior on the **ECOSYSTEM**...
- **HEROES, HEROINES, EXTRAORDINARY LEADERS, VILLAINS, GREEK GODS, COMMUNITY HELPERS,** etc. ...
- Spanish words related to **TRAVEL**...
- Ways we use **FRACTIONS**...
- Most significant events in the **20th CENTURY**...
- Words that begin with **B** or **F** or **Gr** or have **THREE SYLLABLES**...

Teammates Consult

Purposes
- To structure the learning experience so all learners participate
- To promote development of communication skills
- To cause students to think before they "fill in the blanks"

Process
The teacher selects or prepares a set of questions that the students are to work with collaboratively to find the answer. The complexity of the information and the level of understanding required by the question determines the level of difficulty of the task. At no time during this process are students both talking and writing.

- Students work in teams of three to five.
- All students put their pencils or pens in the center of their team's work space. Providing a pencil holder, such as a can or beaker, formalizes this step.
- A student reads the first question.
- Student teams seek the answer -- from text material, notes, and discussion.
- The student sitting to the left of the reader checks to see that all the group members understand and agree with the answer.
- WHEN THERE IS AGREEMENT, all students pick up their own pencils or pens and write the answer in their own words on their own papers.
- When the students are finished recording their answers, the writing implements are returned to the container in the middle of the work space.
- Groups then move on to the next question and repeat the process.
- Students take turns reading the questions.

Remember!
All writing implements are in the container while discussion is ongoing! This is a great way to keep students from just "filling in the blanks" based on a brief look at a text or on what someone else said. You may want to give each group red, yellow and green "signal" cups or cards so that they can let you know when they are functioning smoothly (green), struggling (yellow) or stuck (red).

Think-Pair-Share

Process
- Ask a question.
- Ask students to think quietly about possible answers to the question; this is usually only thirty seconds to one minute, unless the question is quite complex. **(THINK)**
- Have students pair with a neighbor or a learning buddy to discuss their thinking. The discussion usually lasts two to three minutes. **(PAIR)**
- Ask students to share their responses with the whole group or with a table group. Not all students have to share their answers with the large group. **(SHARE)**

Some teachers use hand signals, pointers, bells, cubes, etc., to mark transition points during the cycle. When appropriate, students can write notes, web or diagram their responses during the "Think" or "Pair" time. Students can either explain their own thinking, their partner's thinking, or the consensus they reached together. **Think-Pair-Share** can be used 2-5 times during an instructional period.

Benefits to Students
- Provides the processing time called for in 10:2 theory
- Builds in wait time
- Provides rehearsal
- Enhances depth and breadth of thinking
- Increases level of participation

Benefits to the Teacher
- Provides opportunities to check for understanding.
- Provides time for the teacher to make instructional decisions.
- Provides time for the teacher to locate support materials and plan the next question.
- Allows the teacher to intervene with one or two students without an audience.

3 - 2 - 1

The 3-2-1 process provides a structure for student meaning making and summarizing of key points in a learning experience. The stems for 3 - 2 - 1 can be created to match the kind or level of thinking you want students to do about the material being studied.

3 most important events in this person's life

2 questions you would ask this person if you could talk with him/her

1 way in which you are like this person

At the end of a discussion, a reading, a video or a field trip students might be asked to write:

3 things that really interested you

2 things you'd like to know more about

1 idea that you will write about tonight in your journal

Joanne Mayers-Walker, ESL teacher, Lee High School, Fairfax County Public Schools, Springfield, Virginia, asked her second language learners following a film on the Civil War to respond to:

3 important facts or events I would like to discuss

2 questions I have about the film

1 event similar to an event that happened in my country's history

Three Column Charts

Purposes

- To help students access prior knowledge through brainstorming
- To identify areas of student interest or concern
- To aid the teacher in planning lessons as well as checking for understanding
- To track student learning throughout the unit
- To identify areas for further student research/study

Process

- Use this strategy prior to, during, or at the close of any unit of study. The process can be done individually, in small groups, or as a class activity.
- Announce topic and column titles; post on charts, or have students record in table groups.
- Have the teacher or students record student responses to the stems. The student who offers the idea tells the recorder which column to put it in.
- During the brainstorming phase, emphasize getting lots of ideas rather than debating or discussing the ideas as they are generated. Debates, clarifications, and discussion of ideas occur once the brainstorming is over. The teacher does not clarify any confusions or react in any way other than to record the data. Conflicting data may be recorded.

Choose any ONE of the following SETS of column headings or create your own.

	What I Knew...	What I Now Know...	What I Still Don't Know...
OR	What I know...	What I don't know...	What I wish I knew...
OR	Productive...	Somewhat productive...	Unproductive...
OR	Most important...	Somewhat important...	Not important at all...
OR	Already know...	Want to know...	Learned...
OR	In reading vocab...can read, use in writing & use in discussion...	In reading vocab...can read, but don't use it...	Never heard/saw it before...

Through the Eyes Of...
Through the Voice Of...

Powerful learning can occur if we have students make meaning of their learning through real world connections and the use of complex thinking skills. Assuming the persona of a character from literature or a person in history and/or creating products for such people causes students to process the learning at a much deeper and more enduring level.

Discussions Over Time & Place

- Place an essential question in the square in the middle of the page.
- Place the names of characters from various pieces of literature, people from various countries, people from various time periods, or any set of people who would have differing viewpoints on the question under study.
- Students speak, discuss, debate, or write about the question from the perspective of one or more of the persons.

Tom Loftus, Greece Central School System, Greece, New York, uses the essential question, "Is the world a fair and just place?" He has his students discuss and write about that question from the perspectives of The Pearl Buyer from Steinbeck's *The Pearl*, of Cora and Juana from Langston Hughes' "Cora Unashamed," and Romeo and Juliet from Shakespeare's *Romeo and Juliet*.

Simulations

A simulation is a learning experience in which students create an "as if" environment. Simulations cause learners to move into another time period, another place, or assume the perspective or role of another person. Such learning experiences move from the contrived nature of readings and worksheets to situations that help students make personal meaning of the concepts being studied.

Simulations can be brief and spontaneous ("Pretend you have just landed at the Cairo airport") or highly structured and ongoing (a recreation of the Renaissance or a simulation of life in a rainforest). The latter requires considerable preparation and orchestration. Fortunately, there are many commercially prepared simulations available to supplement your creativity and that of your students. Before creating or selecting and using a longer simulation, be sure to ask yourself if it is worthy of the instructional time that will be consumed. Be sure that you review the standards and check your pacing plans to ensure that this engaging exercise is the best use of time.

Through the Eyes or Voice Of continued...

Simulations provide students opportunities for cognitive and social development. Be sure to do an analysis of the plans for extensive simulations to identify the needed academic and social skills, and take action to ensure that students can be successful in this experience you are designing.

While simulations and role plays can be very powerful learning experiences, it is easy to fall into the activity completion trap where the focus is on completion of the activity, rather than on the learning outcomes. The feeling tone can go off the chart into the "fun" zone and the purpose of learning can be lost.

Role Audience Form Time

The RAFT technique, which is explained in many journals and attributed to various sources, requires students to create scenarios about the content being studied. RAFT allows students to consider the information from a variety of perspectives and use a wide range of formats to present information to limitless audiences. This brain compatible approach causes students to rethink, rewrite, and discuss an event or concept in another place or time, or through the eyes or voice of the famous or familiar.

Laramie Brown, Director of the Teacher Learning Center, West Irondequoit Central School District, Rochester, NY, created the following RAFT for her middle school science students.

> Problem: The Green Grocer, having learned that "vegetable" is a street term without scientific meaning, decided to classify the produce in his store into groups representing the six plant parts. The follow ad appeared in the local newspaper.
>
> ## Immediate Help Wanted
>
> Local grocery market needs knowledgeable STOCK PERSON to reorganize produce into display groups representing the six plant parts. Interested individuals must demonstrate their ability to identify plant parts by selecting five examples of each of the six plant parts (total 30) and submitting a response in one of the following forms that would represent the new produce market design.
> 1. Labeled diagram of produce department
> 2. Graphic organizer
> 3. Memo explaining the new plant classification in paragraph form
>
> Direct all responses to: Green Grocer Produce Manager within two days.

Through the Eyes or Voice Of continued...

Great Impersonators

When students are asked to draw, much to the dismay of art teachers everywhere, some of them immediately say, "I can't draw!" An amazing thing happens when you have them draw "through the eyes of..." AND they learn a little bit about art in the process.

- Locate either the ART DECK cards, which include 52 paintings by 13 impressionist artists, postcards from art galleries, or paintings off the internet.
- Give each group of students a set of paintings by a given artist and have them study how the artist paints...the genre, the colors, the use of space and light, etc.
- When they have had time to explore the artist's style, have each member of the group select a colored marker. Whenever that marker is used on the work they are going to create, the person holding that marker has to be the one to use it.
- Give the students a stem or set of stems based on the current area of study. Their task is to draw the concept "through the eyes of" the artist whose work they have been studying. The artistic renderings and the explanations thereof are amazing!

The Hats

A middle school teacher from Churchville-Chili School District, Churchville, New York, has collected an assortment of hats that her students wear when they are assuming the persona of a historical figure in role plays, simulations, and RAFTs. The props seem to help her students go to the next level of creativity.

And That All Time Favorite...
Let's Play Teacher

Set this up any way that works in your classroom and watch them be **just like you!** Glasser is clear that the best way to have students remember what we want them to remember is for them teach what they know to someone else. Turn on the video camera for this one.

Ticket to Leave

Purposes

- To have students sort through all they have learned
- To have students make personal meaning connections with the concepts studied
- To provide the teacher with formative assessment data

Procedure

- Use at the end of an instructional period.
- Have students use either their own paper, an index card, or a "ticket" you have drawn and copied for this purpose. Alternatively, students could draw or tell their thinking.
- Select an appropriate stem and provide time for students to write their responses. The stem will be determined by the kind of thinking you want the students to do.
- Stand at the door and collect the "tickets" as they leave.

Possible Stems

- List the most interesting thing you learned today and tell why you chose it.
- When you get home, what will you tell your parents you learned today?
- Write one reason why today's lesson may help you in the future.
- List as many occupations as you can that need the skills we practiced today.
- Describe one thing you accomplished that you feel good about today.
- Write one question you have related to the content studied/process used today.
- Write one question that would be a good test question on this material. Write the answer on the back.

Kathy Adasiak, a French teacher at Irondequoit High School in Rochester, New York, stands at the door as her students leave and has them use the target language to tell her such things as their birthday, favorite color, or age, or to use a simple sentence to identify or describe a picture she is holding. She finds that the flash cards for primary students available at teacher supply stores are useful for this process.

Carol Cummings, Jon Saphier, Maryann Haley, Bruce Wellman and Laura Lipton include this strategy in their publications.

Walking Tour

Purposes

- To introduce complex texts, provocative ideas, or discrepancies
- To emphasize key ideas of content material
- To raise curiosity and increase speculation about a subject

Process

- **Compose five to eight charts** that represent the content material, pictorially or verbally. Use photographs of places or objects, direct quotes from the text, or other means to convey one idea per chart. For example, for a study of France, charts might contain postcards, phrases in French, and/or a map of France. *Hint*: **If the tour is used to introduce complex concepts or a complex reading, isolate the primary points and create one chart for each point.**

- **Post the charts** around the classroom and number each chart. Divide students into "touring groups" to fit the classroom space, age of students, and complexity of the material.

- **Assign one group per chart** as a starting point. Groups spend two to five minutes at that chart, taking notes on and/or discussing the idea presented.

- **Rotate the groups** until all groups have "toured" each chart. When students return to their seats, allow some time for discussion and reactions.

Variations

- **Jigsaw Walking Tour** - If time to tour is limited, form groups made up of the same number of students as there are charts around the room (4 charts means there should be 4 members in a group). Have group members number off and send one representative to each chart. Students form new groups at the charts and react. They then return to their original groups to take turns reporting on the information on each chart and their reactions to it.

- **Gallery Walk** - Pictures or other works of art are displayed around the room and the students move from display to display responding to questions or statements given as guidelines for analyzing the artwork.

A-B-C... to ...X-Y-Z
The End of the Lesson

There are dozens of ways to use the alphabet and random words to summarize learning.

ABC #1

Randomly assign a letter of the alphabet to each student. Give them one minute to think of a word that summarizes the lesson or captures the essence of the concept being studied. Do a whip around the room to hear the words.

ABC #2

Have students draw a magnetic letter from a basket. Each student must share a word that begins with that letter to summarize the day.

ABC #3

Have students write the alphabet down the left hand margin of their paper and then work in small groups to think of words beginning with each letter of the alphabet related to the topic being studied.

WORDS #1

Have each student quickly jot down a word that captures the essence of the day's lesson. Have small groups combine their words, adding others as necessary, to make a complete sentence. The only rules are that it must be a complete sentence and they have to use all the words jotted down by individuals.

WORDS #2

Give students a key word related to the topic being studied. Have students write it down the left margin of their paper one letter to a line. The task is for them to create an acrostic using each letter.

WORDS #3

Write two to four nouns on the board. Students are to brainstorm how what they have studied today is like one of those objects. An object with moving parts adds to the possibilities. For example, "The US Government is like a television because one channel often does not know what the other is doing."

Where Do I Begin?

Use this page to jot down your reflections and to make a "To Do List" of the actions you want to take to ensure that students are not spectators of the learning process.

Implementing Instruction
Surprise!
You Are a Reading Teacher!

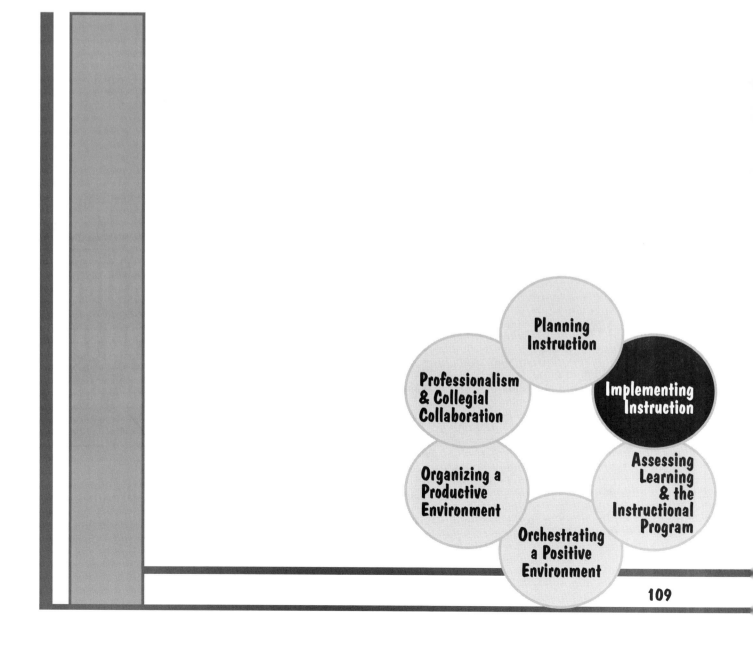

Planning Instruction

Professionalism & Collegial Collaboration

Implementing Instruction

Organizing a Productive Environment

Assessing Learning & the Instructional Program

Orchestrating a Positive Environment

Recommended Sites for Literacy

www.iss.stthomas.edu/studyguides

This study guide and strategies site was created by, and is maintained by, Joe Landsberger, the academic web site developer at the University of St. Thomas (UST), St. Paul, Minnesota. Many strategies are translated into languages other than English.

www.crede.ucsc.edu

This is the site for the Center for Research on Education, Diversity and Excellence. Click on **Research Findings** then on **Language Learning and Academic Achievement** for a report that clearly explains sheltered instruction.

www.ncela.gwu.edu

This is the site for the National Clearinghouse for English Language Acquisition. This site has extensive information and links for research, lesson plans, programs, and practices related to English language learners. Click on **In the Classroom** for a 2002 toolkit for teaching English Language Learners.

Points to Ponder...
We All Teach Reading!

Various forces have converged to bring to the surface what has always been a hidden reality. That is, **we all have to explicitly teach reading and writing.** The delightful diversity and mobility of our learners means that they come to us with different background knowledge and experiences, as well as speaking literally hundreds of different languages and dialects. It is our job to ensure that they are able to make meaning of and use the information that is presented to them in printed text or via technology. The good news is that many of the instructional strategies that we know and use in other contexts are the very same strategies we need to use to ensure reading comprehension and content literacy.

Many well written texts are available for an in-depth exploration of how to teach various types of learners to read and how to teach reading in the content areas. The purpose of this chapter is to identify the essential understandings of the field, to identify and briefly explain widely used reading strategies, and to make connections between those strategies and the strategies we have studied in different contexts.

Reading
Reading is the process of **constructing meaning**, where the reader connects information in the text to what he or she knows. (NCREL)

Content Literacy
Content literacy is the ability to use **reading and writing to learn** subject matter in a given discipline. (Vacca and Vacca)

What It Means to be Literate
According to the New Jersey Core Curriculum, to be literate means that one is able to:
- **Speak for a variety of purposes and audiences.**
- **Listen in a variety of situations to information from a variety of sources.**
- **Write in clear, concise, organized language that varies in content and form for different audiences and purposes.**
- **Read various materials and texts with comprehension and critical analysis.**
- **View, understand, and use nontextual visual information.**

This document goes on to say that literacy is not achieved by adding skills one-by-one, but by using and exploring these interdependent processes of language.

Points to Ponder continued...

Scaffolding

Scaffolding is the purposeful provision of support for learners as they construct meaning and build skills for accessing and using information. Think of the scaffolding you see around the construction of or rehabilitation of a multistory office building.

Sheltered Instruction

Sheltered instruction is the careful use of English in a classroom with students who do not speak English as a first language. Particular care needs to be taken with vocabulary that is academic/school related, content specific, slang, or colloquialisms.

Phonemes, Phonemic Awareness & Phonics

Phonemes are the smallest units of speech in a language. There are 48 phonemes in English. Phonemic awareness means that learners know that spoken language is made up of phonemes. This awareness is essential so that learners can make the sound-letter connections essential to reading. Phonics is instruction in the relationship between sounds and letters, letter groups, and syllables so that students learn to make automatic sound/symbol connections when decoding text.

Reading First

The **No Child Left Behind Act of 2001**, in the section entitled **Reading First**, mandates that every kindergartner through third grader has access to a reading program that contains explicit and systematic instruction in five areas. Those areas are:
- phonemic awareness
- phonics
- vocabulary development
- reading fluency, including oral reading skills
- reading comprehension strategies

Learning to Read & Reading to Learn
via Balanced Literacy

Balanced literacy is most often discussed and used in elementary settings, but it has huge implications for teachers across all content areas and all grade levels. The capacity to read and write well is essential for students not only for demonstrating competency on high stakes assessments, but as they continue on their learning journey as lifelong learners. The balanced literacy process focuses on reading, writing, and word study, and includes **reading to, with, and by children** and **writing for, with and by children.** Struggling readers in our classrooms may be so focused on decoding that they are unable to access and use prior knowledge in a productive way. This means we need to include modeled and shared reading and writing experiences throughout K-12 education. Given that many of us do not consider ourselves knowledgeable about and skilled at teaching reading and writing, we need to develop an understanding of and a sense of competency with teaching the processes of literacy within the context of our teaching assignments.

Reading to students helps them learn sentence structure, develop an understanding of story and text structure, build prediction skills, create mental images, make cognitive connections, and provides them with a strong model of proficient reading in the context of either literature or expository material.

Reading with students helps them develop comprehension skills. Guided reading sessions designed to explicitly meet the needs of a small group of students help students build basic reading skills and become more proficient independent readers. This small group work requires that students know and use systems for working together in other small groups without direct interaction with the teacher.

Independent reading by students helps them build self-confidence, fluency, vocabulary, and provides them with opportunities to practice using reading strategies they are learning.

Writing for and with students provides them with models of spelling and mechanics of writing. These learning experiences also help them understand how reading and writing are connected, as well as in hearing and sequencing sounds in words.

Writing by students helps them not only build confidence as writers, it also provides practice in different types of writing.

This balanced approach can transfer to secondary classrooms in all content areas. Substitute math, science, or social studies for the content focus and keep the instructional variables the same.

Learning to Read & Reading to Learn
via Balanced Literacy continued...

The Providence Public Schools, Rhode Island, website (www.providenceschools.org) suggests that the components of a balanced literacy program include:

- Thinking aloud during the daily message to teach mechanics such as spacing, capitalization, and punctuation
- Read alouds from various genres to promote listening skills and to promote comprehension through discussion and writing
- Word work to build phonemic awareness and skills
- A guided reading block in which the teacher demonstrates a strategy or skill that has been identified as a focal point for a group of three to five students
- Literacy centers
- Shared writing
- Writer's workshop
- Independent reading

St. Vrain Valley School District, Longmont, Colorado, uses "A Balanced Approach to Literacy" that includes:

- Read alouds
- Shared reading
- Guided reading
- Independent reading
- Literature discussion groups
- Modeled writing
- Shared/Interactive writing
- Guided writing
- Independent writing

The flag fluttered in the wind as the puffy clouds drifted by in the morning sky.

Reading to Learn

Strategies versus Skills

McREL in its **Strategic Reading Project** used by Chicago Public Schools makes a clear distinction between **reading strategies and reading skills**. The manual points out that we often teach skills such as finding the main idea, using prefixes and suffixes, or distinguishing between facts and opinions in ways that help students build skills without making meaning of the whole piece they are reading. When students' reading skills are adequately developed (at whatever age) and they are able to concentrate on **reading to learn**, it is essential that we include both **skill and strategy instruction**. As readers develop reading skills, strategies such as those taught in the McREL's project become the focus of reading instruction because students need to learn when to use and when not to use particular reading skills before, during and after reading. The reading strategies on which that program focuses are:

- Prior knowledge
- Inferencing
- Text structure
- Word meaning
- Metacognition

These five strategies provide an excellent starting point for content area teachers tasked with including content area reading and writing in their instructional program. A profile of a proficient and strategic secondary reader is found on page 126.

Where to Find Information:

- **Using prior knowledge: See page 116**
- **Inferencing or "reading between the lines" and "filling in the gaps" See pages 116-117**
- **Recognizing and using text structure: See pages 118-122**
- **Word meaning (vocabulary development): See pages 123-125**
- **Thinking about thinking processes (metacognition): See pages 58, 81-82**

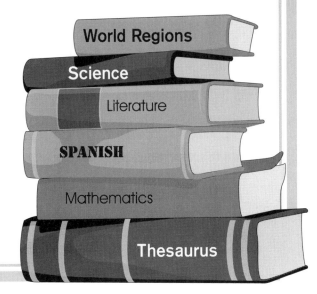

Using Prior Knowledge

Prior knowledge and experiences provide the lens through which we receive and process new information. The reading research is clear about the need to be explicit in orchestrating learning experiences so that students access and use prior knowledge. This is fundamental to student achievement. We need to guide the learning process so that students are connecting new information to prior information, making predictions, and then either refining, realigning, or discarding what was previously known. The challenges are that prior knowledge and life experiences vary from student to student and that some students need far more guidance than others about using prior knowledge appropriately **before learning, during learning, and following learning.** A primary task of any teacher is to level the playing field by carefully designing the prompts, the questions, and the interactions of students with the material and with each other. Chapters II, III, and IV provide a wide array of strategies for accomplishing this.

Reading Between the Lines
Making Inferences

To infer means to reach a mental conclusion by reasoning from evidence. To reach this conclusion, students combine what they are learning with what they already know. The process of inferencing is clearly interwoven with strategic use of prior knowledge. Keene and Zimmermann, in **Mosaic of Thought**, suggest that readers be taught to make three kinds of connections... **text-to-self, text-to-text, and text-to-world.** When we have students speak and write about those connections, we can evaluate the level of their reasoning and intervene as necessary. Another strategy that is useful K-12 is Palinesar's **Reciprocal Teaching** strategy. (See page 133.) It requires students to predict, clarify (look up words), question, and summarize. Page 117 describes how teachers in St. Vrain Valley School District, Longmont, Colorado, have students use **Text Frames** to promote inferencing and questioning.

Students throughout their K-12 education can become discouraged if they do not have decoding skills, sufficiently developed vocabularies, or other reading skills necessary to perform the learning tasks we give them. A new text structure, a new content area, or a second language can cause a reader to fall back to reading word-to-word or not reading at all. Reading to and with learners, modeling our thinking aloud, explicitly teaching reading strategies, and providing opportunities for guided practice are essential components of our work if we want our students to be able to make inferences independently and to know when their conclusions are well grounded in evidence.

Through the Voice of...
Increasing Inferencing & Questioning
In Young Readers

Text Frames are scaffolds for students to use when thinking about deeper levels of meaning in text. They can be used as entries in literature response logs, preparation for literature circles, and as starting points for individual conferences.

It is suggested that teachers model the use of text frames by sharing their own response to text, that questions for text frames may be posted in the room for reference to guide free response writing, and that students should have opportunities to review text frames for writing ideas.

The forms below are small reprints of the **Text Frames** provided to students.

Text Frame: Inferencing

One section of the text that made me stop and think was

Complete one of the following:
   I think the author is trying to say

   It reminds me of

   I wonder

   It made me feel

One question I'd like to ask the author is

Text Frame: Questioning

One question I have while reading this section is

I wonder this because

The author leads me to think that

I think that this question will/will not (circle one) be answered in the next section because

**Ellen Gury, Marsha Hansard, Leslie Kesson, and Jacalyn Colt,
St. Vrain Valley School District, Longmont, CO**

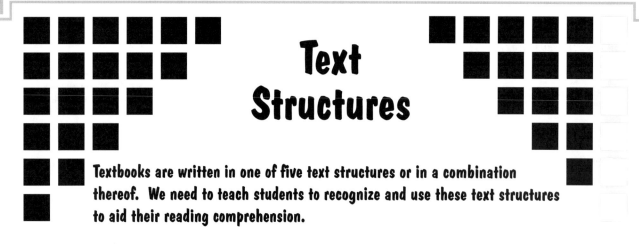

Text Structures

Textbooks are written in one of five text structures or in a combination thereof. We need to teach students to recognize and use these text structures to aid their reading comprehension.

Classifications and taxonomic listings focus on information about different concepts/facts that are classified according to a specific set of criteria. Signal words are "there are several types," and "one subset of this issue is...." The visual which looks like an organization chart or family tree, is a useful graphic organizer for this pattern of text.

Sequential and chronological text patterns present a progression of events in chronological order, or the sequential stages of some process. Information in history texts is often presented chronologically, while information in science is often presented as a sequence of stages. Signal words for this text structure are "first," "next," "then," and "following that." Flow charts are best for capturing the important bits of information in this text structure.

Compare and contrast text patterns identify items with similarities and/or differences. Signal words for this text structure are "similarly," "likewise," "contrary to," and "unlike." Venn diagrams and matrices are useful graphic organizers with this pattern.

Cause and effect text patterns are used when two events or items are related to each other, with some causing an event and some resulting from the event. Signal words for this pattern include "as a result of...," "consequently," and "therefore." The graphic organizer with the "event" in the middle with causes flowing into the event and the effects flowing out is useful with this pattern.

Expository or explanatory text patterns present a series or list of facts, ideas, or variables that may not immediately seem to be related to one another or may seem to jump from one point to another. Mind maps or semantic maps and webs are useful in clustering the information.

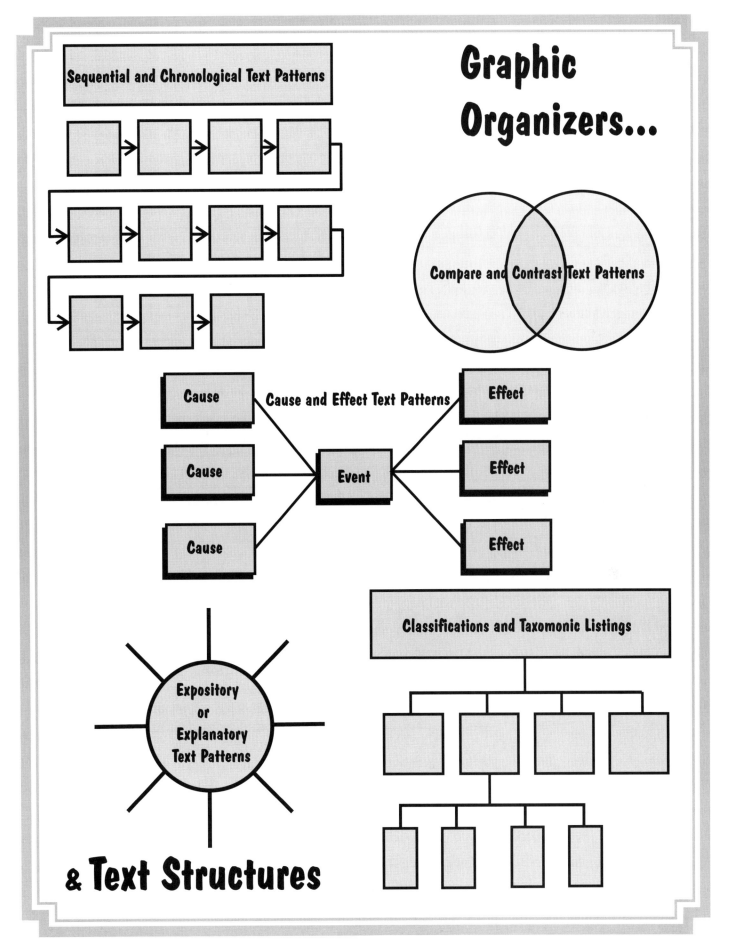

Sequential and Chronological Text Patterns

Graphic Organizers...

Compare and Contrast Text Patterns

Cause

Cause

Cause

Cause and Effect Text Patterns

Event

Effect

Effect

Effect

Expository or Explanatory Text Patterns

Classifications and Taxomonic Listings

& Text Structures

Through the Voice of...
Graphic Organizers

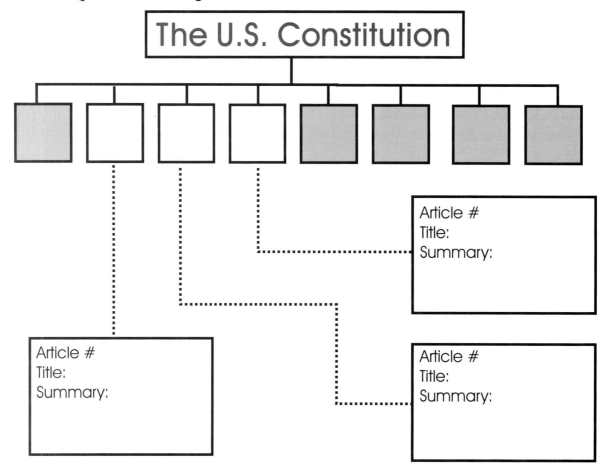

Graphic Organizers as Teaching & Learning Tools

This graphic organizer was designed as a learning log for students to use as they read, viewed, or listened to information on the U.S. Constitution. Such an organizer is an important tool for helping students see how what they are studying in the moment is connected to a bigger concept. The use of this sort of visual tool has a strong research base (Marzano, et. al.) for promoting retention of learning. The use of graphic organizers has been identified as extremely important for English Language Learners. Teachers can explicitly identify and use graphic organizers found in textbooks and can model collecting and organizing information on them with the ultimate goal of having students use them independently.

Each of the graphic organizers used to represent text structures on the previous page provides a good starting point for teaching with and teaching students to use graphic organizers. The graphic organizers found on the following pages provide examples of how teachers use graphic organizers as teaching and learning tools.

Mike Rutherford, 8th Grade Civics, Stone Middle School, Fairfax County Public Schools, Centerville, VA

Through the Voice of...
Graphic Organizers

Writing a Research Paper

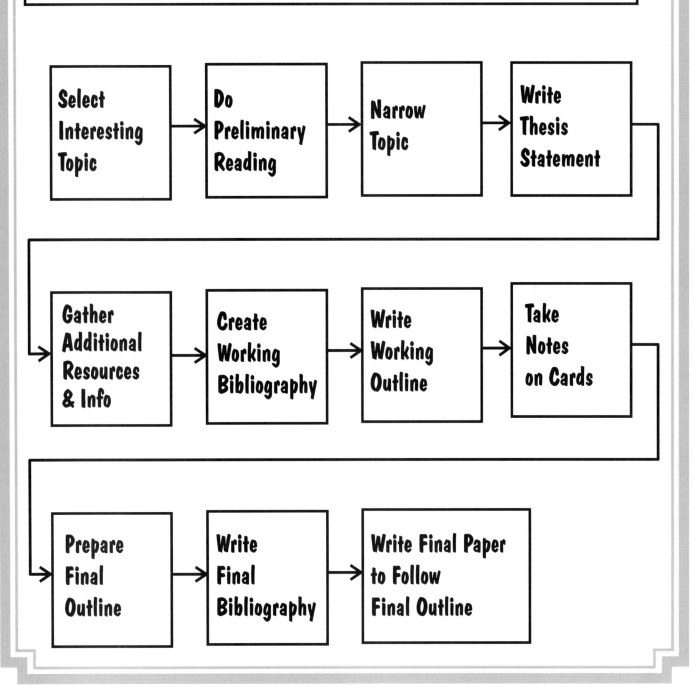

Select Interesting Topic → Do Preliminary Reading → Narrow Topic → Write Thesis Statement →

Gather Additional Resources & Info → Create Working Bibliography → Write Working Outline → Take Notes on Cards →

Prepare Final Outline → Write Final Bibliography → Write Final Paper to Follow Final Outline

Possessive Adjectives in French

Mon
- in front of masculine nouns. e.g., Mon papier
- in front of any noun beginning w/ a vowel. e.g., mon amie
- in front of any word beginning w/ an "h". E.g., mon hotel

My

Ma
- in front of all feminine nouns, except those beginning with a vowel. E.g., ma poupee

Mes
- in front of all plural nouns. E.g., mes papiers, mes amies, mes hotels, mes poupees.

This classification graphic organizers helps students see that "MY" takes three different forms in French. It can also be used with the possessive adjectives ton, son; ta, sa; and tes, ses.

It could easily be used in math, science, or social studies to visually display a great deal of information with only few words.

Vocabulary Development

Looking words up in a dictionary or a glossary and writing down the definition even when followed by using the word in a sentence does not always do the trick! Students need to work with the vocabulary words in context and in connection with other words they already know and use. They need to do so in a way that promotes **mastery** (the capacity to use the word in both their receptive and expressive language), **retention** (the capacity to use the word over time), and **transfer** (the capacity to use the word appropriately in other contexts). Many educators are calling this **word study.**

Graves and Slater, in ***Content Area Reading and Learning***, identify six levels of vocabulary development. While looking up a word in a dictionary or glossary may be appropriate for some of them, it is not the best approach most of the time. When you identify vocabulary words to preteach or to emphasize during teaching, consider the relationship the students already have with the word when selecting the instructional strategy. The levels are:

- Learning to read words already in oral vocabulary
- Learning new meanings (content specific) for known words
- Learning new words for known concepts
- Learning new words representing new concepts
- Clarifying and enriching meanings of known words
- Using words currently in the students' receptive vocabulary (listening and reading) in their expressive or productive vocabulary (speaking and writing).

Instructional Strategies to Use in Vocabulary Development

Word Splash

Dorsey Hammond "invented" the idea of a word splash. See page 125 for an example. Early readers can use a "picture splash." The idea is to have students look at words that are known to them, and decide how they might be related to one another and to the focus of their study. This is not a strategy to use with new words, but rather with words being used in a different context or with a different meaning.

Word Walls

Selected concept/vocabulary words from the current area of study are placed on the wall in the classroom. They may be arranged in a random angled way to encourage students to make guesses about what they mean, why they are important, and how they are related to the topic under study and to each other. Alternatively, they may be grouped by category and even printed on different color paper to explicitly identify the group to which each term belongs. The important point is to have the

Vocabulary Development continued...

words on display for students to refer to in their discussions and while they are writing. This approach is appropriate for all levels of vocabulary development. It is especially useful for English Language Learners and for promoting use of the terms and concepts in written and spoken language of all learners.

Frayer Model

This visual organizer is useful in helping learners separate critical attributes from interesting information about a concept. See page 125 for details on how to set up the organizer. This is a recommended approach for new words for new concepts.

Word Sorts

See pages 93-94 for details on how to set up a word sort or sort card exercise. See pages 85-86 for more ways to have students "handle" the vocabulary terms or concepts. The name **List-Group-Label** is used in the reading literature for the word sort strategy that is useful for helping students clarify and enrich meanings of known words. As the name implies, students list all the words they can think of related to a given topic. They then group the words and label the groupings. These three steps are the first stage in Hilda Taba's inductive thinking model, which was originally presented as an elementary social studies strategy.

Three Column Charts

This strategy, which is explained in detail on page 100, is a good one for helping students identify their own level of use and expertise with words. Use the headings **I Know and Use It in My Speech and in My Writing, I Recognize It and Understand It When I Hear and Read it, I am Not Sure of the Meaning.**

Graphic Organizers

Descriptive graphic organizers, or **mind maps,** are particularly useful in helping students refine their understanding and use of terms, as well as to integrate the terms within a context. Students could create their own mind maps, work with a partner to refine their mind maps, and then create a class mind map on the board. This is an excellent way to review an important and complex concept that has vocabulary that is challenging and/or vocabulary that is being used in a new way.

Inside-Outside Circles

When it is necessary to have students look up words up in a dictionary, and they do not need to work on glossary or dictionary skills, have each student look up one word. Have them write the word on one side of an index card and the definition on the other. Follow the directions for **Inside-Outside Circles** (Kagan, 1994) as presented on page 87.

The Frayer Method

Students list as many attributes of the word as they can think of, then cross out those that are not essential. The remaining essential attributes will help define the new word. This model helps students build skills at crafting rich definitions of concepts and vocabulary words.

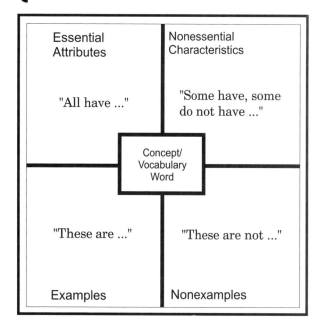

Word Splash

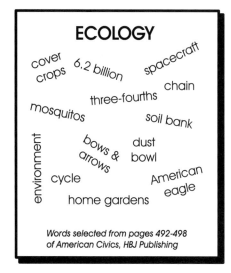

A word splash is a collection of key terms or concepts from a reading. The terms should be familiar to the students. The purpose is to relate the terms to each other and to the new topic of study. It is a particularly powerful strategy when different meanings of some of the words are being introduced. Prior to reading, viewing, or visiting a site, students brainstorm and generate complete sentences to predict the relationships. After the learning experience, they review their predictions and make corrections.

Reading & Writing Across the Curriculum

Willard Daggett, President of the International Center for Leadership in Education, says *"Once a student leaves high school, 90% of his reading will be information reading. Only 10% of his reading will be for pleasure."* This statement from Daggett reinforces the responsibility we have to explicitly teach students how to read informational material in all our classroom settings.

Profile of Proficient Readers

Based on their review of the literature, secondary educators in Fairfax County Public Schools, Fairfax, Virginia, compiled the following list identifying the behaviors practiced by proficient readers across the curriculum. Proficient readers:

- Set a purpose for reading
- Access prior knowledge and relate it to new information
- Construct meaning
- Reread, skim, summarize a chapter
- Paraphrase and predict based on chapter headings
- Frame and reframe focus questions prior to, during and following reading
- Look for important ideas in charts, tables, and graphs
- Test their understanding of technical information
- Identify patterns in the text that serve as examples of main idea
- Use graphic organizers to organize ideas
- Sequence events, e.g., in an explanation of historical facts
- Look for relationships, e.g., between math concepts
- Read ahead for clarification, e.g., of scientific terms and concepts
- Mentally execute directions in a manual
- Have a repertoire of strategies and know when to use which
- Think about reading strategies before, during and after reading
- Monitor their understanding of difficult explanations

Secondary content area teachers can use the components of a balanced literacy program, such as guided reading, modeled reading, and discussion groups, to help their students develop and use these skills. Other essential tasks of the secondary teacher include the teaching about, and providing practice with, content specific vocabulary through the study of commonly used prefixes and suffixes, as well as Latin and Greek roots, and the structure and parts of the textbooks used in the study of the discipline. Information, patterns, connections, and processes that are so clear to teachers who are experts in their field may well escape the learner who is encountering this material for the first time.

Unsuccessful Readers
Behaviors of Unsuccessful Readers...
& What To Do About Them

Unsuccessful readers demonstrate the following patterns of behavior:

1. Poor visualization
2. Little or inappropriate use of prior knowledge
3. No predictions or hypotheses
4. Little self-monitoring of comprehension
5. Few, if any, fix-up strategies*
6. Form hypotheses but fail to evaluate and modify them appropriately on the basis of new information

What To Do...

When students fail to reframe their thinking around incorrect hypotheses:

- Point out words with multiple meanings. Hammond's **Word Splash** is a good tool for helping students realize that words are being used in multiple ways. See pages 123 and 125.

- Point out the writing patterns of authors who use contradictions as a means of hooking new information onto old, incorrectly held ideas (i.e., "Most people think that..., but..."). The problem here is that the topic sentence (or the main idea) is found in the middle or at the end of the paragraph or is never expressly stated.

When students do not use prior knowledge and/or do not monitor comprehension:

- Have students set their own purposes for reading rather than using teacher-imposed purposes for reading. For instance, rather than telling students to "read to find out why Jose was so excited about what was planned for after school," ask students to predict and speculate in their own words about what could be the cause of the excitement. Many teachers' manuals suggest teacher-imposed purposes for reading rather than providing strategies for helping learners set their own purposes for reading.

- Use KWL charts or other **Three Column Charts** to help students become focused on the reading. They are useful before, during and at the end of a reading selection. See page 100 for directions for Three Column Charts.

*The first five points are discussed in an article by Beth Davey, 1983.

Unsuccessful Readers continued...

When students fail to use productive strategies when reading, do not stop with telling them what to do in that particular instance.

- Help students **figure out the sources of information** needed to comprehend the reading. Raphael suggests teaching students to ask themselves the following questions to guide reading comprehension.
  - Are all the parts to the answer in one sentence? Does the reader need to put together information found in various sentences and/or parts of the book?
  - Is the reader expected to combine information from the text with his own opinions and knowledge?
  - Is the reader to use his/her own experience and knowledge rather than information in the text to answer the question?
- Teach students not only the reading strategies, but also **when to use** each strategy.
- Have students analyze the **effectiveness of the strategies** they use with teacher guidance and of those they use independently.
- Use **Reciprocal Teaching**, particularly with struggling readers. See page 133. In Palinscar's model:
  - The student and teacher take turns "teaching" information from passages by way of summarizing, questioning, clarifying, and predicting.
  - Students are taught to access background knowledge, generate questions they want answered, and to make predictions. Additionally, they are taught that throughout the reading they should stop and evaluate their predictions, make new predictions, and identify the information that made them change their minds.
- Use **Think Alouds** as a demonstration of the thinking processes used by successful readers. See page 134 for information on Davey's Think Alouds.
- **Build those bridges!** Explicitly frame questions and prompts to cause students to make connections between what is being studied in class and their life beyond the moment, beyond the classroom, to the past and to the future. See pages 54-60 for guidance in framing questions.

Patterns of Inappropriate Use of Prior Knowledge & Text

Learners enter almost all learning experiences with some prior knowledge. Often it is incomplete and/or inaccurate. McTighe and Wiggins, in **Understanding by Design**, describe understanding as ranging from "naive" to "sophisticated." Unfortunately, many students manage to answer questions at the end of the chapter, complete worksheets, and even pass examinations without really processing the information; that is, they read and respond without making meaning or connecting cognitively with the new information. Therefore, they fail to add to or refine their store of knowledge or their understanding of the concepts being studied. Some of their approaches to "studying" include:

1. Fill in the blank and call it quits!

Some students who are poor readers rely primarily on their prior knowledge. These students tend to read just enough to find information or concepts that resemble something they already know and determine that the material "makes sense to them." They use their prior fund of knowledge to answer the questions and, without even knowing it, attribute that information to the text. In these instances, students may "fill in the blanks" or select the correct multiple choice answer without having ever really processed the significant information in the text.

2. I, too, can learn these highlighted vocabulary words!

Other poor readers focus on isolated words found in the text in order to complete the assigned task. They neglect to identify relationships between words or relationships to their prior knowledge. They often look for "big words" or italicized words to use as answers to teacher questions. They may even manage to satisfactorily complete the assignment without ever processing the significant information in the text. It is really no surprise that students focus on unrelated words rather than main concepts, because it is often new vocabulary that textbook publishers print in bold type or italics. When these students are later asked to explain a concept studied in the text, whether it is in a class discussion or on a written assessment, they have no idea of how to respond in a thoughtful way.

3. If it's listed in Trivial Pursuit or Cultural Literacy, I'll learn to define and explain it!

Even some students who are relatively good, strong readers depend on unrelated facts to answer questions, because they have found that developing

Patterns of Inappropriate Use of Prior Knowledge & Text continued...

lists of facts has led to school success in the past. They usually do not relate facts to one another or to real life experiences, and do not distinguish between details and main ideas. These students, too, are able to complete school assignments without having ever processed the significant information in the text.

4. I already know this stuff!

A great many strong readers also rely too heavily on prior knowledge when trying to make sense of textbook material. It is their belief that the text will always confirm their previously held knowledge. They look for information that matches what they already know and read with the belief that they "already know all this stuff." Even though these students do integrate prior knowledge with the new information, they often distort or ignore some of the new information in order to create the match. As a result, these students complete their reading without having processed the information in the ways the teacher and the textbook authors intended.

The approach we want is...

Learners who are willing to struggle to make sense of textbook material most likely have a history as successful readers. This past success causes them to approach the task of reading with focus and with a willingness to integrate new information, even if that new information forces them to reframe their thinking about the concept being studied. This approach, of course, results in learning at a deeper and more enduring level, as demonstrated by the fact that these readers are able to:

- Recognize and paraphrase the main/most important concepts presented in the textbook.
- Realize that there is the conflict between their previous understanding and the information presented and are willing to reframe their thinking and/or abandon old ideas, as appropriate, to resolve the conflict.
- Are aware of the fact that they are changing their perspective or level of understanding.
- Can identify what information in the text is different from what they previously thought was true.
- Can make personal connections and apply the information in the text to other academic, or beyond the classroom, situations.

Finding A Balance Between
Skill Building & Meaning Making

Just because learners use a
skill or strategy doesn't mean that they know which
skill or strategy they are using!

They need multiple opportunities to reflect upon and
label the skills and strategies they are using.

Just because students use a skill or strategy doesn't
mean that they recognize where else it can be used!

They not only need to use skills and strategies in a
variety of situations, they need to focus on where else
they might be able to use them both inside and
outside the school setting.

Just because learners can name and define the skills
or strategies they're using doesn't mean that they
know how to use them well or efficiently.

Learners also need to reflect on the usefulness of each
of the strategies and skills, and analyze what actions
or behaviors were the most effective and why.

Confidence plus effective effort leads to development of reading skills.

Our task is to help all students build a repertoire of reading strategies, and to
recognize and analyze the processes they use to comprehend what they read. This
task is appropriate for successful readers, as well as struggling readers, because
sooner or later all readers have to tackle material that is complex and confusing
for them. Reflection and analysis now will be a useful tool for all readers either in
the present or in the future.

English Language Learners

Establishing Cognitive Empathy

The range of literacy in their first language, as well as their proficiency with English as their second or perhaps third language, varies widely across our English Language Learners (ELLs). For purposes of understanding how it feels to be a non-English speaker in an American classroom, imagine for a moment you have just arrived in Beijing, China. Without the added pressures of the academic arena, think how you would feel (or felt) when no one understands what you are saying and it seems like every single person is simultaneously speaking loudly and rapidly in a language in which you are not fluent, and are limited to hello, good bye, thank you and please. Consider being faced with directions in Cantonese or Mandarin Chinese for a simple task such as, "Take out your notebook and copy the notes from the board." This would most likely cause you to turn and run for home, or to quickly seek out those who speak your language, or even better, your dialect.

There were 4.4 million English Language Learners (ELL) enrolled in Pre-K -12 public education in the 1999-2000 school year. This represents more than 9% of the student population (Antunez, 2002). Seventy-seven percent of the ELLs in American schools have Spanish as their first language. Whatever the learners first language, we need to be careful to not confuse the lack of English skills with the lack of capacity to learn. We must not think that speaking with an accent means a lack of literacy/fluency.

What a challenge! What an opportunity!

The good news is that best practice for English speaking students is best practice for English Language Learners. Additionally, we need to fine tune our **cognitive empathy**, check our **figurative language,** be proactive in **identifying gaps** in students' life and academic experiences, consider the **differences in language structures**, and identify where each ELL is on the literacy spectrum both in his first language and in English. Do not for a minute lump all English Language Learners into one group. Some ELLs are accelerated learners who know and understand amazing amounts of information and can read, write, and speak with great proficiency in their first language, while some ELLs have not been in an academic setting before. The first step is identifying what our ELL students know and can do, in any language. The second step is figuring out the best way to lead these students to English proficiency at the same time they are tackling challenging academic learning across the disciplines.

Carefully design lessons focused on the desired outcomes and surround not only ELLs but all students with multiple sources of information, as visual as possible, and written at various levels of complexity. Remember your cognitive empathy! Pictures on menus in Beijing are really helpful!

Reciprocal Teaching

Predict   Clarify   Question   Summarize

Reciprocal Teaching is designed to help students develop expertise with the thinking and process skills of predicting, clarifying, questioning, and summarizing. It is a strategy that can be used with K-12 learners. It works equally well with literature and expository texts. Anne Marie Sullivan Palincsar developed **Reciprocal Teaching** as a variation of **ReQuest**, which was developed by Anthony Manzo. Both strategies have as their ultimate goal students independently setting a purpose for reading, asking questions throughout the lesson and summarizing.

These skills are best taught separately and then integrated into the model. The classroom teacher can model thinking aloud about each, use each of the process skills as prompts in **Think-Pair-Shares,** and as the focus of informal one-on-one discussions and quick checks for understanding.

There are several versions of the technique. In the original version, the teacher and a student take turns being the "teacher," hence the name. In this way the classroom teacher is able to model desired behavior, and the student "teacher" practices the processes immediately. Over time the strategy can be frequently used by a teacher working with a small group having students assigned various process responsibilities and different students functioning as the "teacher," In the elementary setting, small group guided reading sessions can be transformed into a reciprocal teaching structure. In the secondary classroom, the strategy can be used to structure small group work.

After students have developed familiarity with each of the four process skills, identify text to be read. Have students predict what the text will be about based on the cover, the headings, the first sentences, on what they know about this text or the author, or what has happened/been presented in previous chapters. Read a small section of material with the small group having the "teacher" clarify, question, and summarize. Have the students take turns being the "teacher" who leads the process. Continue the process alternating small sections of the reading material with pauses for predicting, clarifying, questioning, and summarizing.

Since the ultimate purpose is independent use of the process skills and strategies, in the most sophisticated version students would work in small groups with all students having prepared for the discussion by writing out their responses to each of the four processes. One student would be designated the "teacher" or leader of the each discussion group and the classroom teacher would circulate around listening in on the discussions.

Think Alouds

A think aloud is a strategy in which the teacher assumes the role of a student "thinking aloud" about how to comprehend a passage or how to work through complex or confusing tasks or problems. The purposes of this strategy are to point out potential pitfalls and common misconceptions or behaviors of learners and to model strategies, ways of thinking, and working through the problems.

Our students think that we were born knowing how to read in three languages, write bibliographies, and twenty page research papers. Why? They think so because we always seem to do it right the first time. When we demonstrate, we show our students how a task is done; we seldom demonstrate the trial and error nature of accomplishing tasks. To help fill that void, "think alouds" were originally discussed in the reading literature (Davey, 1983) as a way to help students with reading comprehension; their use has been extended to demonstrating the perils and pitfalls of any multi-step or obscure task. (Saphier, 1990)

Process
- Identify points you want to make with a **think aloud** prior to presenting it. As an instructional strategy for reading, you might use the most commonly neglected strategies and/or other problems you have identified as interfering with reading comprehension.
- Assume the role and talk out loud about your thinking and feelings as you attempt to do the task.
- Do not interact with the audience (your students).
- In addition to modeling the reading strategies discussed in this chapter you might want to **think aloud** about the following:
  - **Confusion about what you are supposed to do**
  - **Failure to recall all of the steps in the directions**
  - **False starts**
  - **Weighing alternatives**
  - **Reviewing what you've done in similar situations**
  - **Remembering what you've read or been told to do**
  - **Possible frustrations**
  - **Thinking of places to get help**
  - **Persistence and recognition of effective efforts**
  - **Feeling of success**
- When you are finished with the role play, **have students identify the strategies** you used in working through the task.
- Coach students, or have students coach each other, in using the same process.

Where Do I Begin?

Use this page to jot down your reflections and to make a "To Do List" of the actions you want to take to enable you to explicitly include instruction in literacy strategies in every lesson.

VI

Assessing Instruction & Learning
Assessment 101

A. How Do I Make Sure That They are Ready to Learn?
B. How Do I Make Sure They are On the Learning Journey with Me?
C. How Do I Make Sure That "They Have Caught What I've Taught?"

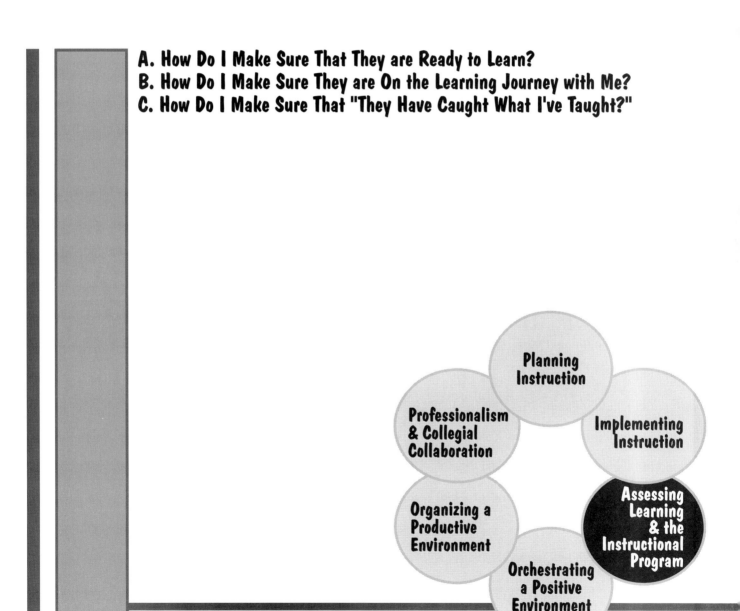

Planning Instruction

Professionalism & Collegial Collaboration

Implementing Instruction

Organizing a Productive Environment

Assessing Learning & the Instructional Program

Orchestrating a Positive Environment

137

Recommended Sites on Assessment

cresst96.cse.ucla.edu

This is the site for the National Center for Research on Evaluation, Standards, and Student Testing. Click on **Assessments** in the Library section. There are several sophisticated performance assessments available there.

Points to Ponder...

IT hasn't been TAUGHT...

If IT hasn't been CAUGHT!

Leaders cannot be called leaders if no one is following. The same is true for teachers. Presenting or telling information is not teaching. In order to call ourselves teachers, we have to have someone who is learning from the learning experiences we orchestrate. A significant component of our teaching repertoire has to be checking to see if our students are with us on the learning journey, or if we are going on the trip alone.

Strategies to find out where to "pick them up" for the learning journey are essential. Many of the active learning strategies we use to help students make meaning of the work can provide us with important assessment data. When we do a task analysis, access prior knowledge, surface misconceptions or naive understandings, we gather a great deal of information about what students know and at what levels they can use that knowledge and those skills. In fact, we may find that we do not need additional preassessment, but simply need to use the data we collect through those exercises.

In order to facilitate learning, we have to adjust the design of the learning experiences based on the data we collect not only at the beginning of the learning experience but throughout the work. In many instances the data is right in front of us but we are not seeing it as "data" that can inform our decisions.

This chapter describes **systems** for finding out where to begin instruction, **systems** for checking to see if our students are coming with us on the learning journey, **systems** for students to use in monitoring their own progress, as well as **tips** on how to design both traditional tests and performance tasks for use as summative assessments.

An Assessment Continuum
from Formative to Summative

It is difficult to distinguish between assignments and assessments in today's classroom because assessment is not an end of the unit event, rather it is integrated into the instruction program. Formative assessment begins even before we begin teaching with preassessment. We gather formative data throughout the unit of study, often in informal ways, to inform our teaching decisions and improve student learning. Each assessment option listed below is either discussed in this chapter or in other sections of this book. Please note page references below for information found in other chapters.

Preassessments

Checks for Understanding

Observations/Anecdotal Records

Student Questions/Comments (In-class and in Journals) See pages 81-83.

Teacher Questions & Prompts (In-class) See pages 54-62.

Assignments (including Homework)

Peer Assessment

Self Assessment

Quizzes

Tests

Performance Tasks

Preassessment Strategies

The good news is that many of the strategies we use to engage learners in active learning can be used as preassessment strategies. Even better news is that we do not have to do two exercises. We just need to pay attention to the assessment data that surfaces while we are accessing prior knowledge, surfacing misconceptions, and naive understandings.

It is wise to do the preassessment a week or two before the beginning of a unit of study. That way there is time to locate the resources we need and to adjust the learning experiences we have planned for the unit.

Active Learning Strategies as Preassessment Strategies

- Anticipation Guides   Pages 68-69
- Corners (Kagan, 1994)   Page 77
- Frame of Reference   Page 78
- Graffiti   Pages 79-80
- Journal Entries/Reflections*   Pages 81-84
- Line-Ups (Kagan, 1994)   Pages 89
- Questions: Teacher and Student   Pages 54-62
- Signal Cards   Pages 144-145
- Slates and White Boards   Page 146
- Sort Cards   Pages 93-95
- Stir the Class   page 96
- Three Column Charts   Page 100

* You can use the essential questions for the upcoming unit as the prompts for journal writing.

Additional Sources of Preassessment Data

Anecdotal Records, discussed on page 143, provide a rich source of assessment data. Other ways to gather preassessment data include having students draw their understanding of, or create a graphic organizer about, the concept before the learning experience begins. If you have students complete another drawing or graphic organizer at the conclusion of the learning experience, they will have a clear representation of their learning. More formal ways of gathering and assessing student knowledge and skill prior to learning include pretests, standardized test information, portfolio reviews, and interviews.

Checking for Understanding

> ## This is NOT checking for understanding!
> ### "Are there any questions?"
> "Are you all with me?"
> ## "Am I going too fast?"
> ### "This is an adverb, isn't it?"

If the above are negative examples, what is checking for understanding? It is asking questions that can only be answered if students understand. Using Howard Gardner's definition of **understanding**, this would mean that **students are able to use knowledge and skills in new situations in appropriate ways.** While recall of significant information is an important part of learning, "checking for understanding" is not the same as checking for recall or memorization. It is essential that we be clear in our own minds what we are asking students to do. John Goodlad found in his research that two-thirds of all questions asked in classrooms were at the recall level. That is why it is essential that we build skill as designers of questions that, by their answers, really let us know whether or not the students **understand.** See pages 54-60 for information on the **design of questions and levels of thinking required by the questions and tasks we design.**

Another classroom dilemma is that one we all experienced as students. We sat in classrooms where the teacher asked many questions to the entire class and called on one student to answer. Given the number of students and the limited amount of time, the chances were pretty good that any one student was called on only once during the period. There are two big problems with that approach. One, the teacher only knows if the one student who answered the question knows or does not know the answer, or has or does not have an informed opinion on the point being discussed. Two, the rest of the students can tune out if only volunteers are called on or if the teacher makes it a practice to call on all students one by one. After students have answered they are off the hook. Why do we, as teachers, even consider continuing this practice year after year?

There are ways to check across many students on the same concept or skill in a relatively short time. As we incorporate 10:2 Theory into our practice (See page 228), a strategy that is easy to implement is **Think-Pair-Share.** This strategy meets the needs of the introverted learner who wants time to think before talking because there is a short **"think"** time before any answers are accepted.

Checking for Understanding continued...

The extroverted learner's needs are addressed too because the students talk in **"pairs"** to discuss their thinking. Checking for understanding can occur during this component as you move around the room and listen in to the conversations. In the **"share"** component, random students can be called on to share their thinking, their partner's thinking, or any questions the two of them have.

Anecdotal Records/Observations

Clipboard cruising with computer labels, index cards, or observation checklists attached is a great way to gather informal assessment data. The advantage to computer labels is that, if you choose to do so, you can use the class list to put the name of a student on a label. That way you can track who you have observed by the blank labels and make a point of getting to students you might otherwise neglect because some students require or demand so much attention. Whichever record keeping device you use, you may choose to cluster the information on individual student data pages to be used later for instructional planning and conferencing, or you may want to group the cards, labels, etc. by level of competence demonstrated to plan differentiated lessons as needed.

Moving around the room and **listening in on small group discussions** and **checking over shoulders** to see how student work is progressing is an ongoing formative assessment strategy that requires no paperwork or grading. The trick is, of course, remembering who needed help with what or who might help someone else.

Additional Checking for Understanding Strategies

- **Signal Cards** — Pages 144-145
- **Slates** — Page 146
- **Sort Cards** — Pages 93-94
- **Think-Pair-Share** — Page 98
- **Journal Entries** — Pages 81-83
- **Tickets to Leave** — Page 104
- **Homework** — Pages 147-149

Many other active learning structures found in Chapter IV can be used for checking for understanding.

Checking for Understanding with Signal Cards

Provide students with cards to signal understanding of concepts, or directions, or a sense of "I'm lost!", and you send the message that it is all right not to understand everything the first time around.

You can use as many cards as you want, but a good place to start is with red, green and yellow cards which have universal meanings. Green is **GO**, Yellow is **CAUTION**, and Red is **STOP** in both traffic signals and in soccer around the world. Students can monitor their own learning and signal:

- **"Stop, I'm lost!" or "Slow down, I'm getting confused" or "Full steam ahead!"**
- **"We are working together productively" or "When you get a moment we'd like some help" or "We're dead in the water."**

Additionally, other meanings can be assigned to the cards in order to do checking for understanding of concepts and information under study. For instance the three cards could represent:

- **negative, positive, or zero**
- **complete, run-on, or fragments of sentences**
- **saturated, semi-saturated, or unsaturated**
- **future, present, or past tense**

Whatever meanings you assign the cards, the possibilities are endless!

Gerry Zeltman, teacher of English at Rush-Henrietta High School in Henrietta, New York reports that his senior students are far more willing to admit confusion and ask questions when they have a set of cards with which to signal. Several elementary teachers suggest that library card pockets taped to the student's desk work well for keeping track of the cards.

Through the Voice of... Checking for Understanding
Using Signal Cards to Check for Understanding

Read each statement aloud. Have students raise signal cards to indicate which statistical measure was used to analyze the data.

GREEN = mean, RED = median, YELLOW = mode, WHITE = range.

1. The most frequent test score was 85%.

2. The average class score was a 75.

3. Half of all students spend more than $500 per year for clothing.

4. The most popular spectator sport at our school is football.

5. The difference between yesterday's temperature and today's temperature is 30 degrees.

6. More mozzarella cheese than cheddar cheese or American cheese is eaten each year.

7. The average number of books read by each student over the summer was 3.

8. The basketball team scored 44 points on Friday night and 64 points on Saturday night, a difference of 20 points.

9. Out of all the peaks in the mountain range, 3212 feet is the middle peak.

10. The class selected chocolate chip cookie dough as their favorite flavor ice cream.

Mean? Median? Mode? Range?

Created by a wonderful teacher somewhere!

Checking for Understanding with Slates

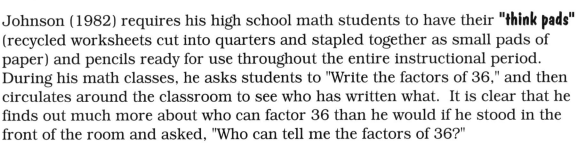

Students are provided with **slates, white boards or pads of recycled handouts** cut into fourths on which to record their thinking during a lesson and given the appropriate writing tool.

At appropriate times students can "show" their thinking by holding up their slates for teacher review or the teacher can circulate around the room to check to see who understands or can use what information.

Johnson (1982) requires his high school math students to have their **"think pads"** (recycled worksheets cut into quarters and stapled together as small pads of paper) and pencils ready for use throughout the entire instructional period. During his math classes, he asks students to "Write the factors of 36," and then circulates around the classroom to see who has written what. It is clear that he finds out much more about who can factor 36 than he would if he stood in the front of the room and asked, "Who can tell me the factors of 36?"

This kind of checking can be done frequently throughout the explanation of any multi-step process. Asking for student response after almost each teacher statement provides an opportunity to identify where and with whom the learning breaks down. While most often used in elementary classrooms, teachers of physics are also strong advocates for this active learning tool.

Checking for understanding in this way, before students do homework or other independent practice, helps ensure that the students are not practicing errors or experiencing frustration during their independent work.

As a variation, you can engage students in helping with the checking process by assigning the same problem to all students. As a student finishes, she signals for the teacher to check her work. If it is correct, this student and others who follow can join the teacher in checking the work of others. This shortens the process and gives all students a chance to successfully complete the practice problem before moving on to the next step.

Homework
Making It Worth the Effort...Yours & Theirs

Lee & Pruitt created a classification system of categories of homework. The four categories they identified were practice, preparation, extension, and creative. Their analysis of homework practice revealed that most of the homework we assign falls in the practice and preparation categories. Common sense and our own experiences as learners tell us that extension and creative homework assignments are much more likely to engage students in the learning and minimize the ever present problems of incomplete or copied homework.

Guidelines for Practice and Preparation Homework

- Design assignments to yield a **success rate of at least 80-90%.** If students have not mastered the basic concepts, do not give them an assignment that will send them home to work incorrectly. Review the assignment before giving it to students. Identify major concepts and important vocabulary, anticipate difficulties, and prepare students to deal with them.

- Give the assignment orally and in writing. Use a consistent, easily seen location to post assignments. Present assignments so that there is time to clarify instructions.

- When students have difficulty with an assignment, teaching has to take place before they are asked to do more of the same work.

- Have students keep a **homework or learning log** containing each assignment's directions, connection to the learning objective, and completion time, or why it wasn't completed. If the assignment is incomplete, have them enter what they tried and where the process broke down. Log entries may be accepted as an alternative to the regular assignment as a good faith effort to learn through trial and error. See Tools for example of an Incomplete Assignment Log.

- **Avoid assignments such as:**

  "*Read Chapter 3.*" (Students may read the chapter without purpose or comprehension.) or "*Read Chapter 3 and answer the questions at the end of the chapter.*" (Students may complete the assignment without comprehending a word.)

  Instead use "Read Chapter 3 and identify the three most significant factors related to ___. Be prepared to discuss (with your discussion groups at the beginning of class tomorrow) the factors you selected and your rationale for selecting them as the most significant." This communicates what success looks like and gives a purpose to the work outside of class.

Homework continued...

Guidelines for Extension and Creative Homework

- Build in opportunities for meta-cognition and real world connection making.

- Ask students to react to, instead of just reporting on, what they are learning.

- Journal entries, interactive notebook processing, RAFTs, surveys, and interviews are productive extension assignments.

- When possible, give students opportunities to make decisions and have choices about how they will process and demonstrate their learning.

- Performance assessment tasks, projects, and other multifaceted work can provide students with the opportunity to integrate multiple concepts and to hook bits of learning to essential understandings.

In Cases of Student or Teacher Homework Angst, Check for:

- Unplanned or irrelevant homework. If there is a homework policy and student skills and knowledge in the current area of study are not sufficient for students to work independently, assign a review of key ideas or extension homework such as reflection, journal entries, and other connection making exercises.

- Assignments given at the very end of class with no time for clarifying purposes or explanations of confusing directions.

- Assignments that seem like busy work and that aren't moving students closer to competency with the standard on which they are working. They may already know how to do what they are being asked to do, or this type of activity hasn't been productive in the past.

- Assignments that call for knowledge and skills not currently in the students' repertoire where there is, therefore, little chance for successful learning.

- Promptness and appropriateness of feedback from classmates, an answer key or you.

- Explicitness of instructional purpose. Do not give homework as punishment and do not say omit homework because of good behavior.

- How much reliance there is on parent participation. Some parents cannot or do not for a multitude of reasons help their children with homework. Children should not be penalized for lack of parental support and, on the other end of the spectrum, others should not be rewarded for work done by parents.

Homework continued...
Maximize Feedback & Minimize the Grading of Homework

Be sure that you and the students are examining homework for evidence of learning rather than for completion of activities. Too much time and energy is put into doing and grading homework for it to be about whether or not students "did" their homework. The formative assessment data we gather from homework results is far more important.

Have students complete an error analysis (See Chapter X: Tools) or react to their homework learning experiences in their journals or interactive notebooks. (See pages 81-84.)

At the beginning of the instructional period, have the students work in pairs or groups to reach consensus on practice homework. When students cannot agree, they should circle any points of confusion or disagreement. You circulate and intervene with the small groups as necessary. Only mass confusion is dealt with in large group. When papers are collected, they are all correct. The students have done the work and you have no papers to correct!

There is no need to "test" students on facts they have to memorize. Instead have the students draw the objects or some graphic representation of the facts to be memorized as a homework assignment. Have the students exchange drawings and label those of a classmate. Students check each other's work. This practice can continue until the tidbits are memorized and can be used later for cumulative review. If drawing won't work, have the students create mini-tests or flash cards to teach and test each other. There are no papers to grade!

When students write a summary statement of their thinking or of their readings as a homework assignment, have two students meet to share their summaries and to combine their thinking into one paper. The consensus paper is collected. The number of papers to be collected is cut in half!

When teaching a new operation in math, a new sentence structure, or a new science concept, have students make up one to five problems that illustrate the new information. When they arrive in class, have them exchange problems or you can collect them at the door and redistribute them randomly. Students work the problems they have received; then the problems are returned to the creators for checking and correction. Once again, no papers for you to grade!

Self Assessment

"We must constantly remind ourselves that the ultimate purpose of evaluation is to have students become self-evaluating. If students graduate from our schools still dependent upon others to tell them when they are adequate, good, or excellent, then we've miss the whole point of what education is about."

Art Costa and Bena Kallick, 1992.

In a learning-centered classroom, students are continuously engaged in assessing their own work and giving their classmates feedback on their work. They, of course, have to be taught to give feedback and to self-assess. They then need to be given opportunities to self-adjust based on what they learn from the self-assessment.

Tools we can use in the classroom that will help students learn how to self-assess include:

Performance Assessment Task Lists See pages 155 and 166.

Rubrics See pages 156-158 and 165-166.

Error Analysis See tool on page 311.

Three Column Chart

See page 100 for a description and possible column headings, template in Chapter X: Tools, and page 151 for an example of how Renee DeWald, chemistry teacher at Evanston Township High School, Evanston, Illinois, uses the three column chart to help her students self assess before their final examination.

Checklists See page 154.

Sort Cards See page 93 for directions on how to set up sort cards.

Journal Entries

See pages 81-83 for information on journals and interactive notebooks and pages 147-149 on homework that cannot be copied.
Possible self assessment entries include:
- Reflections on how I contributed to the project.
- How I studied...how well it worked. What I will do differently next time.
- What was on the test that surprised me. How might I have known it was that important.

Through the Voice of... Self Assessment

Chemistry
1st Semester Exam Objectives

The final exam consists of a lab practical and four questions. The lab practical will be given on Friday and the questions during final exam week. The questions focus on the "big ideas" from first semester - Chemical Reactions, Heat, Atomic Structure, and the Periodic Table. You may use one page of prepared notes on the official note paper provided.

You should be able to:	I can	I think I can	I can't
1. Use common laboratory equipment correctly			
2. Make accurate measurements in the laboratory			
3. Convert volume in ml to liters			
4. Apply the ideas expressed in scientific laws (conservation of mass, energy, atoms, definite proportions, multiple proportions, periodic law, Le Chatelier's Principle)			
5. Given the name, write the formula of an ionic compound			
6. Write the formulas of common acids (hydrochloric, nitric, sulfuric)			
7. Calculate percent composition			
8. Calculate the molar mass of a molecule			
9. Convert moles to mass			
10. Calculate molarity of a solution			
11. Given molarity and liters, calculate moles			
12. Write and balance a reaction equation			
13. Compare the number of moles of two substances (mole ratio or factor-label)			
14 Given mass, temperatures, and specific heat, calculate heat in joules and explain			
15. Identify atoms that utilize s and p orbitals when bonding			

(+15 more objectives)   **Renee DeWald, Evanston Township High School, Evanston, IL**

Through the Voice of... Self Assessment

Bingo

Process

- Teacher distributes Review Sheet listing key terms, people and events.
- **STUDENTS IDENTIFY THE ITEMS ABOUT WHICH THEY ARE UNSURE.**
- Students place unknown items on a Bingo-type card.
- Teacher calls out clues, and students find and mark the item(s) on their cards.

The Odyssey Bingo

Laertes	Aiolus	Eumaios	hekatomb	Argives
Ino	Elpenor	Orestes	Alkinous	hybris
Nausikaa	Halitherses	Seareach	Peisistratos	Aegisthus
Demodokos	Phemios	Mentes	paradox	Kirke
Medon	homeric simile	Akhaians	Helios	Polyphemos

Emily Stamos, Evanston Township High School, Evanston, IL

A Self-Assessment

Name:

Group:

Task:

My roles and my participation in the group consisted of the following:

I am proudest of these components of my work on this project:

I can improve my work and my participation in the following ways:

After reviewing the criteria and considering the feedback I have received, I feel that I earned the following grade:

The reasons for this grade are:

Through the Voice of... Self Assessment
4th Grade Writing Checklist

DATES

1. **Heading**
   a. signature
   b. full date
   c. title

2. **Oreo Cookie**
   a. topic sentence
   b. ending sentence
   c. lots of details

3. **Paragraphs**
   a. indent
   b. more than 1 sentence
   c. separate paragraphs

4. **Sentences**
   a. complete
   b. no run-ons
   c. make sense

5. **Edit**
   a. show edit in another color pen/pencil
   b. spelling (3)
   c. sense
   d. capitals
   e. periods

6. **Sentence Starts**
   a. variety of sentence starts
   b. no "ands" to start sentences

7. **Cursive**

8. **Neat**

9. **Margins**

10. **Spaces between words**

11. **Apostrophe (') used correctly**

Stacy Holahan & Margie Cawley, Sherman Elementary 154 School, Rush-Henrietta School District, Henrietta, NY

Mirrors & Magnifiers Newsletter
Performance Assessment Task List

Components	Possible Points	Self-Assessment	Teacher Assessment
Includes all required elements	10		
Visually appealing	5		
Displays imagination and creativity	5		
Informs, teaches, or reviews the key ideas	10		
Accurate scientific information	40		
Characteristics of light			
Reflection and refraction			
Mirrors and lenses			
Cooperative participation in group	10		
Ideas well organized and presented clearly	10		
No grammatical or spelling errors	5		
Engaging presentation	5		

Total Points: 100

Background information on the task:
Students worked in cooperative groups of five or six students to create "Mirrors and Magnifiers" Newsletters that explained the major concepts they studied during the unit. The newsletter was to include articles, both narrative and expository, diagrams, pictures/comics, interviews (with scientists in these fields, and a question/answer section (an advice column). Each group gave an oral presentation of its newsletter to the class.

Joyce Richmond & Stephanie Hoff, Grade 4 teachers, Bowen School, Newton, MA

Reading Rubric for Grades 2-3

Reader	Growing Reader	Awesome Reader
I forget to make predictions.	I make predictions sometimes.	I make predictions most of the time and change them as I read.
I forget to make pictures.	I make pictures sometimes.	The words help me make clear mental pictures.
I forget to ask questions.	I ask questions sometimes.	I ask questions most of the time.
I forget to make connections from the story to something else I know.	I make connections sometimes.	I make connections most of the time with my own life or with other books I have read.
I can retell the beginning and end of the story.	I know what story grammar is and I try to use it while I read.	I can retell what I have read using the elements of story grammar.
I forget to read chunks of words.	I read chunks of words sometimes.	I read chunks of words most of the time.
I forget to help myself to: -finish the sentence. -reread the sentence. -use the print. -skip the word. -self-correct.	I help myself sometimes to: -finish the sentence. -reread the sentence. -use the print. -skip the word. -self-correct.	I help myself most of the time. I can talk about these strategies: -I finish the sentence. -I reread the sentence. -I use the print. -I skip the word.

Jeanne Harper and Julie Masterson, Honeoye Falls–Lima School District, Honeoye Falls, NY

Students could use this rubric to self-assess on a regular basis. They could make journal entries about their performance. Because each component is addressed at each level of the rubric, the rubric could be rewritten in analytical format and students could self-assess on each component.

ENGLISH II
Responsible & Active Learner Rubric

5
- I am always prepared when called on and am always on task.
- On a daily basis, I frequently and voluntarily take risks, assert opinions and support them, ask questions, and listen respectfully to others.
- My written and oral comments and questions demonstrate a thorough and careful completion of assignments.
- I do not wait for the teacher to initiate discussion; instead I bring up ideas for the class to consider.
- Through oral participation and inquiry, I consistently demonstrate a genuine desire to learn and to share ideas with my teacher and peers.
- I demonstrate an attitude of cooperation, not competition, by responding to my peers' comments and observations.
- I take an active role in my own learning.

4
- I am usually prepared when called on and consistently on task.
- Although I may take fewer risks, I still assert opinions, support them, ask questions, and listen respectfully to others.
- My written and oral comments and questions demonstrate I have completed my assignment. Sometimes I initiate topics for discussion without waiting for the teacher to ask questions.
- Through less frequent oral participation and inquiry, I generally demonstrate a genuine desire to learn and to share ideas in my own learning.
- I usually demonstrate an attitude of cooperation so that ideas and understanding can evolve.

Nan Wampler, Worthington Kilbourne High School, Worthington, OH

Through the Voice of... Self Assessment
ENGLISH II
Responsible & Active Learner Rubric

3
- I generally speak only when called on and may not be prepared to answer with detail or substance.
- Only rarely do I voluntarily participate or ask questions.
- My written and oral comments indicate that I might not have thoroughly completed my assignment.
- I hesitate to share ideas and to take risks, and I may even stray from the assigned task.
- I may disrupt class discussion, sleep in class, or blurt out rather than wait to be recognized.
- I may not always listen to and respect the opinions of others.
- I infrequently take an active role in my own learning.

2
- I speak only when called upon and am often either unprepared or shallow in my responses.
- I do not ask questions and am unwilling to share ideas with my teacher or peers. My comments indicate that I have not completed your assignment.
- I often stray from the assigned task, display poor listening skills, and may be intolerant of the opinions of others.
- I may frequently disrupt class discussion, sleep in class, or blurt out rather than wait to be recognized.
- I infrequently take an active role in my own learning.

1
- I speak only when called upon and sometimes not then.
- I am usually unprepared in my responses and do not ask questions or share ideas with my teacher or peers.
- My lack of comments indicate that I have not completed your assignment.
- I may even try to interrupt the flow of the discussion and distract the attention of my peers.
- I may also display poor listening skills, am intolerant of the opinions of others, wander frequently from the assigned task, disrupt class discussion, or sleep in class.
- I do not take an active role in my own learning and may try to disrupt the learning of others.

Assessing with Balance

There is no one right way to assess learning.

Performance assessments assess complex thinking and problem solving skills, and, because they are designed to be realistic, are generally more motivating for students.

While performance assessments tell us how well students can apply their knowledge, multiple choice, matching, true-false, etc., tests may be more efficient for determining how well students have acquired the basic facts and concepts.

Asking a student to perform an interesting or complex task/activity does not make it a good assessment. If the task is not one which when completed measures use of concepts identified as significant, it is worthless. Not only must the task focus on essential understandings, key concepts, and big ideas, it should cause students to demonstrate skills that transfer to other situations and problems.

Another issue of balance is matching assessments with the standards of learning, with the time spent on the concept, and with the levels of thinking students were asked to do in classwork and assignments. Unbalanced assessment creates unnecessary frustration and failure.

We need to be knowledgeable about, and skilled with, the selection or design of, and use of, both performance assessments and traditional paper and pencil assessments. The following pages focus on that knowledge base.

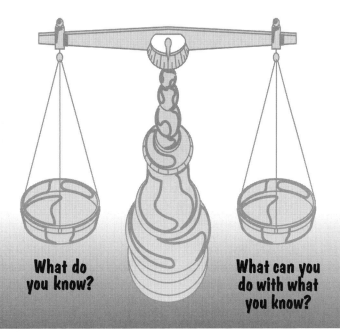

What do you know?

What can you do with what you know?

Classroom Test Design

When selecting or designing a paper and pencil summative assessment it is essential that the test fairly and comprehensively represent the learning standards being addressed in the instruction, what was actually taught and processed, as well as the time and emphasis placed on the material during instruction. Current best thinking is that the assessment should be designed immediately after the standards and/or objectives are identified. Instruction is then planned to lead students to competency on the summative assessment.

When selecting paper and pencil assessment items, there are two broad categories. Each promotes and measures a different kind of student thinking and gives the teacher different kinds of information about student learning. One category requires the student to select the best answer from a list of alternatives or to recognize a correct or incorrect statement. The other broad category requires the students to supply or create an answer that may be short or long in design. The **Select the Answer** type item is efficient for measuring recall of facts and, when skillfully designed, can measure organizational, analytical, and problem solving skills with the topic being studied. The **Supply/Create the Answer** type item is not as efficient for measuring recall of facts, but is quite useful in measuring complex learning, promoting higher level thinking about the material being studied, and demonstration of what the student can do with what he/she knows.

Guidelines for the Design of Test Items
True-False
This type of test item is useful when there are not three or four plausible distracters to use in the design of a multiple-choice item.
- Avoid absolute words like all, never, always, and usually.
- Make sure items are clearly true or false rather than ambiguous.
- Attribute opinion statements to a source.
- State items in a positive, rather than negative, voice.
- Write all items at approximately the same length.
- Write approximately half true and half false items.
- Limit true-false questions to ten.
- Make each item focus on only one key concept.
- Consider asking students to make false questions true to encourage higher order level thinking.

Classroom Test Design continued...

Matching

This type of test item is efficient at measuring competency with factual information when the emphasis is on the relationship between two components.

- Limit list to no more than ten. Use multiple sets of ten if necessary.
- State the basis for matching in the directions.
- Use homogeneous lists. (Do not mix names with dates.)
- Place directions and all items to be matched on the same page.
- Create more responses than stems.
- Consider the possibility that responses can be used more than once.
- Place responses in alphabetical or numerical order.

Multiple-Choice

Multiple choice items eliminate the prospect of random guessing that is inherent in true-false questions. This type of test item can go well beyond the recall of factual information. It takes thoughtful planning to write multiple-choice items that ask the learner to identify correct applications of facts and principles, to interpret cause and effect relationships, and to explain why a sequence or condition is the way it is. This type of test item allows the test designer to determine the level of discrimination required. Good multiple-choice items are the most difficult test items to write.

- Clearly state the problem or main idea in the stem.
- Avoid irrelevant information in the stem.
- When possible, state the stem in a positive voice.
- Use reasonable incorrect choices; make them plausible without creating "trick" questions.
- Make choices the same length.
- Avoid "all of the above," "none of the above," and "both A and B."
- Place one word options and short phrases in alphabetical order and numerical options in numerical order.

Classroom Test Design continued...

Short Answer, Fill In the Blank, or Problems

This type item is useful in measuring knowledge of terminology, of specific facts, of principles, and of methods or procedures. It is also useful for measuring skills at making simple interpretations of data, at solving numerical problems, at manipulating mathematical symbols, and at completing and balancing chemical equations.

- Limit blanks to one per item.
- Make answer blanks equal length.
- Place blanks at the end of the item.
- Avoid use of language directly from text.
- State item in a way that only one answer can be correct or be prepared to give equal credit to different but equally accurate answers.

Essay

- When creating essay questions, focus on the key concepts studied during the unit. Use Bloom's Taxonomy or McTighe and Wiggins' Facets of Understanding to design items matched to the level of thinking cited in the benchmarks or indicators.
- Decide whether to ask for an extended response or a restricted response. An extended response asks students to respond in a more global way and requires them to decide what to include in the answer. They are often required to give a rationale for their decisions. A restricted response requires a much more specific response like: "State two causes and two effects of deforestation."
- Define point value and criteria for evaluation and communicate it to students before the test begins.

Classroom Test Design continued...

Potential Problems with Test Item Design

- Ambiguous statements
- Excessive wordiness
- Difficult (or different) vocabulary
- Complex sentence structure
- Unclear directions
- Unclear illustrations or graphics
- Crowded or cluttered presentation
- Unintended clues
- Lack of match to standards, benchmarks, or indicators
- Students asked to use a process they have not practiced

Ways to Promote Learning during Traditional Testing...

Extra Inning

Collect test papers at the end of the period and announce that students will be able to have an extra inning tomorrow...ten minutes at the beginning of the period. They are to go home and study whatever they could not remember or figure out during the test. As promised, the next day they can work on their tests for an additional ten minutes. If you want to track what they struggled with have them use a different color ink or pencil. Do they get full points? Absolutely! We are into learning here and even those who had everything correct the first time are checking one more time!

Two Minute Warning

Two minutes or so before the end of the period announce that students can get out any materials they have with them to look up that nugget of information they need to support an argument or to clarify a point. Watch them get better at taking notes and knowing where to look in their texts and notes. Unlike during an open book test, when they have only two minutes they have to be really organized.

2 x 2

Correct two tests simultaneously. Mark only those questions that both students answered correctly. Return the papers for the two students to go over. They have to discover if they are both incorrect or which one is correct and submit a new consensus answer to the problem.

A special thanks to David Baker and David Brinley, math teachers in St. Vrain Valley Schools, Longmont, CO, for these ideas.

Award Winning Performance Assessment

The Performance Task

Questions to consider in the design of the task:

- **Coherency:** Do the component parts of the task flow logically from one to the other while moving toward completion of the task?
- **Rigor:** Is the task designed at the appropriate level of thinking and matched to the age and grade of the student?
- **Authenticity:** Does the task call for the creation of a product that could be used by a real audience?
- **Validity:** Does the task measure the essential understandings it seeks to measure?
- **Engagement:** Is the task both interesting and worthy of the time and energy it will take to complete? (Wiggins, 1998)

The Task Analysis

- Identify the background knowledge, the levels of understanding, and the skills necessary for successful completion of the task.
- Identify the knowledge, levels of understanding, and skills the entire group or subsets of the group are lacking.
- Based on the task analysis, design the learning experiences in a purposeful and proactive way to prevent frustrations and problems with learning.

The Assessment Criteria

- Criteria can be presented in either a holistic or analytic rubric, a performance assessment task list, or a checklist.
- The essential variables are that the criteria be presented to the students prior to the beginning of the task in a precise and public way.

The Role of Exemplars

- Exemplars are powerful motivators. Teachers find it helpful to provide not only exemplars of work that meets standards, but also to provide examples of work that does not meet standards.
- Providing students with multiple samples of work and having them sort the work into the categories of exceeds, meets, and does not meet standards helps them more explicitly identify the essential components of acceptable work.

PERFORMANCE TASK

TASK ANALYSIS

CRITERIA

EXEMPLARS

Assessment Criteria

No matter what format is used, the criteria should always be PUBLIC, PRECISE, and given to students PRIOR to the beginning of the work!

A Rubric is...

an objective set of criteria, expressed as a scale, used to assess levels of student performance in comparison to clearly articulated standards. A rubric is distinguished from other forms of criteria by the fact that each performance level on a rubric is accompanied by a narrative describing the products that meet each level of performance.

Creating a Rubric

Experienced rubric designers suggest that when creating a rubric, start with the "meets expectations" descriptors.
Ask yourself:
- What are my expectations or specific goals for this task?
- What behaviors will a student who has mastered the skill display?
- What level of performance do I hope all students will attain?

After that it is natural to move to "exceeds" and "does not meet" descriptors.

If you have done a task analysis and identified the knowledge, skills, and levels of understanding required by the task, you have done the work of identifying the components of a rubric.

Rubrics are more easily designed where there is a collection of student work to separate into piles representing "exceeds," "meets" and "does not meet" work. When the work is sorted into these categories, identify the characteristics each group has in common. If no student work is available, a performance assessment task list may be the best approach.

A frequent problem with rubrics is the lack of parallel construction. That is, designers neglect to include in the description of each level all of the component parts identified in the "meets expectations" descriptor. If, for example, organization is addressed in "meets expectations" it must be included in the "exceeds" and "does not meet" descriptors.

Rubrics can be either holistic, giving one rating for the work, or analytic, giving individual ratings for components of the work. Holistic rubrics are fine for summative assessment where the student will not be given the opportunity to learn from the feedback. See an example of a holistic rubric on pages 157-158. Analytic rubrics are much more useful to students in identifying areas for improvement, because students can clearly see the relative success they met with each component. See page 156.

Assessment Criteria continued...

The same rubric can be used over time as a **longitudinal rubric** to capture the growth a student makes with a set of skills. Consider using rubrics this way to measure growth in reading, writing, problem solving, or social and communication skills.

Rubrics can be **generic, genre, or task specific**. It is in the best interest of our students for school staffs to create or select rubrics to assess processes like communication skills, problem solving, expository writing, etc. so that all students and staff develop an understanding of what excellence looks like.

Rubrics are available from many sources. Be careful of rubrics found on the internet and in some textbook publishers manuals. They may lack clearly measurable descriptors or may include components you do not wish to measure.

A Performance Task Assessment List is...

a set of criteria with each criterion assigned a specific number of points. Performance Assessment Task Lists provide an alternative to rubrics and are quite useful for low stakes assessments. These assessment tools resemble the check lists teachers used to attach to student projects or papers after the students turned in their work. It is the fact that they are presented to the students prior to their beginning work on the task that makes them much more powerful than they were in past use. Educators in Pomerang Regional School District 15 in Connecticut have worked collaboratively to develop and refine this assessment tool to include student self-assessment as part of the process. See page 155.

Steps in the Development of Performance Task Assessment Lists

- Design student tasks that focus on the content knowledge needed to demonstrate mastery, and on the process skills and work habits students need in order to be successful.
- Do a task analysis both during and following task design.
- Make a list of the components of the performance task.
- Assign points to each component to match the significance of the component and the areas of need of the student(s).
- Provide/create models of work (both acceptable and unacceptable).

When using performance task lists with primary students, the ratings may be "terrific," "okay," and "needs work."

One of the powerful aspects of performance task lists is that they can be used to differentiate instruction by simply changing the components listed on the task list or by adjusting the number of points assigned to a specific component.

Where Do I Begin?

Use this page to jot down your reflections and to make a "To Do List" of the actions you want to take to ensure that you use on-going and balanced assessment.

VII

Planning Instruction Beginning with "Ends" in Mind

How do I translate "Beginning with the 'ENDS' in Mind" to planning & pacing for the year, the unit, & the lesson?

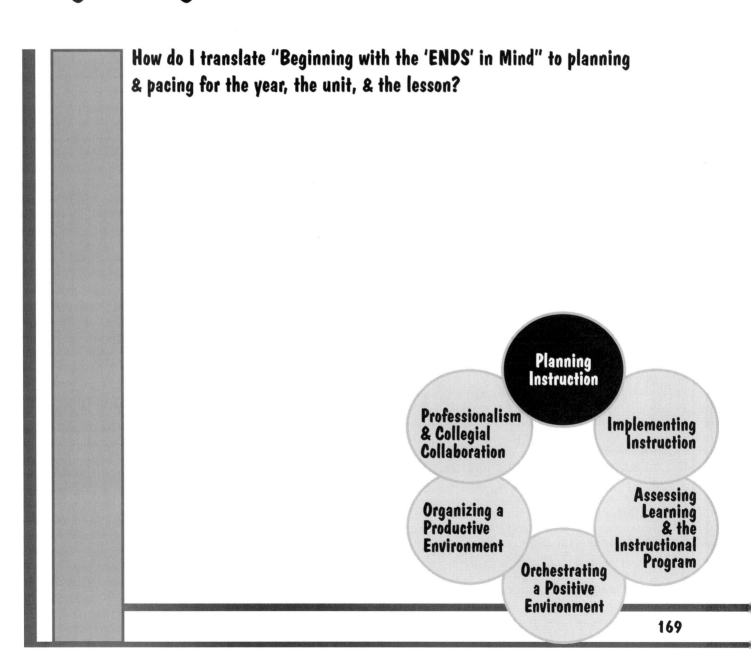

Planning Instruction

Professionalism & Collegial Collaboration

Implementing Instruction

Organizing a Productive Environment

Assessing Learning & the Instructional Program

Orchestrating a Positive Environment

169

Recommended Sites for Lesson Plans

www.eduref.org Click on **lesson plans**. Browse lesson plans by subject.

www.sdcoe.k12.ca.us THE site for standards-based web delivered units based on core literature studied K-12. You can also search for "cyberguides".

webquest.sdsu.edu THE WebQuest Page at San Diego State University

Click on **examples** and then select content area and grade level. You can also search for "Bernie Dodge."

www.edhelper.com Scroll past information on worksheets to the categories box on left side.

www.nytimes.com/learning

www.teachers.net

www.school.aol.com

Points to Ponder

Positive Planning Practices & Potential Pitfalls

YES! You do want to plan the **FIRST DAY OF SCHOOL**, but that is not the end you want to have in mind. Focus first on the whole year and plan backwards. You want to plan the first day with a picture of what you want your students to know and be able to do by the end of the year. Careful planning and preparation are essential for each and every day. Having said that, it is understood that there is a certain anxiety about the first days and the first weeks of school.

- See Chapter I and Chapter VIII for important ideas on how you want to plan for a learning-centered environment for the **FIRST DAY** and **EVERY DAY!**

- See pages 187-188 for a description of the essential understandings you most want to have come from your interactions with your students on the **FIRST WEEK OF SCHOOL** and which activities would be most useful in moving toward those essential understandings.

In order to accomplish what we want and need to accomplish, the following guidelines are offered:

- Don't even think about using one of those plan books with two inch squares! Review the materials you have on hand from your preservice days to identify formats that will allow you to record your plan for the year, the units, and the daily lessons.

- Don't think for a minute that you will have planning time during the "preplanning" days at the beginning of the year. You will be in meeting after meeting, followed by professional development opportunities! Labor Day weekend is truly a time of labor for teachers!

- Buy or print out an academic year (July 1st through June 30th) calendar. If you are fortunate enough to be hired and to know your teaching assignment prior to July 1st, then you will be able to do the very best planning. See suggested activities to be completed during the summer on pages 189-190. These summer planning activities were suggested by teachers with 0 - 3 years experience.

- Do not plan on starting with chapter one and working your way through! Preview the entire text and check its alignment with learning outcomes for your district. You will be sorry if you don't do this because you will run out of time for important lessons!

Planning in a Standards-Based Environment

The headings in this section come from the **Facilitators' Manual for Developing A Common Ground** developed by Centennial Boces, Longmont, Colorado. The team of educators who developed **A Common Ground** were early scouts in the standards movement. These statements represent the goals teachers have in mind when developing their knowledge and skills in planning.

Standards guide all classroom decisions.

This statement represents where we want and need to be. Across the USA educators have access to standards developed at the state, and often at the local level, that should guide instructional decision making. The reality is that few educators can say that they are **standards-based**. What they can say so far is that they are **standards-referenced**. That is, many teachers refer to the standards to see if they can justify what they had planned to teach based on teachers' manuals or on programs purchased by the district or by what they have "always" done. Teachers who are new to the profession, however, seem to more readily engage in practices that are **standards-based** because they have no "old habits," units, lessons, or activities to give up.

The stages of being **standards-based** are as follows:
- Knowing that the standards exist
- Knowing where to find a copy
- Reading the standards
- Posting the standards
- Occasionally referring to the standards during planning and with students
- Checking to see if what is being taught can be found in the standards
- Beginning to understand the power and focus the standards provide and working to identify the essential understandings that are embedded in and that transcend the standards as they are written in the documents.
- Being able to say "I am **standards-based** because I used the standards to design assessments and instruction, and I used student work to judge whether or not the instruction was well designed for this content with these learners."

Planning in a Standards-Based Environment continued...

The first six bullets on the previous page are more representative of **standards-referenced** than they are of **standards-based.** Teachers have to include the last two before they can say that they are **standards-based.** The next five headings further clarify variables that must be in place before teachers can accurately say, **"Standards guide all classroom decisions."**

The focus is always on student learning.

"I have so much to cover" continues to be the cry of many teachers. It is true that the amount of information and the number of skills they are asked to ensure that the learners master is mind-boggling. Given that, we teachers have to be thoughtful and focused about **how we spend the currency of education: time.** We need to make sure that every single learning experience students engage in is not only an interesting activity, but also the right exercise for moving their learning forward. Just because exercise is next in the textbook, or because our teammates have been using it for years, is not sufficient reason for having our students do it. The next exercise, or the long projects, may be just what is called for as the next lesson, but we have to ask the following questions:

- **Is this the right lesson for these students right now?**
- **Given the school-year time frame, is this learning experience worthy of the time it will cost?**
- **Is there another way to approach this learning that might work better for these learners or be more efficient in moving them along?**

In our first years of teaching it is difficult to know the answers to these questions, so it is essential that as we move through those first years we keep good reflective/analytical records of what worked and what did not work but about the cost in terms of time. That way we can be even more purposeful in the years to come.

Expectations for learning are the same for all students, even those who have traditionally performed at low levels.

At the same time the standards movement was sweeping across the land, IDEA made legally imperative what was already our moral responsibility. It requires that all students must have access to the same rich curriculum and be held to the same level of understanding as all other students. The implications are huge. The percentage of students who have been labeled as "special needs" and the percentage of English Language Learners (ELLs) is staggering. This mandate and

Planning in a
Standards-Based Environment continued...

these students are the reason we hear so much about **differentiation of instruction.** The reality of differentiation is that it has to start with a strongly focused curriculum based on the standards, and teachers must have the attitudes, skills, and knowledge to design and lead learners in one version of a good lesson before they can differentiate. To differentiate means to provide multiple pathways to learning that are equally valid and meaningful. Learn one way to do the job well first!

The final determination of the effectiveness of instructional practices is whether or not they result in higher levels of achievement for students.

Are we making progress? We need to first gather and analyze **preassessment** or baseline data about what our students know and can do as they enter the learning experience. The analysis of that data leads to an instructional plan which includes the ongoing gathering and use of **formative data. Summative assessment data** informs us and the learners about whether or not the students are moving toward mastery of the identified standards. **The question is not did they complete all the assignments and do their homework, but rather, did they learn what they were supposed to learn, did they retain it over time, and can they use it in ways that demonstrate that transfer has occurred.**

Assessment results are used to inform the teacher about the effectiveness of curricular and instructional decisions.

This fifth category is different from the previous one in that it forces the issue of using not only **classroom data** but **external data** to inform our practice. The data we glean or that we are given may reveal that the pacing of instruction needs to be adjusted, that the curriculum needs to be re-examined, or that instructional practices need to be revamped to promote retention and transfer. We can look at assessment results across schools, departments, and classes so that we can examine and redesign instruction to more closely align with what is working most effectively in similar settings. We can look at the data longitudinally across the year and over several years. **When we reach the point where we do this work collaboratively, we should see astonishing results in student achievement.**

The Planning Process in a Standards-Based Environment

Planning in a standards-based environment is often called "backwards" because we "begin with the end" in mind. In fact, we almost always begin with the end in mind when we plan vacations or weddings or purchase new automobiles. It is the way our colleagues in business and industry do project management/action planning. **In school, teachers have always planned with "the end in mind." Often though, the end we had in mind was to work our way through the book, chapter by chapter, or through the year, project by project.**

In a standards-based environment, we must be clear about "the end" we have in mind and be certain that we are working together from prekindergarten through twelfth grade to lead students to the achievement of commencement level standards. It is within this context that we focus on the standards, benchmarks, and indicators that have been identified as the ones students are to master during the grade or courses we teach. The end in mind cannot be a particular activity or project, chapters in a book, or completion of a packaged program. We have to be clear about how what students are doing in the classroom is tied to the outcomes we seek this year and throughout their K-12 educational experience.

Just like we have a clear picture of that perfect vacation, car, wedding, or ad campaign, we need to have a clear picture of what it looks like when our students are competent with what we want them to know and be able to do. Just as that vacation, wedding, or ad campaign will not happen without an action plan, we need an action plan for guiding our students to be able to demonstrate the learning we have in mind for them.

The first step in this planning process, both inside and outside the classroom, is identifying the outcome we want. The second step is creating our vision of what it looks like when get there. Next we analyze the outcome and vision to figure out what we have to do in the third step in order to accomplish the first and second steps. It makes no sense to start the third step without **THE END** in mind.

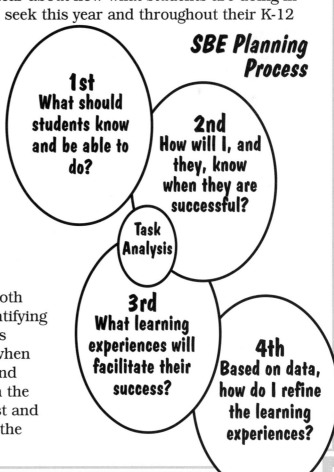

SBE Planning Process

1st What should students know and be able to do?

2nd How will I, and they, know when they are successful?

Task Analysis

3rd What learning experiences will facilitate their success?

4th Based on data, how do I refine the learning experiences?

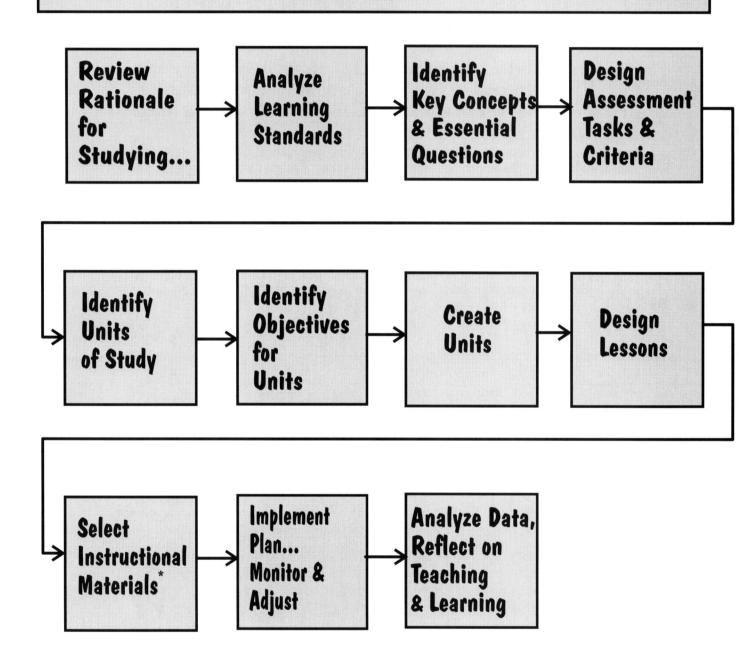

Planning Instruction for the Year

All decisions are based on district standards combined with your knowledge of the DISCIPLINE(S) you teach and of the STUDENTS who are to learn this curriculum.

Review Rationale for Studying... → Analyze Learning Standards → Identify Key Concepts & Essential Questions → Design Assessment Tasks & Criteria

Identify Units of Study → Identify Objectives for Units → Create Units → Design Lessons

Select Instructional Materials* → Implement Plan... Monitor & Adjust → Analyze Data, Reflect on Teaching & Learning

* "Select Instructional Materials" is placed at this point in the sequence because the focus must be on teaching to the learning standards in ways that match the students needs, interests, and backgrounds rather than how much time to spend on each chapter in the textbook. The textbook can be a valuable tool but we must remember that we teach students not textbooks!

Identifying & Communicating
Essential Understandings

What Are They & Why Bother?

Essential understandings, key concepts, and big ideas are both embedded in and transcend standards, benchmarks, and indicators. They become the questions/statements we post on large banners across the front of the room, the titles of bulletin boards, and the focus of performance assessments. When we identify them, and communicate them to students, they become the ribbon that ties all the bits and pieces together and helps us all stay focused on the most essential understandings.

If we design assessments that allow our students to memorize in order to pass the test, they miss the essential understandings, key concepts, and big ideas. As a result, they quickly forget the information that they stored in their short term memories for testing purposes. These essential understandings provide the umbrella for the design of performance assessment tasks. These understandings are the points we want students to hold on to and remember long after they are out of school. An additional benefit of having students focus on essential understandings is that they will be better able to answer questions on high stakes assessments. Even if they have never heard of the details in a test item, they can eliminate choices that do not match the key concept addressed in the stem.

Posing these essential understandings as questions promotes curiosity and inquiry. They can, however, be presented to students as statements. On the following pages are examples of essential questions and statements, key concepts, and big ideas as developed by teachers, as well as practical examples of how teachers are translating them and communicating them to students.

A dilemma we face is that different states and different districts call different ideas and different levels of information essential. Many documents do not include "understandings" but focus instead on knowledge and skills. While seeking to identify the big ideas or essential understandings, follow the directives of your district.

McTighe and Wiggins in *Understanding by Design* offer a widely discussed version of essential or enduring understandings that gets at the heart of the matter. This book is recommended reading when you are ready to investigate the big ideas of what you are teaching.

Through the Voice Of...
Essential Understandings

- All living things need to adapt to their habitat to survive and thrive. (Grade 4 Science)

- All living things need each other to survive. (Grade 4 Science)

- How does the study of language help us understand and experience the world around us? (Languages Other Than English)

- What makes a book worth reading? (Middle School English)

- How do geographical, economic, technological, religious, and social variables affect the course of history? (Grade 5 History and Social Science)

- There are positive and negative consequences of revolutions. (Grade 5 History and Social Science)

- Math is a language. Effectively communicating mathematical ideas is a critical component in solving real-life problems. (Geometry)

- Numbers tell the story of a business. (Accounting)

- Is the world a fair and just place? (High School English)

- How does literature affect your life, and how does your life affect your interpretation of literature? (High School English)

- The three big ideas of Chemistry are structure and properties of matter, atomic structure, and chemical reactions. Everything we study will fit in to those categories. (Chemistry)

- Observations lead to model building that helps explain past observations and predict future events. (Grade 2 Science)

- The study of mathematics is the study of how to organize information to solve problems. (Mathematics K-12)

- Why war? (Middle School Social Studies)

- All life on earth is interdependent. (Grade 4 Science)

- Data that occurs in real world situations can be examined for patterns and trends. These patterns may exhibit linear or non-linear relationships. (High School Math)

- How do we balance our need for a certain quality of life with the need to maintain a healthy ecosystem? (High School Biology)

- A system involves parts working together to form a dynamic whole. (Grade 1 Science)

- A revolution, which is a sudden or momentous change in a situation, can be political, cultural, economic, or scientific. (Middle School Social Studies)

Communicating
Essential Understandings
Key Concepts, Big Ideas ... & Standards

Tom Loftus, high school English teacher, Greece Central School District, Greece, New York, created **essential questions bookmarks** for students to use in the books they were reading. Having the questions in hand helps him, and his students, stay focused on why they are reading the text.

Jan Swanson, St. Vrain Valley School District, Longmont, Colorado, printed the English Language Arts district standards to be used as **section dividers in student notebooks.** She printed one large standard area, with indicators, on a page of colored paper and the students filed their assignments behind the standard it addressed. By doing this, the students were building a body of evidence of their work around a given standard.

Donna Begley, Induction Coach in St. Vrain Valley School District, translated **kindergarten standards into kid friendly language** for teachers to post and to share with students: The language arts standards read:
- I can name the letters and the sounds they make.
- I know how to read some words.
- I can tell you what happened in the story.
- I can answer questions about a book I have heard or read.
- I know how to handle books.
- I remember poems and songs.
- I know which words rhyme.
- I know which words start the same and end the same.
- I can write words to go with my pictures.
- I can write my name with a capital letter at the beginning.
- I follow three directions at a time!
- I am a good listener to all kinds of stories!

Renee DeWald, chemistry teacher, Evanston Township High School, Evanston, Illinois, displays an overhead at the beginning of the year, and at the beginning of each unit of study, of a **classification graphic organizer** that reveals that everything the students study in chemistry is related to three key concepts: the structure and properties of matter, atomic structure, and chemical reactions. The students keep a copy of the organizer in their notebooks and complete a **concept map, a type of a descriptive graphic organizer,** as they study component parts of these key concepts. Additionally, Renee and the other chemistry teachers at ETHS have developed and given students **essential questions that become essay questions for each unit of study.**

Through the Voice of...
Communicating
Key Concepts

ART

Creativity
*ideas
*expressions
*reality
*story
*beauty
*effort
*sketchbooks

Skills
*materials
*practice
*neatness
*craftsmanship

Seeing/Knowing
*art history
*self-evaluation
*group critiques
*resources

Composition

Elements	Directional Dominance	Principles
*line		*rhythm
*color		*unity
*shape		*emphasis
*space		*contrast
*color		*balance
*texture		
*value		

Debbie Novak, Evanston Township High School, Evanston, Illinois

Guiding Questions for
Unit Design
in the Standards-Based Classroom

1st STEP: What should students know and be able to do?

1. On which content standard(s) will the students be working?

2. What are the key ideas, major themes, big concepts, or essential understandings embedded in, or which transcend, the standards listed above?

3. Given the essential to know key concepts and ideas identified in #2 how will this unit be different from what/how I taught and asked students to do in years past? If this is a new unit, skip this question.

4. When and where (inside and outside of school) have the students encountered information about and had experience with these key concepts/big ideas before? Think horizontally and vertically across the curriculum.

2nd STEP: How will I, and they, know when they are successful?

5. What would it look like when students can demonstrate that they understand the big ideas and have the essential skills? That is, what are some ways they might demonstrate their capacity to use the newly learned concepts/information appropriately in a new situation?

6. What task/products would best demonstrate student understanding? Should I use a rubric or a performance task list, and what criteria should I include?

7. What does a task analysis reveal about the skills, the knowledge, and the level of understanding required by the task?

8. Do I already have sufficient preassessment data or do I need to gather more? If so, what method shall I use? What does the preassessment data tell me about the skills and knowledge on which the entire group will need to focus? Are there individual students who will need additional support if they are to have a realistic opportunity to demonstrate mastery? In which areas will they need support?

Guiding Questions for **Unit Design** in the **Standards-Based Classroom** continued...

3rd STEP: What learning experiences will facilitate their success?

9. How will I "Frame the Learning" so that students know what they are going to be doing, what they will know and be able to do as a result of those activities, how they will be assessed, and how everything they are doing is aligned with the standards?

10. How will I help students access prior knowledge and use it productively, either building on it or reframing their thinking as appropriate?

11. What methods of presentation and what active learning experiences can I use to help students achieve the standard? Could I provide multiple sources of information and exercises that would help all students to make real world connections and use sophisticated thinking skills?

12. What assignments, projects, and homework will help students see the relevance of the learning? How might I provide multiple pathways to learning?

13. What classroom activities/observations, as well as formative quizzes and tests, would provide me and my students information on their progress toward the standard?

14. What materials and resources do I need to locate and organize to provide multiple pathways to learning? How should I organize the classroom and the materials to provide easy student access?

15. What else might I do to to provide challenging and meaningful experiences for both struggling and advanced learners? Are there other human, print, or electronic resources I might consult to refine/review my plan?

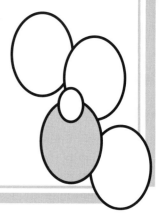

Guiding Questions for **Unit Design** in the **Standards-Based Classroom** continued...

4th STEP: Based on data, how do I refine the learning experiences and/or the assessment?

16. How did students do on the performance task? Were there some students who were not successful? What might account for that? What could I do differently next time?

17. What else do I need to consider in my advance planning the next time I am focusing on this standard?

18. Did all of the activities guide students toward mastery of the standard? Are there activities that need to be added, modified, or eliminated? Am I using these activities because I have always used them or have I analyzed them to be sure that they are the most effective and efficient tools at my disposal?

19. Overall, was this unit effective for addressing the standard(s)? Are there other standards that I could incorporate into this unit or are there other units of study where I can have the students revisit these standards or essential understandings?

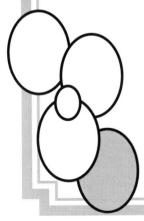

adapted from the Facilitator's Guide and Workbook for *Common Ground in the Standards-Based Education Classroom* prepared by the Northern Colorado BOCES SBE Design Team

TOP TEN QUESTIONS
to ask myself as I design lessons

1st What should **students know and be able to do** with what they know as a result of this lesson? How are these objectives related to national, state, and/or district standards or proficiencies?

2nd How will **students demonstrate what they know and what they can do?** What multiple means of assessment from the assessment continuum can I use? What will be the **assessment criteria** and what form will it take?

3rd Questions 3 -10 address the third step.

3. How will **I find out** what **students already know (preassessment),** and how will I help them access what they know and have experienced both inside and outside the classroom? How will **I help them** to not only **build on prior experiences** but **deal with misconceptions** and reframe their thinking when appropriate?

4. How will new knowledge, concepts, and skills be introduced? Given the **diversity** of my students and my **task analysis**, what are **my best options for sources and presentation modes** of new material?

5. How will **I facilitate student processing (meaning making)** of new information or processes? What are the key questions, activities, and assignments (in class or homework)?

6. How will **I check for student understanding** during the lesson?

7. What do I need to do to **differentiate instruction** so the learning experiences are productive for all students?

8. How will I **"Frame the Learning"** so that **students know the objectives,** the **rationale** for the objectives and activities, the directions and procedures, as well as the **assessment criteria** at the beginning of the learning process?

9. How will I build in opportunities for students to make **real world connections** and to learn and use **varied and complex thinking skills.**

10. What adjustments need to be made in the **learning environment** and in **instruction** so that all students can work and learn efficiently? How is **data** being used to make these decisions?

Task Analysis

Task analysis is **ESSENTIAL** between Step Two to Step Three in the SBE Planning Process so that we can be purposeful about selecting the learning experiences in Step Three.

1st Be absolutely certain that the **task** is **worthwhile** and **valid!**

2nd Analyze the task by noting and listing (either on paper or mentally) all the **skills,** the **knowledge,** and the **levels of understanding** students need to have in order to be successful at moving toward mastery of the standard and at completion the task.

3rd Identify **which students have mastered which parts of which skills and know, at the necessary level of understanding, the knowledge needed to be successful.** If unknown, decide how to find out (design and use a preassessment) or determine how to circumvent the need for the skill.

Once you know who knows and can do what, plan instruction and learning exercises that address the various levels of expertise of the group or individuals. When planning for differentiation, do not fall into the trap of using "normal" and "different." Provide multiple pathways to learning.

Remember that differentiation starts with good lesson design. The next step is to adjust instruction based on informal and other formative assessment you gather along the way. Provide support systems and scaffolding as needed. See pages 39-42 for suggestions for special needs students and pages 127-134 for reading strategies to use with struggling readers and English Language Learners (ELLs).

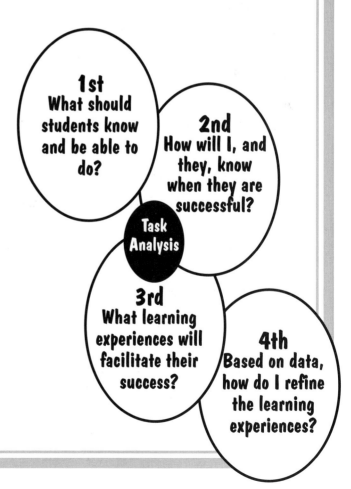

1st What should students know and be able to do?

2nd How will I, and they, know when they are successful?

Task Analysis

3rd What learning experiences will facilitate their success?

4th Based on data, how do I refine the learning experiences?

Getting Started with
Differentiation

Differentiation of instruction does not mean that you individualize instruction or provide something "different" from the normal lesson for a few struggling or advanced students. It means that you think proactively and, from the beginning, the "normal" lesson includes more than one avenue for success. It means that you think about the diversity of your learners when you are planning and don't ever again fall into the trap of thinking that "One size fits all."

1. What do you expect your students to know and be able to do when they study _____?

2. What assessment opportunities might you give students to demonstrate what they have learned about the above concept?

3. Given the task analysis, what is the information and the learning processes with which all students should work? List a few instructional strategies and practice and/or processing activities that would promote learning those items.

4. What might you do to extend and expand the thinking of students ready to, and/or interested, in going beyond what you've planned? Include both inside and outside of class possibilities.

5. What do you know about your struggling learners that you need to address up front? What about your ESL students? Your special education students? List specific examples of instruction strategies, adaptations, and support systems that would be helpful to several of them.

6. What might you do to reteach or help students having difficulties in understanding this concept? Include both inside and outside of class possibilities.

Planning for the First Week of School

Beginning with the End in Mind, the Essential Outcomes of the First Week are:

- A preview, in an age appropriate way, of the essential understandings, key concepts of the course or the grade level
- A preassessment of the levels of student knowledge and skills in each content area
- A preview/overview of the primary texts and instructional materials
- An overview, as appropriate, of end of the year assessments
- Some nifty nuggets of knowledge so that when parents ask, "What did you learn today?" the students have a ready answer
- An overview of classroom organization and procedures
- Getting to know your students as people and as students
- Building community by having students get to know each other
- Helping the students know you as a person and as a professional educator
- Ensuring that the students, in an age appropriate way, are informed about school policies and the rationale for them
- A preview/review of the rights and responsibilities of educators, students, and parents in an age appropriate way
- Establishing the classroom rules or norms together, or communicating the rules you have developed, perhaps in collaboration with your team or mentor. Include modeling and practice of the rules.

Given These Outcomes, the Preparation & Planning You Need to Do includes:

- Learn about all the items listed above.
- Figure out your options for orchestrating all of the above.
- Make a schedule for implementing your plan.
- Complete the planning for all of the above so that you can be at the door in a positive, prepared, and professional state of mind to greet your students as they arrive.

Keep Your Eyes on the Goal!

Be positive, professional, and passionate about teaching, learning and your learners, and be as prepared as you humanly can be given that you may have never done this before! People skills and organizational skills reign supreme!

Planning for the First Week of School
Continued...

No matter how much experience a teacher has, getting ready for the school year requires a great deal of planning and work. The work of the veteran teacher may be invisible, as over time, more and more of it goes on in your head; you run mental movies of what you want to do differently and figure out how you might do that. In the beginning, the planning and preparation is much more visible because you are gathering information and materials to set up the classroom and your own professional library and office. Pages 194-250 provide guidance for what information to seek and help for setting up organizational systems. The completion of this advance work during the summer allows you to concentrate on creating a learning-centered environment and on teaching and learning from the minute the students walk in the door.

There is an incredible listing of **101 Things You Can Do the First Three Weeks of Class** on the University of Nebraska Lincoln website. That it is directed to college professors in no way makes it less useful for K-12 educators. The focus is on best practice in a learning-centered environment to include getting to know your students, letting your students know the curriculum and the assessments, the logistics, each other and you.

The directions to access it are complex but it is well worth the effort. Bookmark the site for future reference!
- Go to www.unl.edu
- Click on Faculty/Staff
- Click on Faculty Resource Index
- Click on Teaching Tips

Through the Voice Of...
Summer Planning Advice
June

- Take a vacation.
- Mentally prioritize and plan.
- Read through district learning standards.
- Do an overview of the curriculum.
- Obtain copies of student texts and teacher's manuals.
- Read for content background.
- Begin to map or chunk the year.
- Collect/organize "stuff."
- Read for best advice on discipline plans and develop a plan.
- Learn about district, school, and department assessments.
- Locate/create rubrics.
- Decide on organizational system.
- Check out organizational software.

July

- Do background reading.
- Have entire school year mapped and outlined.
- Plan first unit.
- Develop lesson plans: Have first two weeks planned, done, final!
- Put masters in plastic covers.
- Prepare expectations sheet, class policies letter, etc.
- Go to garage sales to find "stuff."
- Shop for "back to school" clothes.
- Develop student supply list.
- Find visual aids for classroom.
- Read for fun.
- Enjoy the summer weather and recreational activities.
- Sleep a lot.

These ideas on how to prepare for the upcoming school year were contributed by fifty-five "new" teachers in St. Vrain Valley School District's 1st Annual Why Didn't I Learn This in College Summer Institute. Participants had 0 to 3 years classroom teaching experience.

Through the Voice Of...
Summer Planning Advice
August

- Find a place to live.
- Locate an office/cubicle space for my stuff.
- Transport school stuff from ...trunk, home, under bed, file cabinets...to school.
- Organize files, folders and notebooks.
- Finish detailed lesson plans for the third week.
- Order supplies through school office.
- Get personal school supplies.
- Buy/create thank you notes.
- Develop questionnaire for students.
- Select/plan team building activities for students.
- Inventory check.
- Locate furniture for classroom.
- Develop substitute plans and folder.
- Send letter to students and their families.

Put test keys on colored paper

The Week Before School Opens

- Meetings, Meetings, Meetings!
- Read up on school policies.
- Learn how your computer works and what programs are on it.
- Set up grade book on the computer.
- Get a good bathroom pass.
- Organize/decorate classroom.
- Buy/make name tags or tent cards and seating charts.
- Get to know co-workers/teammates.
- Have coffee and lunch with other teachers.
- Make copies of forms.
- Review school calendar.
- Do laminating.
- Check out equipment from media center.

These ideas on how to prepare for the upcoming school year were contributed by fifty-five "new" teachers in St. Vrain Valley School District's 1st Annual Why Didn't I Learn This in College Summer Institute. Participants had 0 to 3 years experience.

Where Do I Begin?

Use this page to jot down your reflections and to make a "To Do List" of the actions you want to take to plan instruction in a standards-based environment.

VIII

Organizing a Productive Environment Organizational Systems for Me, the Learners, & the Classroom

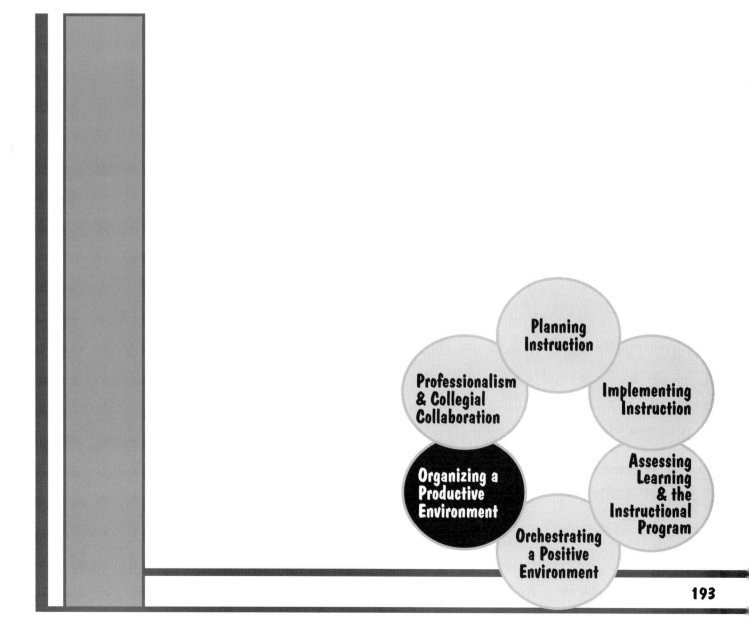

Planning Instruction

Professionalism & Collegial Collaboration

Implementing Instruction

Organizing a Productive Environment

Assessing Learning & the Instructional Program

Orchestrating a Positive Environment

On
The
Web

Recommended Sites for Organizational Systems

www.learnnc.org

Click on **New Teacher Support** for an excellent Beginning Teacher Handbook with tools for setting up a classroom.

www.nea.org/tips

Click on **Works4Me Tip Library** for a vast array of tips from teachers around the country.

www.sitesforteachers.com

This site lists over 250 sites for teacher use.

www.iss.stthomas.edu/studyguides/

This site provides study tips for students. Many are translated into several languages.

teachernet.com
teachervision.com

Points to Ponder...
Systems Design So That You Can Maintain Your Sanity & Focus Your Attention on Teaching and Learning!

When reading this chapter about organizational systems, you will need to consider the **context in which you work**. You will need to translate the ideas presented to fit your own situation, which can range from small school to large school, from regular ed to special ed, from urban to suburban to rural school, from high to middle to elementary school, from a school well equipped with technology to one with little or antiquated technology. You may encounter amazingly sophisticated and potentially complex systems already in place, you may find yourself working on a team that has a way it has "always done it" or in a "you are on your own to come up with an organizational system" situation.

First jobs in any field include a **steep learning curve.** As mentioned in the first chapter, you are unique as an educator in that you not only have to learn your job and get yourself organized, you have to immediately figure out how to organize a group of young people into a smoothly operating learning community. Because of these dual responsibilities, any organizational systems you can put into place for yourself before the opening of school will pay off handsomely.

You cannot imagine the **paperwork** that is going to flow through your hands and potentially cause chaos in your life. Even if there are systems in place within your school, team, or department, you will have to implement those systems. This chapter focuses first on the kind of paperwork generated by schools and school systems, and then on the professional paperwork you will need to collect and organize for yourself.

Following the focus on **systems for organizing your professional life** you must take a look at setting up systems for organizing the paper flow and materials within the classroom and with the parents of your students. This is when you start to generate mounds of paperwork yourself. As you translate all the words that you have been given in writing and orally into instructional and organizational plans for the classroom the paper flow gets even crazier! You can do this! You just have to come up with a system that works for you. *A system that works for you is defined as a system where you can find what you want when you need it.*

The last part of this chapter focuses on **organizing and leading a learning-centered classroom.** The philosophical underpinnings of the first part of the chapter will greatly influence how you put procedures into place and how you and the students interact with each other to promote learning by all.

In the Beginning
Starting the Year Out Right

Take Care of Yourself

Sleep as much as you can the week before you report to work. Unless you are a triathlete you are going to be more tired on the Friday of the first week of school than you have ever been in your entire life. It does not matter how long you have been teaching or how organized you are, the first week is absolutely exhausting.

Especially in the first years, you will spend many hours beyond the school day preparing lessons, preparing paperwork, and critiquing student work. There is absolutely no way to escape that reality. If you do not do that level of preparation, your classroom life will be so draining that you will be even more tired. It is, however, essential that throughout the year you identify times when you will not think about your professional life, and instead concentrate on your physical, emotional, and social well-being. There is little chance that a teacher can lead a lively social life Monday through Thursday, because there is no way you can "party" during the week and face kindergartners, 4th, 8th or 12th graders the next morning. During the week do fit in a stop at the gym, a walk in the park, an early dinner with a friend, or an hour or so at a book store with a coffee shop.

Setting Up Your Office

Figure out what you want to have with you during your first week in your new professional home. While the school system will provide supplies and equipment of a generic sort, bringing your own personal/professional items will make your desk or your office space feel more like you really belong there. Items might include a few favorite books, a picture or poster that makes you smile, a plant, a pencil holder, or other such storage items. If you are a plant person, purchase a low maintenance one for your desk, the top of the file cabinet or the window ledge. If you share a room, ask for a corner to call your own or make whatever corner or cubicle where you keep your materials look and feel like a professional home.

If the school system/school does not provide them, make computer generated business cards for yourself. You can find sheets of business cards with templates provided at any office supply store. For ideas about format, look at the samples at the photocopy center at the store. While you are at it, create letterhead that you can use in your printer or the school copier for the messages you want to send home to parents or to colleagues.

In the Beginning
Starting the Year Out Right continued...

Dress Like the Highly Educated Professional You Are

Identify what you want to wear each day for the first week of school. In fact, consider what you are going to wear to the staff work days before school. First impressions are very important! Maximize yourself. If you are teaching at a high school and look young enough to be confused with the student body president, make sure that your clothes say loudly and clearly, "I am an adult and a professional educator."

You need a minimum of five professional outfits. Jeans are appropriate for picnics, rodeos, yard work, and "hanging out." If you want to wear jeans and tennis shoes to work, you'll need a different venue like horticulture or a dot-com. You never know when a parent in a three piece suit is going to show up. If you are not dressed as a professional, you are at a distinct disadvantage. Do not say that you cannot afford to dress professionally. Jeans and tennis shoes are quite expensive. You just need to shop in a different department. If ironing isn't your strong suit, dig deep and pay a dry cleaner.

R E S P E C T!

It is a cruel hard fact that you may encounter some students who do not "like" you and the parents of some of your students who may disagree with decisions you make. In the end, what you want to be able say is that both the students and parents **RESPECT** you. Respect is something that has to be earned. Educators along with physicians, lawyers, pilots, nurses, and all other professionals interacting with the public (in a role supposedly commanding respect by virtue of the educational level and the level of responsibility connected to the position) have learned that you do not get respect by just showing up.

Consider the people you respect and identify the behaviors and characteristics they exhibit. In particular, think back to your teachers and professors and contemplate the behaviors and characteristics that earned them that respect. Next figure out which of those behaviors and characteristics you want your students to use when they describe you. If you are really brave, go ahead and identify the behaviors and characteristics that caused you to lose respect for a teacher or other person and figure out what you might do to avoid those behaviors.

Be Positive, Prepared, and Professional!

In the Beginning
Starting the Year Out Right continued...

Take the Initiative: Teaching is Hard Professional Work!

The complexity of teaching is without equal. Even though you spent some time as a student teacher with one or more veteran teachers and you no doubt learned an incredible amount during that time, that veteran teacher had done the work of creating the learning environment and planning and implementing the organizational systems for himself, the classroom, and the learners before you showed up to be the student teacher. Now you not only have to design and implement lessons focused on moving all students toward the achievement of high standards, you have to come up with your own organizational systems that will work for you and your students.

The more organizational thinking, planning, and work you can do before school starts, the better off you will be. Hang out in office supply stores to study your options for organizing your papers. If you can access summer school classrooms, stop into as many as you can. Take a look at how they are set up and think about the pros and cons. When possible, ask for the rationale for unusual set-ups or creative ideas you do not understand. See pages 203-211 and pages 231-235 for systems suggestions.

Do not wait for someone to give you materials and information. Seek them out. If what you want is not available, come up with a substitute or find it for yourself. If we worked on a factory assembly line, what we could add to our work space would be quite limited for safety and efficiency reasons. As professionals, we have a great deal more leeway in the tools we use to enhance our work...as long as we do not use materials that have been identified as or might be inappropriate for the children with whom we work.

Find a Mentor

Don't leave home without one! You may or may not be "issued" a mentor and you may or may not build a strong collegial relationship with an assigned mentor. If someone does not take care of initiating this relationship for you, now is the time to be assertive and find your own mentor. Seek out someone who can not only provide emotional support and encouragement, information about how the school operates, the cultural norms, and the school community (Villanni), but someone who can also coach you in how to organize and lead a positive and productive learning-centered classroom. Many school districts have multiple year induction programs. Take advantage of yours if you have one. Even if you are really tired at the end of the day, the collegial interaction and professional development opportunities will restore your energy and focus.

In the Beginning
Starting the Year Out Right continued...

The Way We Do Business Around Here

Like all large organizations schools and school districts have policies and procedures that are to be followed by all employees. In fact schools tend to have more policies and procedures than most organizations because of the issues connected with working with children. Read the School and District Handbooks/Policy Manuals and ask lots of questions! Use pages 199-202 as a checklist of the details you need to know in advance so that once school starts you can focus on teaching and learning. Do whatever it takes to be clear about:

Curriculum Guides and State and District Standards

Find out how to access these documents. Some districts have them posted on the district website, some have hard copies available for you, and some have both.

School Calendar

School districts usually publish their calendars for the following school year in January or February of the previous school year. Access the school calendar early so that you can plan your professional and personal life. Some events will be available only at the school level and may not be available until the opening of schools. Dates to note are:

- grading periods
- testing schedules
- holidays
- professional development days
- teacher workdays
- faculty, department, and team meetings
- athletic events
- special events like concerts, festivals, and homecoming

Daily Schedule & Schedule Changes

Find out which radio and television stations carry announcements of delayed openings and school closures. Identify the

- opening and closing hours
- bell schedule
- specials
- delayed opening procedures
- school closing procedures

> **ASK QUESTIONS!**
>
> Use pages 199-202 as a checklist so that you can keep track of what you know, what you have on hand and to identify what you still need to investigate and locate.
>
> ASK QUESTIONS!
>
> ASK QUESTIONS!
>
> ASK QUESTIONS!

In the Beginning
Starting the Year Out Right: Find Out About...

Attendance Procedures

Student Cumulative Records
- location
- special services records
- access by staff and parents

Student Safety Issues
- fire drill, evacuation, and lock down routines
- suspension and expulsion
- vandalism reports
- student injuries
- student medication
- substance abuse
- safety patrols
- student supervision
- playground regulations and supervision
- adult/guardian/parent access to students

Grading and Reporting Student Achievement
- school/district/state rubrics
- philosophy and procedures
- progress reports
- parent conferences
- interims
- data processing
- grade books
- forms
- students with IEPs
- promotion/retention
- graduation requirements
- class rank

Student Achievement Data
- department/grade results from last year
- data analysis: areas that need to be strengthened
- data on my students

In the Beginning
Starting the Year Out Right continued...

While we study the content we are to teach, learning theory, and pedagogy, there are not usually courses offered on how schools operate. If you want to be able to concentrate on teaching and learning it is helpful to figure out the logistical side of your work before you are settled in the classroom. A unique characteristic of teaching is that you cannot just pick up the phone at any time during the work day and call the human resources or finance departments with your questions. Given that you are with students throughout the day there is simply little opportunity to pose your questions and have them answered during the school day.

To that end it is smart to find out the following information early on. Some of the answers may be provided in a faculty handbook or new teachers' guide. If it is not available in print, two good sources for the answers are your mentor and the front office secretary.

Useful Information for Your Files
- required paperwork at beginning of year, at end of quarter, semester and year
- leave procedures (sick, personal, and professional)
- benefits package (medical, dental, life, and disability insurance)
- investment opportunities
- recertification requirements
- induction program
- professional development opportunities
- tuition reimbursement programs
- criteria for professional performance review
- supervision and evaluation process
- tenure
- specialist services available (in the school and the district)
- referrals to specialists
- substitutes and substitute folders
- materials acquisition
- telephone use and logs
- email
- district/school/class websites
- media center procedures
- materials duplication
- copyright requests

In the Beginning
Starting the Year Out Right continued...

More Miscellaneous but Important Information to Know!
- use of instructional assistants/paraprofessionals
- use of parent volunteers
- use of custodial staff
- staff parking locations and stickers
- staff cafeteria location and procedures
- staff mailboxes
- student transportation
- student dress code
- field trip procedures
- assemblies and pep rallies
- club/co-curricular sponsorships
- recommendation letters
- school pictures
- fund raising
- tickets to concerts/athletic events
- political activities
- school visitors
- exchange students
- professional organizations

Teachers' Lounge

There are unwritten rules that will not be found in the handbook so watch and ask around! For example, it is possible that certain chairs or desks may be "reserved" for someone...and have been for fifteen years.

The oral history of the school and the best jokes may well be found in the teacher's lounge.

Socialization, congeniality, and just plain adult interaction are an important part of our lives. You may well meet a new lifelong friend there.

Be aware, however, that in addition to all the positive relationships and conversations that can potentially be found in teachers' lounges, there is also a possibility that the lounge culture can be one of cynicism, negativism and/or a "us against them" philosophy. The "them" may be the administration, the parents, or the students. IF that is the case, it is in your best interest and the best interest of your students for you to avoid the lounge.

In the Beginning
Starting the Year Out Right continued...

Staff Social Events

Be assertive! Well intended colleagues may neglect to tell you that they always go out for dinner before/after back to school night or that they always have an opening of school breakfast or holiday party!

Whenever possible participate in the pot luck luncheons. They are usually delicious and fun. Sign up early so if you do not consider yourself a gourmet cook, you can bring the paper plates and napkins or hit the bakery for bread or cookies.

Give yourself permission to attend or not attend social events. Be sure, however, to get to know your colleagues on a professional basis as quickly as possible.

In the Beginning
Meet & Greet...We're All in This Together

Create either a file box, a folder, a section in a three ring binder, or a data base on your computer for collecting information about all the adults with whom you work. Note both their professional responsibilities and their personal interests as you purposefully learn about them. Introduce yourself to as many as possible...and remember to send thank-you notes when they contribute to your success and the success of your students!

- School board members
- Superintendent
- Central/district office staff
- Principal and other administrators
- Mentor teachers
- Teachers
- Librarians/media specialists
- Technology coordinators
- Special education staff
- Reading resource teachers
- Athletic staff
- Counselors
- Secretaries
- School nurse
- Custodians
- Cafeteria staff
- Bus drivers
- PTA officers
- Volunteer coordinators/volunteers
- ...and don't forget our parent partners!

In the Beginning
Take a Tour

As soon as you know where you will be working, buy or find a map of the community and the school attendance area. Many school districts provide bus tours of the school district during the August induction/orientation program. In any case, as soon as you know where you will be working, buy or find a map of the community and the school attendance area. Either drive or walk through the attendance area to get a sense of the neighborhood.

You will be very busy after students report so it is a good idea to do a comprehensive tour of the school facility as well.

Use the following list to provide focus for your community tour:
- Note the locations of the public library, the rec center, parks, movie theatres, and shopping areas
- Find the other K-12 schools that either send or receive students to/from your school
- Locate the district office

Use this list for guidance in locating important areas of the school building:
- The cafeteria, the gym and speciality areas like music, art and professional/technical education
- The school grounds
- Front office
- Counselor's office
- Media center/library
- School nurse office
- Photocopy room
- Computer lab
- Cafeteria
- Teachers' lounge
- The field house

Words of Wisdom on
Culture, Collaboration, & Communication

These three, culture, collaboration, and communication, are the keys to not only surviving but thriving in the education universe. There is no other job in the world where there is the potential for you to spend the entire day in the company of five year-olds focused on sequencing, or with fourteen year-olds focused on voice in writing. Judith Warren Little found in her research on student achievement that adult interaction in teaching and learning is an important part of the education process.

Every organization has a **culture.** Terry Deal in his landmark book, ***Corporate Cultures***, describes culture as "the way we do business around here." One of your first responsibilities is to learn and understand the culture of your school, and to know that you can help shape the culture now that you are a part of it. Just as the arrival of a new student changes the culture of any classroom, so should your presence on the school staff. Do not, however, minimize the importance of learning the history of the school and all that has been accomplished in the past. A sure way into the heart of a teacher, or other staff member, who has been around for a long time is to ask sincere probing questions and listen to better understand what has transpired in the past. They will like you and you will be better able to understand why things are done the way they are done.

Healthy educational cultures focus on student learning and include **collegial collaboration.** If the culture in which you find yourself does not yield evidence of collaboration, find the other new teachers, visit another hallway, grade level or subject area. **DO NOT** for one minute think that you have to go this alone. It is not in your best interest or the best interest of your students for you to operate as a sole proprietor. You are part of several bigger systems and need to operate productively in each. As a member of the school community, it is your responsibility to seek out those who share your beliefs about learning and learners, and to ask for and provide support and assistance. **Find a mentor and be a mentor.**

Because you are with your students most of the day, you can feel very isolated unless you use the **communication systems** that are in place in your school and create informal ones that work for you. Technology allows us to communicate quickly and frequently with colleagues both inside and outside our buildings. Reach out! Ask questions! Your district office staff really is there to help. They have years of experience and are always looking for opportunities to get into schools and classrooms.

Dealing with Paper Work

General Guidelines

- Identify the three main categories: **professional, instructional, and personal.**
- Identify a space for each category of paper, label it, and do an immediate sort whenever a piece of paper comes into your life!
- Use a **color file system** to organize not only your desk but your book bag. Choose one color to identify your own personal papers. For example, use yellow folders or small booklets created with yellow covers for your calendar, your hand written or computer generated address book, and for coupons, catalog pages and grocery lists. By sticking with one color you can place personal papers in "something" yellow and know immediately where to look when you need to retrieve it. Use different colors for logistical/professional and instructional.
- An **academic year calendar** is a must! They are usually available in June for the following school year or you can print one out on your computer. A month at a glance will work unless you are in an unique assignment that includes multiple conferences with parents, colleagues, or committees on a regular basis, in which case you will need a week at a glance. Color code or otherwise highlight personal holidays and events and designate important professional deadlines and appointments in yet another color.
- Clean out your book bag/briefcase each weekend!

Sorting

The first level of sorting involves separating action items and informational documents. Papers from both the professional category and personal category can fall into the "action item" category.

Create a **tickler file system** for papers requiring action. Use computer generated file folder labels to set up 36 to 40 file folders, one for each week of the school year. Place papers that require action into the appropriate tickler file. If preparation or mailing time is needed, place the paper in the folder for the week before the due date. Store the tickler files in chronological order in an upright file on your desk or a section of a file cabinet drawer. Green folders to signify **"Go"** can be reserved for tickler files. This technique is widely used by professionals in the business community as a system for remembering not only professional deadlines but important personal events like birthdays and doctor appointments too. It is reasonable to assume that any personal documents you are carrying around with

Dealing with Paper Work continued...

you can be placed in the appropriate tickler file or left at home.

The next level of sorting is separating professional documents, such as memos, bulletins, or notices from instructional papers. It is a recipe for disaster to mix the categories on your desk or in your book bag. Don't go there!

Memos, Bulletins, Notices

Keep office memos and other notices in a container on the top of a bookcase, in a file drawer, or in a three-ring binder away from instructional materials and student papers. If there is not a date on the notice/memo, put one on before filing it so you can tell which is more current as changes occur. We have students put headings on their papers. You do the same!

The next level of sorting is to identify key categories within the logistical/professional category. If you have lots and lots of papers in a sub-category it is time for a three-ring binder. If not, create a clearly labeled folder for each sub-category.

Dealing with the **Paper Flow**
to/from the **School** & the **School District**

You may be able to access and/or store some of this information and these documents on your computer! You can decide whether to keep your files in your school files or at home.

Create files for topics such as:

- Staff development offerings
- Calendars/special events
- Certification and recertification
- Supervision and evaluation system
- Substitute information
- Special education regulations and procedures along with names and contact information for personnel you might interact with around special education issues
- Frequently used telephone, fax, and email addresses
- Contracts
- Payroll
- Benefits information
- Receipts for tax reporting
- Professional organizations
- Bookkeeping such as purchase orders, receipts, book rentals, etc.

Forms save time because you do not have to keep writing the same thing over and over but be careful to not create your own paperwork nightmare!

Locate or create forms for such items as:

- Hall passes
- Referrals to specialists
- Progress reports
- Attendance reporting
- Audio-visual/technology requests
- Grading and reporting forms
- Maintenance/repair requests
- Field trips
- Telephone log
- Conference log
- Student data sheet or card

Dealing with the Paper Flow
Your Instructional Materials

Papers Plus

Organizing our "stuff" is one of the hardest tasks of all! There is no method that will work for all of us, but stuff "stuffed" in the bottom desk drawer, in a closet, or a file cabinet drawer is a definite loser!

Possible organizational strategies are:

- The computer, which can be an important tool if you have developed the expertise to use it in a productive way. You can create **colored covers** and **spine labels for three-ring binders** that can help you distinguish between binders.

- **Stackable crates** are an ideal sorting tool for materials. Ideally, use one per unit you are developing. As you find materials, toss them in the crate for sorting and selecting later.

- Color code materials by class or topic using **colored duct tape**. For temporary coding use **removable sticker dots.**

- **Index cards** are a great way to capture random thoughts or even to design units. Carry them in your book bag or pocket and have them readily available at home. They are inexpensive, weigh nothing, are sturdy, and are easily sorted. You can jot down "to do" lists, things you promised to do, names, or books to remember, or unit design ideas that you can then sort them in multiple ways.

- **Mark originals** with a yellow highlighter and/or place in sheet protectors. It is so hard to remember if you have saved a copy or not, so you end up with fifteen copies of one paper and no copies of another.

- If you use a paper in more than one unit or in more than one class, make a **copy to file** in each place. Otherwise it is never where you need it.

- Post-it notes are great but they sometimes get lost in the shuffle. Consider using 8-1/2" x 11" sheets of paper with only **one topic per each dated page**. It is easier to file them that way.

- **Fold in half all papers to be thrown away** or recycled. When you see one folded, you know that it goes in the recycle bin.

My Stuff!

Dealing with the **Paper Flow**
Your Instructional Materials continued...

Papers Plus

- Buy an **inexpensive fax machine.** You can purchase one for under $90.00. Put it in your classroom and use it as an emergency copier. You will save time and energy, as well as eliminate the frustration of being one copy short of a handout or needing that extra copy for a file or a colleague. Do not plan on making a class set of handouts as that would take too long, but for one or two copies, a fax machine cannot be beat. It does not have to be hooked up to a phone to make copies.

- Consider your **filing system**. It may be that instead of alphabetical order, chunking materials both in file cabinets and on book shelves is best done in categories that reflect the way you use them. You might color code the spines or edges for easy refiling or reshelving.

- **Colored file folders** can be lifesavers. Use a different color for each class, subject, or period. You can use them over and over if you use removable file folder labels made either by hand or on your computer. Just peel off the label and put a new one on.

- **Teacher's manuals** and **curriculum guides** can weigh a ton. Consider taking them apart, three-hole punching them, putting them in three-ring binders and then you can pull out the section you want and take it home with you without lugging a fifteen pound book bag. The trick is, of course, putting the section back where it belongs.

Supplemental materials, or the lack thereof, are the bane of a new teacher's existence. Not to worry! Soon you will have so many supplemental materials the issue will be how to store them where you can find them. For now, beg, borrow, and hit the garage and yard sales. Look all around you. Be brave and tell the shopkeeper that you are a teacher and that you really need that poster, those postcards, brochures, tickets, etc., for your classroom. Check with neighbors who are getting ready to move or have children going off to college. If it can be read, quantified, or used as a prop, grab it!

Dealing with the **Paper Flow**
Your Instructional Materials & Supplies continued...

Papers Plus

- Inexpensive stacking trays from an office supply store can not only provide needed desk top storage, they are great for sorting papers that managed to find their way into piles on your desk.

- Copy the table of contents of your **professional journals**, three-hole punch them and put them in a three-ring binder in chronological order. Identify the binders on the spine and front cover. Place the journals in chronological order in a closet or back shelf. When you want to look up a particular topic, just go through the tables of contents notebook rather than digging through the journals.

Students have a School Supply List...So should you!
These are not for setting up a Classroom Supply Center. These are for your own use!

My School Supply List

Calendar
Standing files for your desk
File folders (letter, legal or both?)
Removable file folder labels
Desk drawer organizer for supplies
Cup to hold writing implements on your desk
Stapler, staples and staple remover
Tape dispenser and clear tape
Masking tape
Scissors
Rubber bands
Paper clips
Ruler
Pencils
Colored markers
Multiple colors of highlighters
Dry erase markers and eraser
Chalk and eraser
Duplicating paper (multiple colors?)
Heavyweight paper
Chart Paper

Overhead transparency film
Overhead pens
Liquid white out or white out tape
Push pins or thumb tacks
Post-it notes in several sizes
Post-it flags
3-Ring binders
3-Hole punch
Thank you notes
Tissues
Small first aid kit
Wet wipes or waterless soap
Toothbrush and toothpaste
Comb and/or brush
Emergency toiletry kit
Sewing kit
Screwdriver
Small hammer
Flashlight
Ziplock baggies in assorted sizes
Ball of string
Small Calculator

Dealing with the Paper Flow
To/From & For Your Students

Where Did All This Stuff Come From?

Classrooms set up for the beginning of school before students arrive look like they could be featured in *Architectural Digest.* They can, however, quickly become cluttered and chaotic with the arrival of students and their "stuff." Pages 231-235 address arrangement of the furniture in the classroom. Here we will focus on storage of and access to instructional materials and the processing of student work.

The first challenge for teachers is to create meaningful and engaging learning experiences. But, an even bigger challenge may be processing all the student work that is generated by those learning experiences. In this, there really is a strong resemblance to a major corporation. The difference in the classroom is that you are both the CEO and the administrative support team. A systems approach is essential in order to make the work flow smoothly and not leave you with a mess after school each day.

If you happen to be one of those people who does not notice clutter in your environment, find a friend who can give you honest feedback about the organization appearance of your classroom. Do not wait until 5:00 p.m. the day of open house/back to school night to get organized.

Student Instructional Materials

For tracking purposes, some teachers give each student with whom they interact a number to use for all their instructional materials and papers. That means student #22 has that number on all "issued for the year" textbooks and workbooks; supplementary materials used in the classroom by that student have the same number. Additionally, that number is the student's number in the grade and attendance books and the student places that number on all papers. That way there is never confusion about what belongs to whom and which "Jennifer" or "Juan" owns or owes for which book or paper. Secondary teachers could number from 1 to 120 or use a 1-3 and 2-3 system to distinguish between blocks or periods.

Dealing with the Paper Flow
To/From & For Your Students continued...

Storage Options for Student Materials
Cubbies & Tubs

A staple of primary classrooms, cubbies and tubs often store not only student materials but jackets and gloves. They can work well for upper grades if there is a need to store materials that are bulky in nature and there is bookshelf or storage cabinet space on which to set tubs. Inexpensive plastic containers with lids are a good alternative for materials that include small pieces. You can find them at The Dollar Store, KMart, Target, Wal-Mart, etc.

Crates

Crates are colorful and they stack. Some even come on wheels. They hold hanging files and all sorts of books and papers. You can use a different crate for each subject or each period. Crates can serve as king size "in-boxes." They are great containers for carrying home a stack of student work to grade. Add an inexpensive set of luggage wheels and you are good to go. How would we get along without crates or luggage carts?

Chair Bags

An elementary teacher in upstate New York had parent volunteers create book bags to hang on the back of the student chairs. Made of sturdy fabric and constructed to have the weight distributed across the top of the chair back, these bags held the materials the students were not using in the present learning experience. The amount of clutter on the tables and on the floor was greatly reduced.

Mailboxes

The idea of student mailboxes in the elementary classroom makes all the sense in the world. You can have students put their papers to take home in their mail boxes, their notes to each other (let's legitimize what has been going on for time eternal!), or you or a helper can put papers to be returned to students, library notices, forms from the front office, etc., in their mailbox. There are literally hundreds of uses for them. Mailboxes work in the front office why not have a classroom office? Units that could be used for this purpose are sold at office

Dealing with the Paper Flow
To/From & For Your Students continued...

supply stores as "literature organizers." Those with 24 compartments sell for under $50.00. In secondary classrooms it is a little bit more complicated because of the number of students. Multiple literature organizers could be purchased, but the cost may be prohibitive. An alternative is to use your positive relationships with students and teachers in the professional/technical department and ask them to build some for you.

Book Boxes

Fiberboard magazine files can be purchased for around $1.00 each. These could be used for organized and readily accessible instructional materials, or as portfolio/folder holders.

Portfolios

Portfolios can be stored in folders, hanging files in crates or file cabinets, or even in pizza delivery boxes.

Distribution of Student Work Papers

If you use mailboxes, you can put the day's papers in the student mail slots and students can pick them up as they come in the door; they can return papers to you the same way.

If you use base groups, a "materials manager" can be in charge of distributing, collecting and returning papers for the team.

Reviewing/Giving Feedback/Grading Student Work Papers

Clipboard cruise with Post-it notes of slips of paper on it. Look over shoulders, observe the work, write a brief note and leave it on the desk. In an elementary classroom have the students leave their notebooks open to a select page and read a few of them while students are at a special.

Select certain letters of the alphabet by first or last name, select certain numbers if using the numbering system, select by base group, or select all the papers of the students with the next birthday in a group for a review that does not involve grading.

Set up portfolios in different color folders and/or assign five to eight different colors to notebooks. You could put sticker dots on each or have students mark them with a colored marker. Collect all the red ones to review, then all the green ones to review another day, etc.

Dealing with the Paper Flow
To/From & For Your Students continued...

Have students keep a chronological table of contents in the front of their notebooks on which they record the date, the assignment, the date due, the date submitted, and you can both track and mark when you reviewed the notebook.

When you collect journals, have each student select one entry that they would like for you to read, select one at random, and read a third one across all students. That way you have student choice, random accountability, and a sense across all students how a particular point was processed.

Students' Personal "Stuff"
Backpacks and Book Bags

The staff at Fox Lane Middle School, Bedford, New York, decided that book bags had become the students' "on the move" lockers holding all their earthly possessions. As such, they became dangerous roadblocks to movement around the classroom. After a brainstorming session they decided to limit students' use of backpacks to the beginning of the class period. Students were instructed to get what they needed out of their backpacks and place them against the back wall. This approach eliminated the potential for tripping over backpack straps.

"Show and Tell" Items

You need to set up a specific place for storage of the precious items brought from home to share with you and with classmates. One sure way to limit the potential for too many items on a given day is to have assigned days or a set number of sign-up opportunities a month.

Projects

A memorable moment for many teachers is the day on which the first big projects are due. In come the students with all their prized creations...some looking like they are as big as refrigerator boxes. Set size limits on projects to avoid a massive storage problem.

Using Technology As an Organizational Tool

Make Your Life Easier!

When thinking about organizational strategies, a computer can be one of your best friends! Using basic word processing, spreadsheet, and database software you can make the organizational part of your teaching life much easier. As you have read in other sections of this book, it is imperative that you establish organizational structures that enable you to best use your time. The trick is to use the computer to establish productive organizational systems from the beginning. For instance, you will use lists of your students' names on a daily basis for everything from keeping track of completed homework to identifying who turned in a field trip permission form. Instead of relying on the office to print you a clean copy of your class lists and then copying it for your use, just make one on your word processor. You can then use this file anytime and even create checklists using check boxes.

The following are some suggestions for using a computer to organize your professional life.

Use the Word Processor for:

• Class Lists

Create **Class Lists** to be used anytime you need to keep track of information pertaining to your students. For instance, turning in projects, emergency care cards, permission slips, order forms, etc. Turn the class lists into checklists that can be used for keeping track of indicator and benchmark mastery, learning objectives, individualized education goals, etc.

Using Technology
As an Organizational Tool continued...

The Word Processor continued

- ### Class News
  Develop a template to be used for reporting class news. Your students can contribute articles and be assigned fun sections for reporting (i.e. Movie Madness, Weather Watchers, What's New, Ask Andy, Learning is Fun, The Teacher's Corner, etc.). This template can be used over and over again.

- ### Personalized Letters
  There are many times when you want to send a personalized letter to your students or the parents of your students. This can be a reality if you use the mail merge feature of your word processor. You write one letter and merge it with a database file that has the names of all your students. The letters are printed, you add your personal signature, and voila, you have a personalized letter to all your students and their families.

- ### Daily Journaling
  This is a great way to keep track of the happenings in the class from a student's point of view. You create a basic template file that is used for the daily journaling. Create a set of questions to be answered by one student each day. These files are then saved according to the date, printed out, and placed in your daily journal. Students who missed class can check the daily journal. These also can be attached to your newsletter and sent home. Your students will love to revisit this throughout the year. It is also a great anecdotal record for you to use the following year.

- ### Graphic Organizers
  Use the basic drawing features of your word processor to create graphic organizers to suit your needs. See pages 119-122 for more information on graphic organizers.

Create Spreadsheets For:

- ### Grades
  Create a spreadsheet to keep track of your grades. Check with other teachers in your school to see if they have already created one or if your school or school system provides grade book software to each teacher.

Using Technology
as an Organizational Tool continued...

Databases
• Class Information

Databases are wonderful tools for organization. Keeping student information like names, addresses, parent names, hobbies, their likes/dislikes, etc. can be easily organized using a database. This file can be used to create a personalized letter via your word processor mail merge feature and to create labels for the mailing!

• Project Management

Create a database of your students with fields for information about a project that they are working on completing. By using a database you can work with your students to customize their project and keep track of the individualized project objectives to which you have agreed.

Use The Internet For:
• E-Learning Platforms

Check to see if your school/school system has an easy to use system to post information on the internet about your class. This would allow your students to have access to your classroom information from anywhere at school, the library, and hopefully from home.

• Data Storage

You can use an online storage service to save all of your files. This allows you to access them from another classroom, the library, or even from home. If you use this online storage, you will have one set place for all of your files! Remember to back up your files weekly!

• Everything You Ever Needed to Know

Your school/school system, regional training center, or state department of education may have instructional resources available to you to use in your classroom. Search their sites and/or ask your fellow teachers if there are sites that they have used.

Search for museums in your area or visit the federal government department websites. They often have resources for teachers to use in the classroom.

Check out **On the Web** at the beginning of each chapter in this book.

Substitute Essentials

Sooner or later it happens! You awaken aching all over and you absolutely cannot get out of bed. Or you have a sick child or are called out of town on an emergency. In order to do what you need in your personal life AND have your students continue to function and learn in the classroom, it is essential to put together a well thought out substitute folder or kit well before you need it.

Schedule
- Staff schedule
- Bell schedule
- Daily schedule (including specials)

Student Information
- Class List(s)
- Special needs (physical or emotional) of individual students
- List of students who go to special classes and the time they go

Lesson Plans
- It is wise to have one to two days of emergency lesson plans ready to go for those times when you are too sick to send in current plans.
- Be sure that what you prepare does not seem like busy work to the students. In fact you may want to let them know that if and when you are away, the substitute may well have them work on study or test taking skills or may provide learning experiences designed to review key concepts previously studied. Set your students and the substitute up for success!

Procedures
- Before school and dismissal procedures
- Classroom procedures
- Attendance and lunch count procedures
- Discipline procedures
- Fire and evacuation drill, tornado, lockdown instructions

Where to Find
- Emergency Lesson Plans (as needed)
- Map of the building to include staff lounge, department workrooms and cafeteria
- Photocopy equipment (access code, if needed)
- AV/IT equipment
- Supplies and materials
- Teacher's Manuals

Substitute Essentials continued...

Who Can Help
- Name of reliable students who can answer questions and explain procedures
- Assistance with technology operation/procedures
- Names of key personnel to include principal, secretary, custodian, team leader/department head and how to reach them
- Name of a teacher who can answer questions and explain procedures

Through the Voice Of...
Sub in a Tub

As a professional substitute for the St. Vrain Valley School District in Longmont, Colorado, I was hired for a long-term substitute position. All of a sudden I was in the position of needing a substitute for myself! I discovered the angst that teachers feel when they have to be away from their classes and do not have plans they feel they can hand off to a sub. To alleviate that problem, I prepared a **Sub in a Tub** which I leave under my desk at all times.

The intended function of the **Sub in a Tub** is to provide a complete one day emergency tool for a substitute teacher. The learning activities included in the tub address the St. Vrain Valley's learning standards. Included are favorite books to be read to the children and review projects or activities for which there was not sufficient time during past instructional periods. Even though the **Tub** required a few hours to prepare, the peace of mind for me when I have an unexpected absence is well worth the effort.

For each activity or subject, there is a manila folder with all the necessary copies/handouts provided. As the year progresses, the activities included are updated to include materials related to current study.

In addition to all the necessary materials for the learning experiences, materials for tent cards or name tags, emergency procedures, a class seating chart, and an all-purpose class list are included.

The final touches in the tub include fifty cents for a coke and a whistle for playground duty!

Marilyn Turner, professional substitute, St. Vrain Valley School District, Longmont, CO

Avoid Mayhem!
Prevention Beats Intervention Any Day

1. Don't talk over them!
Wait until the entire group is quiet and attentive before giving directions.

2. Post the agenda and the learning outcomes on the board in the same place each day.
If you think that they don't notice, just try skipping this routine after it is established!

3. Write out the directions for any activity that has three or more steps or components.
Use the board, chart paper, or a transparency. A flow chart can eliminate a lot of "What are we supposed to do now/next?" questions. Think it takes too much time? How much time do you spend repeating directions over and over?

4. When working with a small group position yourself with your back to the wall, so to speak!
This way you can scan the entire classroom while interacting with the small group. "Eyes in the back of your head" are handy, but let's use those in the front as well!

5. Have extra materials available for student use.
Even adults forget to bring their "school supplies" to faculty meetings and workshops. Conference centers always put out paper and a writing implement for meetings. While we do not want to provide all supplies, you might have two containers with pencils or other writing implements. One holds sharpened pencils, while the other holds broken leads. When a student needs a pencil she simply places one in the "broken lead" container and takes one from the "sharpened" container. Have loaner books covered in fluorescent paper. No down time! No discussion! No problem!

6. Reduce distance and barriers between you and the students.
Arrange the furniture, including empty students desks and the teacher desk, to reduce barriers between you and other students. Try to minimize use of arrangements in which one student is hidden behind one or more other students; that would include rows of student desks. We all know what we did when we sat in class behind someone taller than we were!

Avoid Mayhem!
Prevention Beats Intervention Any Day continued...

7. Use known or easy content to teach a new process, and use a known process to introduce or teach difficult new content.

Combining new processes and new content is guaranteed to cause frustration, confusion, or even chaos!

8. MBWA

Management by Walking Around works in the business world and in the classroom. It even works on the highways. Ever notice how everyone slows down when they see a police car...even on the other side of the roadway, engaged in giving someone else a ticket? It is the power of proximity! Fred Jones puts it this way: "Either you work the crowd or the crowd will work you."

Teacher Induced Mayhem!

- **Activity level thinking.** If we do not begin with clear learning outcomes in mind we can make bad decisions when there are interruptions of instructional time, certain materials, or resources are not available and the activity does not go as planned. If learning outcomes are clear, we can move calmly to **Plan B** and not get excited about the fact that **Plan A** didn't work.

- **Materials and space not ready to go.**

- **"Winging-it."** Unfortunately, we need to read the material we ask students to read, to carefully read the manuals that guide our use of instructional materials, and do the exercises the students are asked to do. If we do not do so, we can get into serious problems with pacing, student attentiveness, student success, etc.

- **Letting "off-the-mark" behavior or backtalk interrupt instruction.** Develop those nonverbal responses of "The Look," wait time, and proximity to deal with such issues; that is all we need 75 to 85% of the time.

- **Unclear directions and expectations.**

- **Unrealistic expectations.** Ten year-olds are ten years old and can only sit still and/or be quiet for so long; the same is true for each age group!

- **Work that is too hard or too easy.** The result is not a pretty picture. Frustrated and/or bored students can really interrupt instruction. The best management program is a strong instructional program!

First, You Have to Get Their Attention!

Jon Saphier in his book *The Skillful Teacher* presents an amazing continuum of attention moves that range from using personal power through humor and charm to using position power through moves like threats and exclusion. There is a time and a place for each of the more than fifty moves, with the exception of sarcasm, on the continuum, but it appears that the ones that work most of the time with most of the students are somewhere in the middle.

One of the most effective ways to gain attention is to ask for it and then **wait!** Inevitably at least some students hear us and they in turn, hush the others. Coupled with **"the look"** and **proximity** plus a commonly understood **signal**, the vast majority of the students will give us their attention the vast majority of the time. And we haven't said a word other than, "May I Have Your Attention?"

Certainly there are times when we do not want to ask for attention but demand it; those times would include events like the building is on fire, there is a poisonous snake on the loose, a world championship fight is brewing, or a tornado headed our way. **We best be careful to save those, "I want your attention and I want it right now!" moments for when we really need them!** Let's spend time and energy on first perfecting a few techniques that get great results and help us avoid unnecessary power struggles.

Wait Time

Do not talk over them! After asking for or signaling for their attention, wait! And if you can stand it, do not move. Kay Toliver in the classic videotape entitled, "Good Morning, Miss Toliver" simply puts her hands on her head, looks skyward and waits. Guess what! They notice and attend. There is no need to say another word. Carry on with the directions you wish to give.

"The Look"

The teacher look is the look we give someone when they get in the express lane at the supermarket with far more items than they are supposed to have. We are surprised when then asked, "Are you a teacher?" Of course, we have perfected "The Look!"

Getting their Attention & Keeping It continued...

Proximity

Have you ever noticed how all the cars slow down when they see a car pulled over by a police car with flashing blue lights? That would be a prime example of the power of proximity. Never mind that the police officer is busy with someone else, we all think we will be the next one! When side conversations disrupt or other inappropriate behaviors distract, simply walk slowly to that area while continuing to do whatever else you are doing. Almost always, if you do not "swoop" into the area, the side conversation ceases and the students assume "ideal student" stances...with looks of innocence, of course. Isn't that the way we deal with the police officer?

Signals

We have used signals forever to let people know that a transition is about to occur. If we are seated and need to terminate a conversation, we tend to either look at our watch, stand, and/or walk toward the door. When we are driving, we use the turn signal to let others know that we are either turning or changing lanes. Some signals, such as sounding the car horn to signal impending danger, are more abrupt.

The same mindset applies to classroom situations. The least disruptive signal is to simply raise your hand. Teach students that when they see you with your hand in the air, they are to finish the sentence they are on and then to raise their hand as well. Soon all have hands in the air and discussions have been terminated. Be patient during the training sessions. Give the process time to work.

Other signals include chimes, train whistles, clapping a rhythm for the students to repeat, lowering the lights, "Give me five!" in which you count backwards 5-4-3-2-1 and all eyes are on you at the end of the count. Some teachers find that a timer, especially a product called Teach Timer that displays the time on the overhead screen, is a useful signal. Others use colored overhead transparencies where green signals that work and small group discussion is ongoing, yellow signifies a one minute warning, and red means, "Stop" and pay attention. In fact, some schools and teachers use a real stop light to let students know when the noise level is acceptable and unacceptable.

Getting their Attention & Keeping It continued...

Keeping Their Attention

The best way to keep students' attention is with **meaningful and engaging lessons.** To maximize their attention, **random order** and **circulation** seem to be the best bets. Use cards or sticks with student names on each and call on them randomly. When their name is called, return their stick or card to the collection so they know that they may be called on again. You might give each student a number of "I Pass" cards so that the pressure does not minimize the learning or risk taking. A New York biology teacher keeps tongue depressors with students names on them in a beaker. She says that when students do not respond to a question beamed to the entire class, someone always calls out, "Get the sticks!" Circulation means simply to keep moving around the room and teaching from various locations so that students never know where you will be next. It is human nature to test the limits if we are some distance from the authority figure. Circulation has the same effect as the police car driving around the neighborhood.

The best management program is a strong instructional program!

Giving Directions

Before you ever open your mouth, be sure you have their complete attention. DO NOT TALK OVER THEM! If they need to get out materials, ask them to do so and then WAIT until they are all on the "right page" before you continue.

1. Plan directions carefully and picture exactly what you want the students to do. Run a mental movie and picture what could possibly go wrong. Make plans for avoiding these potential pitfalls.

2. Do a task analysis and identify which of the behaviors embedded in the task have been done successfully before, which ones the students have had trouble with, and which are new. Review, clarify, or model as appropriate.

3. Use written as well as verbal modes if more than two steps are involved. A flow chart is a powerful tool for reducing questions about what to do next.

4. If sequence is important in completing the task use 1st, 2nd and 3rd instead of 1, 2, 3 or a, b, c.

5. Point out new vocabulary and stress difficult or possibly confusing points in the process.

6. When possible and appropriate, show models of processes, products, and problems.

7. Give students time to think about the task ahead and then check for understanding by having them turn to a neighbor and explain what they think they are supposed to do.

8. If you expect problems, let students coach each other with a sample. In the "olden days" we called this guided practice and it is still a great idea!

Potential Problems:

Pacing and Planning:
If you assign homework as they are walking out the door, only half of them hear you and half of those who do either don't remember or think it is multiple choice about whether or not to do it.

Repeat performances:
Expect recurring problems if you ask any students to do something they struggled with the last time you assigned such a task without any intervention on your part.

Unclear or vague directions:
You know that you were not clear when more than two students or two groups of students call you over for clarification!

Time Templates

It has often been said that time is the currency of education. Each of us has the same amount of teaching and learning time to "spend" and it is up to us to budget wisely to make ends meet. Much has also been written about the importance of time on task. It seems, however, that the additional question has to be, "Is the task worth doing?" As you design worthwhile tasks for your students, keep the following templates in mind as you budget your time on a yearly, monthly, weekly, and daily basis.

Wait Time: Pause three to five seconds after asking a question to give all students time to process the question. Pause three to five seconds again, after a student answers, so you and the other students can process the response and the responding student can add more as appropriate.

10:2 Theory: Pause after small meaningful chunks of information for student processing. Have pairs or trios discuss the most important points, confusing points, connections, etc.

Sequence: We remember best that which occurs in the first few and last few minutes of instruction. Maximize that time. Create lots of beginnings and endings. That which is just after the middle of a list is the hardest to remember. When possible, reorder the list to place the difficult items at the beginning or end.

Movement: Legitimize movement. The brain can only absorb what the rear end can endure. Have students stand for the two minute processing in 10:2. Have students move to meet with a partner or use various signals to indicate understanding or agreement.

Time Templates continued...

Practice: Divide new skills into the smallest meaningful chunks and mass short practice sessions at the beginning of new learning. Always move to real and meaningful use of the skills as soon as possible.

Forgetting: Most forgetting occurs within just a few minutes of learning. Build in recitation, review, processing, and practice immediately. As Madeline Hunter said, "Slowing down is a way of speeding up," because learning increases with immediate processing.

Notice: Warn students of upcoming transitions. Think of the "two minute warning" before the end of football games and do the same in the classroom.

Pace of Speech: The more complex the concept and the more unfamiliar the vocabulary, the slower the pace needs to be. Be particularly aware of the pace of your speech when there are English Language Learners in the class.

Pace of Lesson: Consider the complexity of the concepts being presented and pace accordingly, Given that attention spans are short, provide a variety of learning experiences, and build in movement and processing time. Include large group, small group and paired work.

So that students can learn how to use time effectively, share with them how you make instructional decisions related to time and ask them to consider the implications for their independent study.

"Learning is the constant; time is the variable."
...Vermont teacher

Transition Tidbits

Anticipation:

This is "Murphy's Law" in the classroom. Run a mental movie of upcoming classes with particular attention to transitions, such as the beginning of class, transitions to new learning experiences, and the closing of class. Pay special attention to those transitions that will involve new processes, movement, distribution/retrieval of materials, etc. Clarify in your own mind what you want to happen. With that in mind, plan the directions, identify the needed materials and the potential pitfalls, and act accordingly.

Anticipation and acceptance of the inevitability of mood swings and decreased attentiveness around holidays, special events, or major, or even minor, disruptions is crucial. In these instances, we need to be proactive and plan carefully so that we can engage students in learning experiences that maximize instructional time and capture the learners' interest.

Readiness:

Are you ready? Do you have materials and space ready for the students to do their work? Kounin, Gump, Saphier and the military call this "provisioning." If you are running around at the last minute gathering up what you need to lead the class or the next segment of the class, or if you cannot find what you need, instructional time is lost. There is a high probability that students will become involved in activities other than what you would prefer and it may be hard to recapture their attention. Be positive, **prepared,** and professional!

Realistic Expectations:

Children and adults tend to engage in conversation at transitions whether it is moving from one site to another, distributing papers, or getting out materials. Be realistic about human behavior and teach appropriate conversation behavior.

Procedures:

Often we have to directly teach, model, and practice, even with high school students, how we are going to make transitions. Given that we want to have both small and large group learning experiences, we have to have systems in place to make transitions as smoothly and quickly as possible. Any changes in procedures need to be clearly communicated to students so that those who have difficulty with transitions under any conditions are not caught off guard by a new or different way of doing business.

Transition Tidbits continued...

Sponges, Fillers, & Anchoring Activities:

Planning learning experiences for students to do when they are finished early or while waiting for you is essential. What you identify for such situations needs careful thought because you want to ensure that they are engaged in a meaningful experience, but that the experience does not take on a life of its own and detract from the primary learning emphasis. The activities called "bell work" or "warm-ups" at the beginning of the class can be designed to bridge yesterday's lesson to today's lesson, offer review, or preview opportunities, and create conditions where students immediately locate the materials they will be using in class.

Carol Ann Tomlinson uses the term "anchoring activities" to describe the work students are to go to whenever they have the opportunity. It is essential that the anchoring activity not be busy work and that it be related to one of the outcomes of the curriculum. These anchoring activities can be as simple as having students read their library books or as complex as learning centers or learning packets.

Multitasking:

A key success factor in working with large groups, especially large groups of children, is our skillfulness at doing more than one task at a time. Observe yourself monitoring multiple activities or one activity in various stages or groups. If you either neglect to notice potential problems or overreact to small problems, they can turn into big problems right before your eyes. Jacob Kounin describes "withitness" as our capacity to notice what is occurring and to make decisions about when and how to intervene.

Signals:

The NFL uses the "two minute warning" to let everyone know that a transition is about to take place. That practice in the classroom can minimize the loss of time at transitions. You may wish to establish either a verbal or nonverbal signal that a change is going to happen soon and then another that means that you want their attention or want them to move immediately. A signal that works with all age groups is to simply raise your hand and ask those who notice to also raise their hand as they finish the sentence or thought they were on when you put your hand up. Other teachers use a bell or a whistle or flash the lights. Find one that you think will work for you and your students and then teach it to them. Announcing it won't do the trick; modeling and practice are necessary to make it an established routine.

These transition tidbits include constructs from the work of Kounin, Gump, Saphier, Hunter and Tomlinson.

Procedure Potpourri

TOOL 306-308

Planning procedures and regularly evaluating the effectiveness of those procedures for conducting the business of the classroom is crucial in creating a productive learning environment.

A wise teacher once said, **"A routine is just a dream unless it produces the results we want."** In order for our procedures to become embedded into the classroom life, we have to not only be clear about what we want, but we have to be able to describe and demonstrate what we want and then have students rehearse and practice it. **The direct instruction approach may be the best one for making sure procedures work effectively. That means we would explain the process, give examples or demonstrate, check for understanding, practice with guidance, and then practice independently. As necessary, we would reteach and review the procedure.**

We need to have in mind a system for each of the recurring classroom events listed below. The harder part is to honestly and regularly assess how well each is working over time. If what we are doing is not working, we need to try another approach.

Given the age of the students & classroom conditions, what is the best plan for:

Beginning the school day or the class period
There are often "rituals" for the beginning of class. These may include bell work or starters posted on the board, student self-managed attendance procedures, morning meetings, or homework correction work groups. Student comfort level is increased when there is a degree of regularity in the events of the classroom. This is especially true for students who interact with more than one teacher.

Taking attendance
Do it! Do it quickly and efficiently! Do not take up class time calling roll! Count heads as the first cut. If you use a seating chart you can quickly check it. If you put the seating chart in a sheet protector or laminate it, you can mark absences and tardies right on it and transfer the data to your record books later. If the students are in base groups the students can let you know who is missing.

In the elementary classroom, you might put up a wall chart on which students move their name card or number as they come into the classroom. In the secondary classroom, a quick count of heads lets you know how many students, if any, are missing. If you have assigned each student a number they, too, could move their number card from one designated spot to another to indicate their presence.

Procedure Potpourri continued...

Dealing with tardies

Follow school policy. Identify the cause(s) as soon as possible. Is it a home situation, a distance between classroom issue, a stuck locker issue, a teacher kept the student late situation, or a hanging out with friends issue. Make note of tardies, continue with instruction, and deal with the individual privately after all students are engaged in learning.

Distributing and collecting materials: See pages 213-216.

Student movement

A teacher who posted his classroom procedures at www.iloveteaching.com wrote, "You do not need to ask permission to throw something in the garbage, to get a tissue, or to sharpen your pencil. Just use your common sense as to when you do these activities (i.e., not during group presentations)." He further wrote, "If we are engaged in a long discussion or note taking and you are becoming uncomfortable, I do not have a problem with you getting up to stretch or even standing at the back of the room for a bit. Please do this with some discretion (i.e., Don't say, "Man this is boring!" and stomp to the back of the room.)"

This should be our goal in each of our classrooms. We need, of course, to see what our students can do independently, and then teach and model the parts they have not yet mastered.

Dealing with broken or missing student supplies

Keep sharpened pencils, paper, and when possible, extra copies of texts and workbooks, at The Supply Center. Adults often forget to bring supplies and materials to workshops and meetings. It seems preferable to get them to work on the learning experience than to delay the individual and/or the entire class dealing with missing supplies. You may want to make a note of who consistently does not have materials and have a private chat with them about issues of responsibility. Cover "loaner" textbooks and workbooks with fluorescent paper. That way you will notice should they accidentally be headed for the door.

Dealing with restroom visits and requests for drinks

Whatever you do, be sure to minimize the disruption to the instruction. Honor requests until a pattern of potential abuse appears. At that time, a private intervention is appropriate. There is always a reason, sometimes legitimate and sometimes not. Identification of the underlying cause will help determine the appropriate intervention. In the past drinks of water were not encouraged, but now every adult in the country seems to be continuously carrying around a bottle of water that is deemed by the medical profession to be a good thing. The obvious result, however, of drinking a great deal of water is the need to use the restroom.

Procedure Potpourri continued...

Students asking for and receiving help

A staple of a learning-centered classroom is students helping one another. Some teachers use the "Three Before Me" rule. That means that before a student comes to the teacher for help, they have to have checked with three classmates.

Given that students are going to be helping each other, they have to be taught how to help rather than to provide answers.

When it is essential to ask for teacher help, signal cards or cups are a handy tool. Give each student three cards: red, yellow, and green. When they have a question, which is not stopping them from proceeding, they put out their yellow card which means, "Please help me when you can." When they are unable to proceed at all, they put out their red card. Red, yellow, and green paper cups are handy when small groups are working. When all is well, the green cup is out, yellow means questions, and red means we are really stuck! In a computer lab, a red cup sitting on top of the monitor could mean, "I just lost everything!"

Making transitions: See pages 230-231.

Gaining student attention: See pages 224-225.

Communicating learning outcomes and agendas: See page 48 and page 127.

What to do when work is finished: See page 231.

Leaving the classroom

Hall passes are essential. Your school may have a form that you are to use or you may get to invent one. If you get to create your own, I suggest something relatively large and permanent with your name and/or room number printed on it. That way you do not have to stop and fill in or sign a pass. Set it (them) near the door and when students need to leave they simply pick it up. When the pass(es) is in use, no one else leaves unless, of course, there is an emergency.

Returning from absences: See page 242.

Classroom interruptions/visitors

These interruptions are inevitable. Minimize the disruption. Think-Pair-Share and "Turn to your neighbor and discuss..." are ideal in these situations. Follow school policy for visitors.

Potential Problem Times

Careful thought and attention to detail in advance is essential for these moments. It is best to have **Plan B** ready to roll on a moment's notice, because even those procedures that have been working well up until this time may fall apart here! Do not be surprised and do not take it personally!

- The day(s) before a big holiday or school break
- Homecoming week
- The day of or the day after Halloween
- The day report cards and/or progress reports are distributed
- The first few minutes after a long weekend or holiday
- Friday afternoons before a three day weekend
- The last week of school (especially if the swimming pools are open and/or it's hot)
- Immediately before or after a pep rally or assembly
- Right after a fire drill
- The last few minutes before lunch & the first few minutes after lunch
- The first substitute of the year
- Power outages
- First snow of the year (especially in Florida)

Special Condition...On the Move!

Teaching in multiple locations adds to the organizational issues you have to consider. If you are going from building to building you will most likely be living out of your trunk. Buy colored crates and "wheelies" like those used for carrying luggage. Be sure to purchase a heavy duty model. You can, in fact, buy crates with handles and wheels. Keep all the materials that are used in only one location in one color crate and materials for other locations in crates of different colors. You will probably have one crate that goes everywhere with you so that you can keep those essential supplies and materials organized and readily accessible. If it is not cost prohibitive or too bulky, the best approach is to have multiple copies or sets of supplies so you always have what you need.

If you move from classroom to classroom within the same building, work hard to establish a positive relationship with the people with whom you are sharing the rooms so that you can have a corner in which to store materials and perhaps even a wall for displaying student work. Inexpensive roller shades make excellent transportable charts which you can store in the corner of your storage place and quickly hang wherever you need them. All you need are two small wall hangers in each room where you work.

For the Moment*
Sponges...Fillers...Anchoring Activities...
Bell Work...Starters...

When You Need Them

You need meaningful focused work for students to engage in as they
- enter the room (Starters, Bell Work or Anchoring Activities)
- finish work (Fillers, Sponges or Anchoring Activities)
- experience short periods of transition or down time (Fillers, Sponges, or Anchoring Activities)

These **For the Moment** exercises will help you maximize instructional time, keep students focused on learning outcomes, and give you a moment of two to gather materials at transitions. Two cautions come to mind when planning and using bell work, sponges, fillers, or anchoring activities. Do not create a new paperwork monster for yourself and do not let these activities take on a life of their own that supersedes the main learning exercise.

What Do Students Do

The **For the Moment** exercises should be focused on the learning standards of the school district. Materials can be gathered to provide review, remedial work or extension based on an analysis of both classroom and standardized assessment results. Teachers in several high school math departments in Fairfax County Public Schools, Fairfax, Virginia, use review problems from the previous marking period as a cumulative review in preparation for state testing at the end of the year. Alternatively, you can use the **For the Moment** work as a foreshadowing or even as a preassessment for upcoming areas of study. Literacy and numeracy exercises would be a good focus for any grade and content area.

Where to Find Materials

To find materials, think about where you might find old, no longer used text books and/or old worksheets that could be cut up, or consider how you could have students generate problems and questions as extension homework. The internet is a great source of flash cards, problems, and educational games. Take care to ensure that the content focus is appropriate for your desired outcomes and that the exercises are age and grade appropriate.

*This is one of those teaching strategies that is called by many different names. Madeline Hunter called them sponges, Jon Saphier calls them fillers, Harry Wong calls them bell work and Carol Ann Tomlinson calls a more complex, longer-term version anchoring activities.

Classroom Interior Design

A Good Place To Learn...

The place where you spend most of your day should certainly reflect your personality and be a comfortable place for you to work. The stakes are, however, bigger than whether or not the environment is all that important to you and what makes you feel good about the space in which you are working. You have a responsibility for **creating a space that reflects the learning goals of the work space, the personality, interests and age of the students who learn there and to create a space that is a comfortable and productive learning environment for all.**

If you should be given the opportunity to select the type of student desks you want, ask for **flat top desks with separate chairs**. This type of desk is the most versatile for clustering for small group work, placing in a horseshoe or circle for discussions, or arranging in rows for testing. Whatever furniture you have in the classroom, you want to be purposeful about arranging it to match the sort of student interaction you want.

What to Consider in Setting Up A Good Place to Learn...

Reduce Barriers

A teachers desk and empty student desks are "barriers" between you and your students. Move them, move the students, and/or move yourself.

Reduce Distance Between You & the Students

If the space is large and the group is small, cluster the group in a section of the room.

Monitor Distance Between Student Desks

Ensure that students' desks are arranged so that students can get in and out of their seats and retrieve their materials without bumping into each other or each other's work. To check on placement sit in one chair and leave it out as if a student were sitting in it. Then sit in the chair or desk behind and/or beside it. Try moving in and out of the second seat. It takes more room than it seems like it should.

Check Visibility from Each Seat

Sit at each student location to see what a student sees from that spot in the room. Remove any visual or auditory barriers or distracters from the key instructional points in the room.

Classroom Interior Design continued...

Align Furniture Arrangement with Desired Student Interaction

If you want students to be engaged in a **whole class discussion**, students need to be where they can see each other. The best arrangement for that type of interaction is a circle or horseshoe.

If you want students to work in **small groups** arrange desks to resemble a small table.

If the students are taking a test, the traditional arrangement of **rows** of desks is the desired arrangement. This room arrangement is the most popular because it is the easiest for the custodial staff to clean.

Your Desk

Place your desk against a wall. If you can use it to help form a small conference area it can form that "barrier" that makes the conference site seem more private. Check to see if there is a lockable drawer so that you can put your purse, your cell phone, your laptop, and any other valuables away safely. You do not have to carry the key, as you can put it in a safe place away from the drawer, but you want to minimize the opportunities for unauthorized use.

Computers

Electrical outlets, plus all those cords, coupled with the potential of glare on the screen from outside light, usually dictates where the computers can be placed. It is helpful if the computers can be placed so that more than one student can see the screen, or placed so that they create a learning center. If you have access to room dividers you can place those behind computers to create a fake wall.

Small Table for Guided Reading & Conferences

If at all possible, have a table at which you can conduct small group instruction and also have private conferences with students. Since you want to discuss work and behavior privately, it is wonderful to have a place to do it in the classroom rather than having to go into the hall.

Bookcases, Storage Cabinets, & File Cabinets

The placement of these units will be dictated by their size and the types of materials you store in each. Be mindful of safety issues regarding traffic patterns.

Classroom Interior Design continued...

Supply Center

Set the supply center up where it is easily accessible to both you and your students. The important variable is for you to NOT have to stop what you are doing to get something students need. The supplies in the center would depend on the age of the students, but they might include a stapler, a 3-ring hole punch, scissors, glue, tape, sharpened pencils, markers, and rulers. This could also be the site at which students turn in or pick up papers.

If you are concerned about some students not using materials properly, watch to see what happens. The supply center can become off limits for a set length of time to any one violating the fair use code.

If parents ever ask how they could help and are unable to come to school during school hours because of their own work, let them know you would gladly welcome supplies for the supply center.

High Traffic Areas

Areas near doors, the pencil sharpener, locations for turning in or obtaining materials, and the supply center need to be kept as clear of furniture as possible.

Walls, Bulletin Boards, & Chalkboard

Think vertically! This is where you display standards and agendas and student work. Foreign language teachers are masters at using vertical space to create a feeling of immersion in countries where the target language is spoken. Elementary teachers tend to not only use every inch of wall space, but when the fire marshal permits, they hang banners and student work from the ceiling too.

It is conventional wisdom that learning outcomes and agendas be posted consistently in the same place so that students know where to look for them.

Research on student achievement says that not only should current student work be displayed, exemplars of student work add to the equation.

It would seem that reason and balance should prevail and that the displays should not overwhelm the space and should be focused on student work. When the only wall enhancements are the signs explaining the escape route in case of fire or bomb threats, it is time to add to the decor.

Frame and hang copies of your diplomas on the wall near your desk.

Do not forget to post as large a "master calendar" as you can. Include holidays, school, class, and significant personal events. This is a handy place to note long term assignments.

Classroom Interior Design continued...

Learning Centers

Learning Centers may be literacy centers set up around the room, a technology corner, or book boxes with books on particular topics and/or at various reading levels, exercises in folders, packets, a listening center in a language classroom, a current events corner in a social studies classroom, or learning circuits set up in the media center using print and technology sources. Long a mainstay of the elementary classroom, the notion of learning centers and circuits has become more and more a part of the secondary classroom.

From the literature it is clear that we need to have an information rich classroom in which students can access knowledge from sources other than the teacher and the textbook. The availability of space will partially determine whether you set up actual centers or place "center materials" in folders, crates or boxes that can move to students rather than students moving to them.

Begin planning for center work by identifying one unit you will be teaching three to four months from now, clarify the essential understandings, and begin to collect materials for centers. Check with your colleagues to see what they have that you could borrow. The public libraries are also useful sources of additional materials. Think big...start small.

Systems for Rearranging Room Arrangement

Mike Magathan, middle social studies teacher at Lake Braddock Secondary School, Burke, Virginia, uses different colors of electrical tape on the floor in his classroom. He simply tells the students that the front legs of your desk go on the green dots if we are doing group work, on the red dots if we are doing a whole class discussion, and on the yellow dots if we are testing. This system works like a charm. Ron Axelrod, high school teacher of English and history with Fairfax County Public Schools, shared classrooms because he worked in two departments. As he entered the room, he wrote the type of interaction the class would be engaged in during the first part of the period on the board. If he wrote "discussion," the students, as they entered, moved their chairs/desks into a circle and if he wrote "group work" they moved their seats into clusters. At one minute before the end of the period they quickly moved their desks back to the way they were when they entered the room. Once again, this system worked like a charm! Of course, both Mike and Ron had to explain, model, and practice with their students before these systems "worked like a charm!"

Through the Voice of... Procedures that Work
Together

I have very high standards for my students and I have found that by meeting their needs they are more willing to meet mine.

I have arranged my room so that the desks are in quads of four with as much space between the quads as my physical space permits. At the beginning of the year I seated the students in these quads by simply mixing up students from various elementary schools. As I have gotten to know the students I have regrouped the quads to ensure that students learn to work with all members of the class and to balance the skills, knowledge, and learning styles of the quad members.

I encourage these four students to "look out for one another" by checking each other's work when appropriate, sharing notes with absent tablemates, making sure that each has her name on her paper, checking to see that directions are being followed correctly, etc. This arrangement makes pauses for processing easy and less noisy since the students are in close proximity with their study buddies.

I appoint one person in each quad to be the daily recorder if anyone in that quad is absent. The recorder fills out a sheet outlining the assignments collected or given, tests taken, announcements made, etc. This further promotes the concept of community within the quad and keeps everyone up-to-date on what is happening.

One of the four members of the quad collects papers and brings them to me, which cuts down on time and movement and makes it easier for me to distribute papers to one person in each quad.

On those occasions when I have let them work cooperatively on taking news quizzes, the response has been very positive. In fact, they have voted to do all tests cooperatively! I haven't bought into this concept yet!

This arrangement works well when new students join the class. They can be added to a quad that isn't full and have those students help them learn the procedures we follow in class.

It seems that just by physically changing the desk arrangement, I am better able to remember that I am trying to do things differently. Likewise, I think that students better remember to help each other because of their proximity to one another. By providing students with a support group of their peers, I think I have promoted a cooperative learning environment and the mind set that it is good to work together toward a common goal.

Jan Thompson, English teacher, Appleton Area School District, Appleton, WI

Through the Voice of...
On the Return of Absent Students

Did You Do Anything While I Was Gone?

One of my biggest frustrations has always been how to deal with students returning from absences. I have tried "Study Buddies," but have not felt that they were particularly successful. I have tried writing out what we did, but that proved to be too time-consuming. A colleague mentioned the idea of having a student take notes on what goes on during the class period, placing these notes in a notebook, and then when the absent students return, they can go directly to the notebook and read what they have missed. I thought it was worth a try. I developed a one page form which is filled out by two students in each class. My reason for having two students do it is to assure that all the information has been noted on the sheets.

I have been very pleased with how this has worked, so pleased that I wonder why it took me 20 years to figure out how to do this. The sheets are kept in a folder in the back of the room. Students are pretty well schooled by now to know that if it is their day to be the scribe, they must pick up a sheet, fill it out, and place it in the notebook. I quickly read over their notes, making any corrections or additions, which I seldom have had to do, and place any handouts in the notebook. Students are also well schooled by now to know that they need to look in the notebooks if they have been absent. Only if I forget to put the handouts in the notebook, or if they are really confused, do I need to take time to talk to them when they first return.

In addition to really reducing the stress on me of keeping absentees informed, this system has proved to a valuable piece of feedback for me. By that I mean, when I read over the scribe sheets, I can tell if the students have "gotten" from that day's lessons what I had intended that they should get. It has also increased the listening attentiveness of at least two students in each class each day and provided practice in note taking for those students. It has also placed the responsibility of finding out what work was missed directly on those who have been absent.

Gail Rainey, St. Vrain Valley School District, Longmont, CO

Putting Students into Groups

Thoughtful selection of the materials you use in order to place students into groups can provide brief but powerful learning experiences that can both reinforce and extend the learning outcomes for the lesson, unit or course. If you are working with students who have not had much exposure to the world beyond their own neighborhood, the subjects, the graphics, and pictures you use can have students engaged, for the moment, with information that you may not have time to study in depth.

Cut Ups!

Locate materials related to what you are studying or some related topic. If the paper is fragile, you may want to laminate it so that you can use it over and over. Then simply cut the items up into the same number of pieces as you want students in a group. Deal them out randomly and have students find their component parts.

- **Post cards**
- **Maps**
- **Sentence strips**
- **Cartoon strips**
- **Greeting cards**
- **Advertisements from magazines**
- **Recipes**
- **Formulas**

5, 4, 3, 2, But Not Just 1!

While the following ideas are sorted in ways to form groups of 5, 4, 3, and 2 you may find that you want to use them in other number combinations. Buy a large bundle of 3" x 5" index cards at an office supply store. You can make several sets of cards with which to group students. In order to keep your sets of cards together, you may want to color code the sets with colored duct tape along one edge, sticker dots or simply a swipe of a colored marker.

Groups of 5

- A Dinner Menu: Each group has to have a salad, main dish, vegetable, bread, and a dessert
- Cities in a Country...whatever you are studying
- Countries on a Continent...a great geography review

Putting Students into Groups continued...

Groups of 5 continued...
- Events in a decade...historical, musical, scientific
- Books in a genre
- Activities you engage in during a particular season
- Family groups of sounds, elements, number, grammar, parts of speech
- Rhyming words

Groups of 4
- Decks of cards: In addition to traditional packs of cards there are dozens of decks of cards featuring fantastic artwork, famous African-American leaders, the US Presidents, scientists, notable landmarks, etc. (Hint: Teacher supply stores are a great source for these cards or for ideas about ones you might create yourself!)
- Postcards collected by family and friends while on trips. Students find sites and scenes from the same city, state, or country.

Groups of 2
Create cards with one name on each and then distribute the cards to all students. Have them find their partner and work with that person.
- Famous pairs such as:

Romeo and Juliet	bat and ball	Ben and Jerry's
salt and pepper	stop and go	soup and sandwich
oil and vinegar	Nicholas and Alexandria	cops and robbers
Jack and Jill	supply and demand	search and seizure
hill and dale	Porgy and Bessl	Hanzel and Gretel
sweet and sour	Mork and Mindy	Anthony and Cleopatra
George and Martha	Rogers and Hammerstein	Lewis and Clark
acids and bases	Beauty and the Beast	Ferdinand and Isabella
cease and desist	Mickey and Minnie	Black and Decker

- antonyms
- synonyms
- compound words
- equivalent fractions
- digital time/clock face time
- Learning Buddies

It is Hard to Get Left Out of A Pair!

- When you first have your students work in groups, the best place to start is with partner work. This is true because it is easier for you to structure and monitor, and because when there are only two in the group it is harder for one student to opt out. Begin partner work with short interactions. You may want to let students self-select another student with whom to do 10:2 processing (See page 228) or with whom to do Think-Pair-Share (See page 98) or you may choose to use one of the strategies described on the previous page.

- Announce that they will be working together for two to three minutes and provide a focus question or process direction to define the task for the partners.

- To build in movement, have the partners stand together as they follow your directions or answer the question.

- Circulate and listen in on the discussions to gain information about what the students are learning and/or are puzzled about. This also helps hold the students accountable for talking about the designated topic.

- To build in more structure and accountability you may want to:
  - Have students write before they go to work with their partner.
  - Ask one or two pairs to share with the class what they discussed or decided.
  - Have a student explain what their partner said.
  - Have them take turns talking for one minute each followed by a thirty second round of summarizing key ideas for each student.
  - Use popsicle sticks or name cards to randomly call on students to summarize the partner discussion.

- If you are concerned that they might talk about the wrong topic, please know that these same students were probably thinking about the wrong topic while they were sitting at their desks. At least this way, you know what they are thinking about and can make an appropriate intervention.

Learning Buddies

Long Term Partnerships

As an alternative to constantly forming new partnerships many teachers have found great success with establishing multiple partnerships to use over the long term. The length of time may be a unit of study or a grading period. As depicted on the following page, the appointment sheets can be matched to the age level of the students and the content area being studied.

Students are given a graphic with slots for five to twelve "appointments." After explaining the sign-up process, have students move around the room and sign up classmates at the designated appointment slots. At each slot, two students record each other's name.

Allow about four to five minutes for the sign-up period or the partner selection process will begin to look like the NFL draft.

Issues to consider when creating and using long term partnerships:

- If a student is absent during the sign-up period you can represent that student.

- If at the end of the sign-up period some are not finished or cannot find a partner, hold a quick silent auction to pair up students. If no partner is available, the student becomes a wild card!

- If a student loses her appointment sheet, if her partner is absent, or if she is a wild card, have her come to a predetermined "meeting place" to pair up with someone else. If no one else comes to the "meeting place" she simply joins another pair.

- If you are concerned that there are some students who might not be sought after as partners, you can structure the sign-up process by dividing the class in half and have two lines face each other. The two facing each other at the beginning of the process sign up at the first announced slot. Then one line moves down one space and the students now facing each other sign up as partners at the second announced slot. Continue the process until all slots are completed.

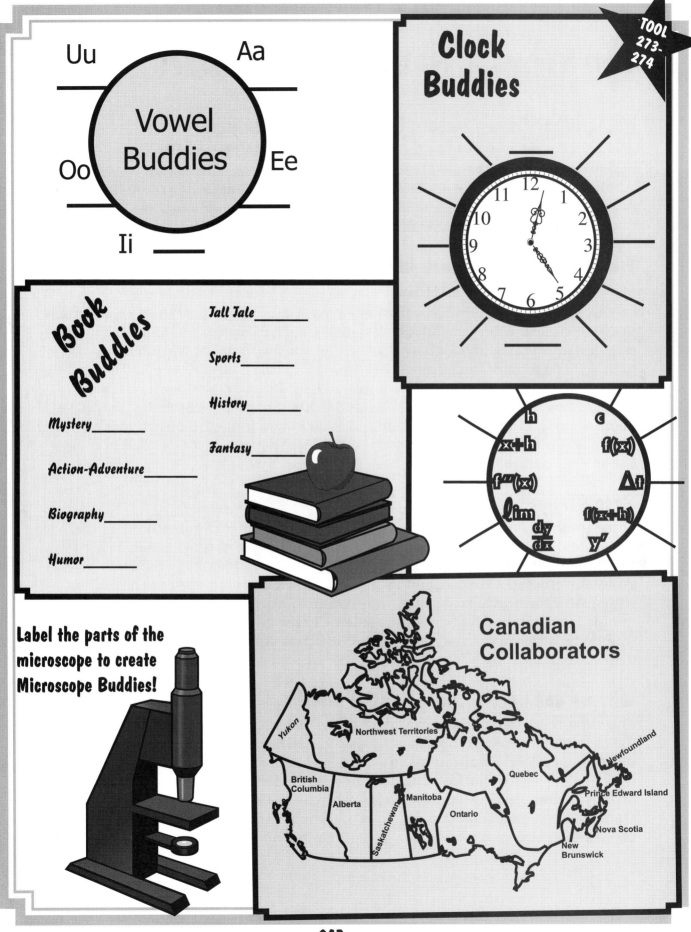

Uu   Aa

Vowel
Buddies

Oo   Ee

Ii _____

Clock
Buddies

Book
Buddies

Tall Tale _____

Sports _____

History _____

Mystery _____

Fantasy _____

Action-Adventure _____

Biography _____

Humor _____

Label the parts of the
microscope to create
Microscope Buddies!

Canadian
Collaborators

247

The Whys & Hows of Group Work

Doing What Comes Naturally...Learning by Talking

According to the results from the Myers-Briggs Type Indicator (MBTI), 75% of all humans are talk processors; that is, we learn by talking. Given that, when we "shhh" a classroom full of students, we are in effect telling them to stop thinking. At the very least, we need to build in opportunities for them to process their thinking with another person every few minutes.

Why Don't We Hear More About Cooperative Learning?

Marzano, et. al., in their 2001 book cite **cooperative learning** as one of the ten research-based strategies they endorse for use because it is proven to substantially increase student achievement. Several meta-analyses have been done on cooperative learning and all have vouched for its success. So, why do we not hear of many "cooperative learning" workshops around the country? It could be that we made it sound too difficult to implement and we did not figure out how to deal with grading of group projects. Or it could be that teachers believe that they have taken the best of the components and included them in their instructional planning; in fact, the concept of cooperative learning may be embedded in many classrooms across the country.

Base Groups

Some teachers find that base groups can promote a sense of community in the classroom. The groups may meet daily or only a couple of times a week. While the students interact in many different group configurations, they return to this group for progress reports and to summarize their learning; they are also responsible for keeping each other up-to-date. At the elementary level, base groups may start and end the day together. These groups are "cooperative" in the traditional sense of the word and may or may not do "cooperative learning" as it is defined today.

Why we don't do it...the potential pitfalls.

The main reasons we do not use small group work and/or move students around the classroom to new groupings is that we are afraid that we will lose control of the group, and we are afraid that we will lose time in the process. Transitions are tricky business, but can be structured in ways that students move quickly and orderly to new learning settings. Pages 236 - 241 offer tips on how to lead students in making smooth transitions and the next two pages offer information on how to structure the small group work so that all students participate.

Structuring Small Group Work

TOOL 312 TOOL 313 TOOL 314

Many of the instructional strategies explained in this book have students working in small groups. For example, Reciprocal Teaching, Numbered Heads Together, Teammates Consult, Consensus Conclusions, Graffiti, and Inside-Outside Circles and even Think-Share-Pair and Learning Buddies require that students know and use appropriate interaction and communication skills.

As part of establishing a learning-centered classroom, you need to identify the essential interaction and communication skills required for the students to work well together. During the first week of school you will need to gather data about what skills are already in place and which ones will have to be taught.

Consider the following lists of skills and decide which ones are essential for the grade you teach, and identify three to five on which to focus at the beginning of the year. The data you gather the first week of school may cause you to reconsider, but at least you have a plan to adjust.

- Moving into groups quickly and quietly
- Giving positive nonverbal feedback
- Avoiding put-downs
- Disagreeing with ideas not people
- Checking for understanding
- Staying on task
- Waiting to talk without interrupting
- Using please and thank you
- Ignoring distractions
- Respecting the opinions of others
- Asking probing questions
- Asking clarifying questions
- Encouraging others to participate
- Sharing materials
- Making eye contact
- Summarizing
- Agreeing to disagree
- Checking for agreement
- Taking turns
- Listen to the speaker
- Paraphrasing
- Using low voices
- Staying with the group
- Not interrupting
- Using names
- Building on ideas of others
- Reaching consensus

You can construct T-Charts with students on which you list what you would see and hear if they were using one of the skills listed above. You may also want to use the Small Group Work Observation Form to track skill use. You can structure small group work by using the active learning structures found in Chapter IV or use Talking Tokens described on the next page. See Tools for forms for each.

Each of the above skills can be assigned as a role. Additionally, you may identify other roles such as materials manager, illustrator, timekeeper, scribe, or reporter. It is important to ensure that the roles rotate throughout the students so that all build expertise with each.

Talking Tokens

If the goal is equal participation you might:

Give each student one to three chips with each student's set of chips a different color from the other students. When a student talks in the group, they "spend" a chip and place it in the middle of the table. When a student has spent all of his chips he cannot talk again until everyone else in the group has spent their talking chips. Once all the chips are spent, they are retrieved and the process begins again.

If the goal is for students to develop skills at participating in/contributing to group work you might:

Assign different responses to different color chips. For example, each student might have a blue chip which means "Ask a Question," a red chip which means "Give an Idea," a green chip which means " Encourage Participation" and a yellow chip which means "Summarize Progress." The students have to make each of the four responses during a designated time period.

One alternative to colored chips is for you to simply create task card sets for each student and have them "spend" their task cards during the group work. See Tools for an example of task cards.

Another alternative is for you to announce that you will be "Clipboard Cruising" and that the responses you will be listening for are as listed above. Announce to the students which skills you are noting on a particular day. Make note of student use of those skills and share your findings at the end of the class.

If the goal is to assign roles within the group you might:

Have each student in the group select a different color chip from their collection. You then announce what role each color represents. These roles might include scribe, timekeeper, summarizer, encourager, cleanup person, materials manager.

If the goal is to have students "jigsaw" the information/learnings from their table groups:

Have all the students holding a certain color chip meet together to trade information and to compare and contrast their findings.

Where Do I Begin?

Use this page to jot down your reflections and to make a "To Do List" of the actions you need to take to create systems for organizing yourself, your classroom and your learners.

IX

Parents as Partners

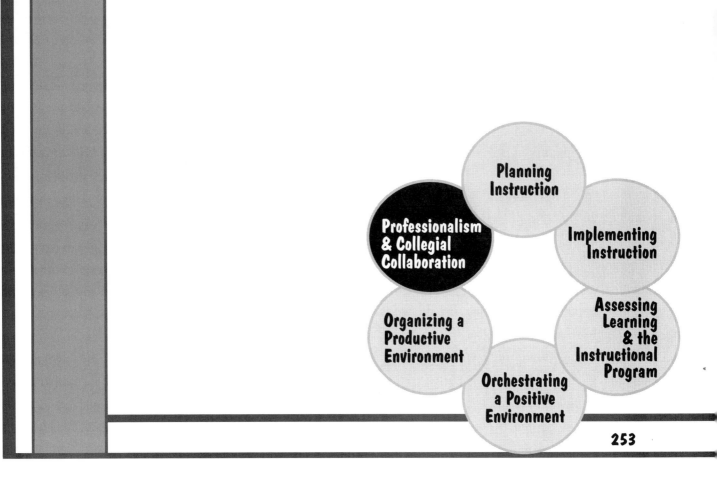

Planning
Instruction

Professionalism
& Collegial
Collaboration

Implementing
Instruction

Organizing a
Productive
Environment

Assessing
Learning
& the
Instructional
Program

Orchestrating
a Positive
Environment

Recommended Sites for Parents as Partners

www.nea.org/tips   Click on **Works4Me Tips Library**.

www.ed.gov   Click on **Parents and Family.**
                         Also click on **Publications and Products.** Then scroll down
                         to **Publications for Parents.**

Points to Ponder...
"Parents are People, People with Children"

As expressed in the words above from the song, "Parents Are People," recorded by Harry Belafonte and Marlo Thomas on the classic record *Free to Be... You and Me,* parents are indeed people who happen to have children. Unlike driver's education where there are extended opportunities to practice driving and get feedback on how you are doing before you take the test, parenting is a summative assessment from the beginning.

Just like students need different levels of support in order to learn well, so do parents. It is conventional wisdom that parents are their children's first teachers. The reality is, that not everyone is cut out to be a teacher. While most parents either do "what comes naturally" or read all the right books and implement successfully, some well-intended people work really hard at parenting and manage to do many things wrong. Teachers are in no position to give parenting advice. What we can do is, as needed, give teaching and learning advice in a helpful, nonthreatening way. In fact, weekly newsletters could include suggestions on how to reinforce at home the learning objectives you are addressing at school.

Given that almost 10% of our students are English Language Learners, we can assume that even a larger percentage of the parents have English as a second language. While many of these parents are determined that their children will be well educated, cultural variables and values may sometimes seem to be barriers to the focus on education. Add to this the number of parents of special needs students, and it becomes clear that a significant proportion of our parents have incredible parenting challenges. You must also factor in the fact that families look different from household to household. We must keep all of these differences in our hearts and heads when we think about and plan for how we will interact as partners with parents. Not every family is the Brady Bunch! Also keep in mind that as Larry Lezotte says, all parents are sending us the best children they have!

This brief chapter focuses on establishing positive relationships, creating productive communication systems, preparing for those special events (parent conferences, Back to School Night and open house) as well as some guidance on dealing with problem situations.

Communication Systems
for Building Positive Relationships

Answering Machines & Email

Answering machines are a teacher's best friend. Mike Rutherford, former 8th grade civics teacher at Stone Middle School, Centreville, Virginia, set up the least expensive phone line, turned off the ringing mechanism, and recorded a homework hot line message each day. For less than $25.00 per month, he had daily contact with parents...without ever actually talking to them! During long weekends or holiday weeks, he recorded a daily civics trivia question that students called in to answer for bonus points! Parents could, of course, leave a message and he could respond at his convenience. Additional benefits include the fact that absent students can check assignments, you can include reminders about long term projects, and upcoming assessments, as well as include information about upcoming school events.

While professors at many colleges and universities only accept assignments via email, we cannot rely solely on technology because not all of our students and their families have ready access to a computer. If your student population is such that email access is assured, you can rely heavily on that means of communication. Even if not all students and families have email access, it is still an efficient way to communicate with those who do have that access. Be ever so careful about what you say and how you say it, though, because once you send that message it is gone, gone, gone and the recipient can forward it to absolutely anyone.

Parent Handbook

The staff at Buckman Heights Elementary School in Greece Central School District, Greece, New York, put together a School Community Handbook that serves as both the teacher handbook and parent handbook. If your school does not have a parent handbook, consider creating one for your classroom, team, or department. At the very least, print all communications from you to parents on the same color paper and suggest that they prepare a file in which to keep all school documents. You might even have the students decorate a file folder or 9" x 12" envelope for the family to keep important school papers in. Keep a copy of each school-family communication in a folder or notebook during the first year or two. That way you will have almost everything you would want to put in a "Parents As Partners" handbook by the third year.

Communication Systems
for Building Positive Relationships continued...

Weekly Newsletter

Linda Denslow, 2nd grade teacher in Rush-Henrietta Central School District, Henrietta, New York, sends home a "Peek At The Week" that includes a brief tidbit about a significant learning activity for each day and a note to parents asking for help with particular learning goals. An example of a tidbit is,"We have an assembly at 9:30 with puppet people called 'Willow Girl'. Our Scholastic News will focus on nocturnal animals and our centers will look at different animal qualities." On the reverse side she includes a brief homework assignment for each evening. Even though the entries are brief, they are just what is needed to start a dinner conversation around, "What did you learn today?"

Early Home Contact

Each student who enrolls at New Trier Township High School in Winnetka, Illinois, receives a **home visit** from the teacher who will be her Advisor throughout her academic career at the school. This long standing practice is the ultimate in early home contact. If it is not the norm in your school to make home visits, then settle for an introductory **telephone call**. The purpose of the call is to introduce yourself and to say how happy you are to have the student in your class this year. With answering machines you can count the call complete if you leave a message!

A **letter** sent home introducing yourself and the curriculum the students will be studying is also a good starting point. Do not fill this first letter with rules and regulations, but with enthusiastically presented information about the learning that will occur. In fact, you might include a form for them to fill out with information about their child that they think you should know, and perhaps even a questionnaire about how they would like to collaborate with you in the education of their child.

Overview of Learning Standards

Heather Clayton and the fifth grade team at Rogers School, West Irondequoit Central School District, Rochester, New York, put together a handbook on the fifth grade writing program for parents and students. They included in the handbook a listing of the New York State writing standards and district outcomes for writing. They also included the rubrics they would use to assess student writing, an exemplar of each genre to be addressed, as well as titles of the units and the schedule for addressing each genre. "The Write Stuff" handbook served as an invaluable communication tool throughout the year.

Communication Systems
for Building Positive Relationships continued...

Good News Calls!

It makes them smile all over! When a student has a great moment at school, make a quick call home to let the parents know. Simply say, "I thought you would like to know that ...!" The great moment could be perfection or progress. The dividends are huge in building relationships, especially with the families of those students who have not had much positive news from school.

Websites/Webpages

Some schools have informative, easily accessible, and up-to-date websites with teacher/class pages. If your school has such a site, get your page up right away and have your students help you keep it up-to-date.

Videotapes

When Pam Readyough was principal of Orange Hunt Elementary School in Springfield, Virginia, she asked parents to enjoy concerts and assemblies instead of videotaping. In return, the school made a videotape of the performance and parents could check it out to view or to make their own copies. The same can be done in the classroom. When students are presenting projects, set up the video camera to capture the learning and excitement. Teachers and students in West Irondequoit Central School District, Rochester, New York, capture their work on videotape and then broadcast it on the local public television station.

Parent Conferences

Parent conferences are a part of our professional lives that can be an opportunity to establish or extend a positive and productive partnership in the education of the children.

Plan on putting your best foot forward and be sure that both your feet and the rest of you are clothed in the most professional attire you have in your closet...or you can borrow! This is not the time for jeans, tee shirts, and tennis shoes, or any garments in need of ironing!

The following list looks long, but most of the items are common sense. If people have always said that you have wonderful manners and are a terrific listener, then all you will need to do is continue to use those admirable skills, determine the desired outcomes for the conference, and make an agenda for the meeting.

The reality is that while you may be nervous because you are the teacher and want to appear perfectly prepared and professional, the parents are just as nervous, if not more nervous, than you. Keep that in mind when you meet with them! Also keep in mind that they are hoping to hear that either their child is en route to Harvard or, at the very least, has turned a new leaf and now has the potential to be a super star student. Remember each student is someone's baby!

Before the Conference
- Extend a personal invitation to both parents.
- Check for the need for a translator.
- Be explicit about the purposes of the conference.
- Allow enough time for meaningful discussion, and be sure all parties understand the beginning time as well as the closing time.
- Get your papers organized in advance. This includes student work, rubrics, standards of learning, and assessment results. Copy segments of your grade book, or create a form, so parents cannot see the grades of other students, and remember that they really want to SEE the numbers/grades you have recorded.
- Make a "conference plan." What end do you have in mind and what topics you think would help the team get there?
- Check names. Children's names may be different from parents AND if you have more than one "Smith" or "Gonzales" be sure you have the right family matched with the right student.

Parent Conferences continued...

At the Conference

- Greet parents near the entrance to the school.
- Eliminate physical barriers. Do not sit behind your desk and do not make parents sit in small primary student chairs.
- Be mindful of your body language.
- Open the conference on a positive note.
- Ask for their opinions and reactions throughout the conference.
- Focus on strengths, interests, and anecdotes that capture the learner and the parents "being right."
- Be specific with your comments.
- Back any generalization up with data or artifacts.
- Listen carefully to what parents say. Pause, probe and paraphrase!
- Focus on solutions and emphasize collaboration.
- Be careful of the professional language you use with the parents. If there are certain terms you need to use, consider the conference one of many opportunities to inform and educate the community.
- Check for understanding and agreement throughout the conference and at conference closure.*

After the Conference

- Write up a brief summary for your records. You may think that you will remember, but you won't! Jot down any pertinent information or impressions you received from the parents.
- Record and assess your behavior and the results you obtained from the conference. If you are pleased, make a note of what caused that to happen. If you did not obtain the outcomes you wanted, make note of your thoughts on what went wrong.
- If you have any strength left, write a brief thank you note or email message to express your appreciation of their time and interest, as well as the opportunity to work with their child.

*If the conversation becomes confrontational, keep both feet on the ground, use your active listening skills as your default response and use your assertiveness skills as necessary. See pages 263-264 for further guidance in discussing difficult situations with parents.

Back to School Night/Open House

Parents come to **Back to School Night** or **Open House** with the following questions:

- Who is this person/these people to whom I/we have entrusted my/our child?
- Does this person/these people realize how special my/our child is?
- Does this person/these people know what she is talking about?
- Is this person/these people a good role model for my child?
- Has this person/these people established a safe, nonthreatening, but challenging learning environment?
- and hopefully, What is my child going to learn this year?

Teachers often prepare for **Back to School Night** or **Open House** by planning to tell parents the following:

- The school rules
- The classroom rules and consequences for not following them
- The forms that need to be completed
- Expectations for parental support at home
- Desires for parental support at school

When you review the two sets of expectations, you can see the potential for a missed connection. It is, however, quite possible to accomplish both sets of outcomes. You will need to develop a thorough and thoughtful "lesson plan" for the evening.

The bottom line is be prepared, positive, and professional!

Miss Classroom Manners Says & Communication Skills

Whether or not this is the first big open house you have ever held in your home or in your classroom, it is certainly one of the most important. To get started in your planning, be sure to review "Miss Classroom Manners Says" on pages 23-24 and "Communication Skills" found on pages 20-21.

Personal Invitations

Even though the event is advertised school-wide, send an invitation or flyer home to let parents and guardians know how much you are looking forward to meeting them. Depending on the age of your students, you may want to have students write a letter to their parents inviting them to the open house.

Back to School Night/Open House
continued...

Focus of Information

Focus on student learning rather than on rules and regulations. Prepare a packet of materials on the rules and regulations for the parents to read later at home. During the evening, share orally and in writing an overview of the learning outcomes for the year, the learning experiences that students will be involved in, and how they will be assessed. If at all possible, have student work on display. In the elementary classroom, you can have the students leave a folder of work on their desks. Have copies of the textbooks and supplementary materials used by students available for parent review. A video of students working is a great way to let parents experience classroom life.

Expectations

Given that you are working to establish a partnership, the expectations have to include the expectations of all parties. While you certainly want to communicate your positive and appropriate expectations for both the students and their parents, you need to also clearly articulate what they can expect from you as an advocate for their child's education.

Who Are You?

What are your beliefs about education and learning? Why are you excited to be a teacher? What life experiences or people have influenced you? What are your hopes and dreams as a human and as an educator? You can be really brief but do reveal enough about yourself to let the parents know what you stand for and that they can count on you to be a partner with them in the education of their child. Let them know that you are **prepared, positive, and professional!**

Student Information

If you have not already done so, this is a good opportunity for you to ask parents to provide information about their child that might not be available from another source. You might ask about interests, successes, fears, concerns, and influential people in the child's life.

Parent Interests

Develop a system for finding out about the interests of the parents and asking them how they would like to partner with you in the education of their child. You may want to develop a survey that asks about their hobbies, their travels, their collections, their careers, etc., and whether or not they are willing and able to share their knowledge and skills with the class.

When There is a Problem

We have to send the message that we are all in this together!

Very few people are parenting experts and those who are so acclaimed often have really difficult children. As teachers we must not assume the role of parenting expert and place blame on the parents just because we have an education degree. Most of us who are parents might not win gold stars in parenting ourselves if our friends and neighbors were polled. The reality is that many of us do not have to "parent" when we get home from work at the end of a long day, so we are hardly in a position to judge the quality and quantity of time the parent spends on "our" homework.

There is no certification required for parenting, and it may be the only work harder or more complex than teaching. At least if the child is really difficult, we only have them for one year. The parents have a lifetime to deal with the issues.

So why do parents sometimes seem so defensive and so protective of their child? Because they are parents! When that child was born, he or she was perfect and was going to accomplish wondrous things. Figuring out how to celebrate the wondrous accomplishments while dealing with the inevitable crises is an eternal struggle. Figuring out how to be an advocate for your child without being an enabler is a constant source of confusion for even the most dedicated parent.

This, of course, does not excuse parents from being our partners in the education of their child. We must, however, continue to invite them to be our **partners** rather than the recipients of complaints, mandates, and/or implied accusations. Very few parents send their children to school with the hope that they will learn absolutely nothing and systematically drive us crazy. Nor do they relish the idea that **"the teacher"** is calling. Often what we are seeing is the continuation of a vicious cycle. The parent of the child who has problems in school may well have had problems of their own when they were in school and so are a little suspicious of, and perhaps a bit afraid of, schools and educators. Their best offense is a good defense, so we can often feel attacked. Our job in this situation is to break the cycle. The other scenario used by defensive parents is that any child of theirs is extraordinarily brilliant so the problem must be the school. In any case, we need to take the high road and find room for collaboration.

When There is a Problem continued...

It is worth repeating here. If you have made positive home contacts earlier in the year, the potential for negative interactions is minimized because you have already established that you and the parents are partners in the education process.

If despite your best efforts you need to lead a difficult conference use the following guidelines:

- Keep both feet on the ground. If you are upset, say that now is not a good time to discuss this. Wait until you are calm to call or to continue a discussion.
- When you need to call home to explain a problem, write out a script of what you are going to say before you call.
- Pause before you pounce. Do not say something, write something or email something you will regret later.
- Do not lecture or nag.
- Try as best you can to identify the cause of the problem and match your intervention to the perceived cause.
- If you are a parent, empathize as a parent.
- Ask what they have tried so far.
- Ask what has worked best in the past.
- Use inclusive language such as, "We have a problem" and "Are you hearing/seeing what I hear/see?"
- Use attribution retraining. See page 18.
- Use collaborative problem solving. See page 34.
- When it seems appropriate, ask if they would like suggestions on what they might try at home. Do not give unasked for advice.
- Also ask if they would be interested in something to read. If they say no, then you at least know that you offered help as a collaborator rather than as a parenting expert.
- Review communication skills on pages 20-21 and translate it to communicating with adults.
- Review dealing with unmet expectations on pages 32-33 and translate it to communicating with adults.
- Consult your colleagues. If the problem or interaction seems bigger than you can solve alone, do not hesitate to ask another staff member to advise you prior to the conference and/or to sit in with you. Staff members to consider including are the guidance counselor, the social worker, the school psychologist, a special educator (as appropriate), or an administrator.
- When there is progress in a negative situation, call home to report the progress.
- Always thank the parent for working with you...even if you would like a little more help! See page 22 for options.

Where Do I Begin?

Use this page to record your ideas on how you will go about establishing positive and productive relationships with the families of your students. What do you want to do to keep the communication channels open all year long?

X

TOOLS for
Teaching & Learning

All the pages in this chapter are black line masters and may be reproduced by classroom teachers for use in their planning and with their students. All other uses, including commercial or workshop uses, are prohibited without written permission of the author.

Planning Instruction

Professionalism & Collegial Collaboration

Implementing Instruction

Organizing a Productive Environment

Assessing Learning & the Instructional Program

Orchestrating a Positive Environment

Recommended Sites for Tools

www.flashcardexchange.com

This site has flashcards for use across grade levels and in many content areas.

www.proteacher.com

www.abcteach.com

This site provides over 5,000 reproducible forms and other tools.

www.sitesforteachers.com

This sites lists over 250 sites for teacher use.

www.teachertools.org

Click on **Forms and Letters.**

Learner Tools

A Good Place to Learn is...

1.

2.

3.

4.

5.

6.

7.

8.

9.

10.

Scavenger Hunt: Find Someone Who...

Sign. _____	Sign. _____	Sign. _____	Sign. _____
Sign. _____	Sign. _____	Sign. _____	Sign. _____
Sign. _____	Sign. _____	Sign. _____	Sign. _____
Sign. _____	Sign. _____	Sign. _____	Sign. _____
Sign. _____	Sign. _____	Sign. _____	Sign. _____
Sign. _____	Sign. _____	Sign. _____	Sign. _____

My Frame of Reference for...

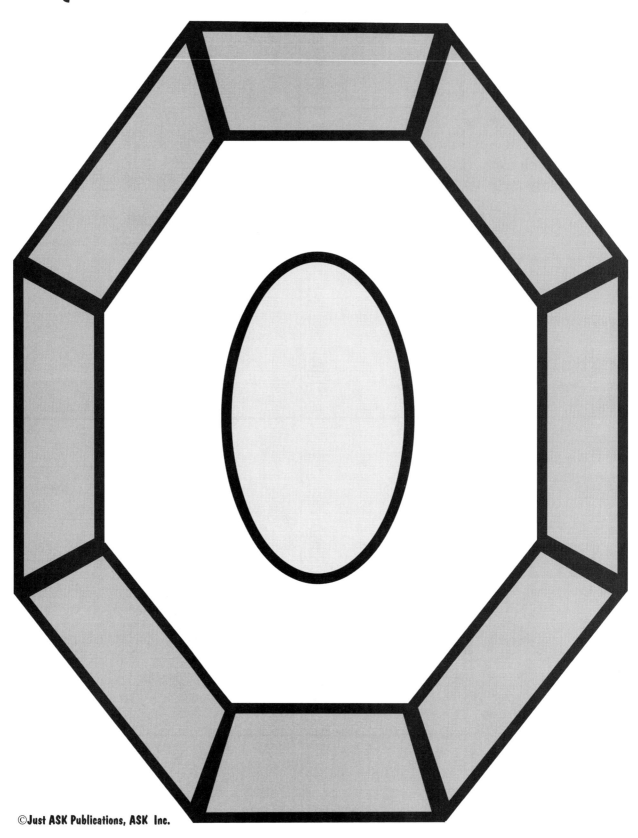

Clock Buddies

Make an appointment with 12 different people (one for each hour on the clock). Be sure you both record the appointments on your clocks. Only make the appointment if there is an open slot at that hour on both of your clocks.

Tape this paper inside a notebook, or something that you
Bring to Class Each Day!

Literature Buddies

Mystery

Tall Tale

Action-Adventure

Sport

Science Fiction

Non-fiction

Humor

Poetry

Horror

Fantasy

Reflections on My Week

Name: **Week of:**

What I Learned This Week:

How I Can Use It:

Areas in Which I Am Making Progress:

What I Learned About How I Learn:

My Goal for Next Week:

What I Enjoyed Most This Week:

THINKING WHEEL

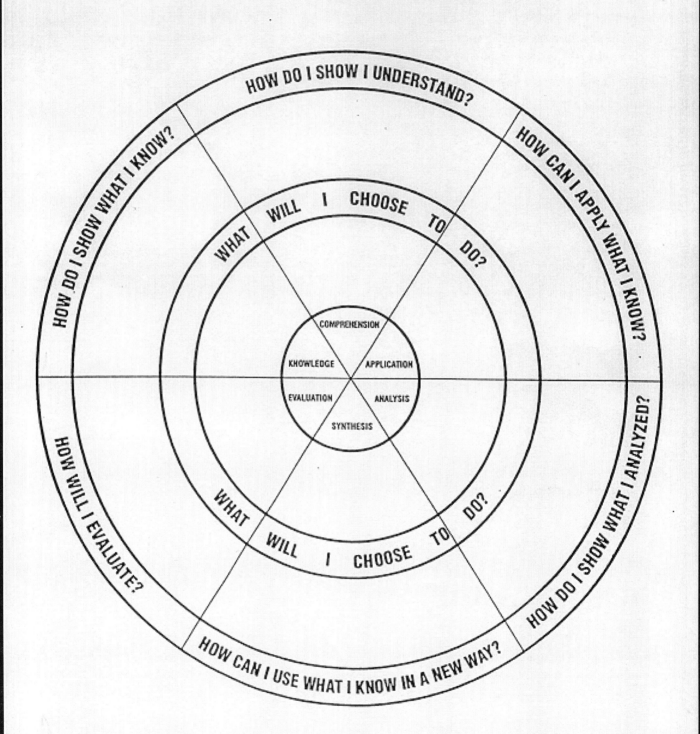

HOW DO I SHOW I UNDERSTAND?

HOW DO I SHOW WHAT I KNOW?

HOW CAN I APPLY WHAT I KNOW?

WHAT WILL I CHOOSE TO DO?

COMPREHENSION

KNOWLEDGE   APPLICATION

EVALUATION   ANALYSIS

SYNTHESIS

WHAT WILL I CHOOSE TO DO?

HOW WILL I EVALUATE?

HOW DO I SHOW WHAT I ANALYZED?

HOW CAN I USE WHAT I KNOW IN A NEW WAY?

Stir the Class on:

1 Your own idea

2 Your own idea

☆**3** Your own really original idea!

4

5

6

7

8

9

10

11

12

13

14

15

16

17

18

19

20

3:

2:

1.

Three Column Chart... a variation on the theme of KWL about...

Assessment on:

The exam consists of:

Indicator: You should be able to:	I can	I think I can	I can't
1.			
2.			
3.			
4.			
5.			
6.			
7.			
8.			
9.			
10.			
11.			
12.			
13.			
14			
15.			

Discussions Over Time & Place

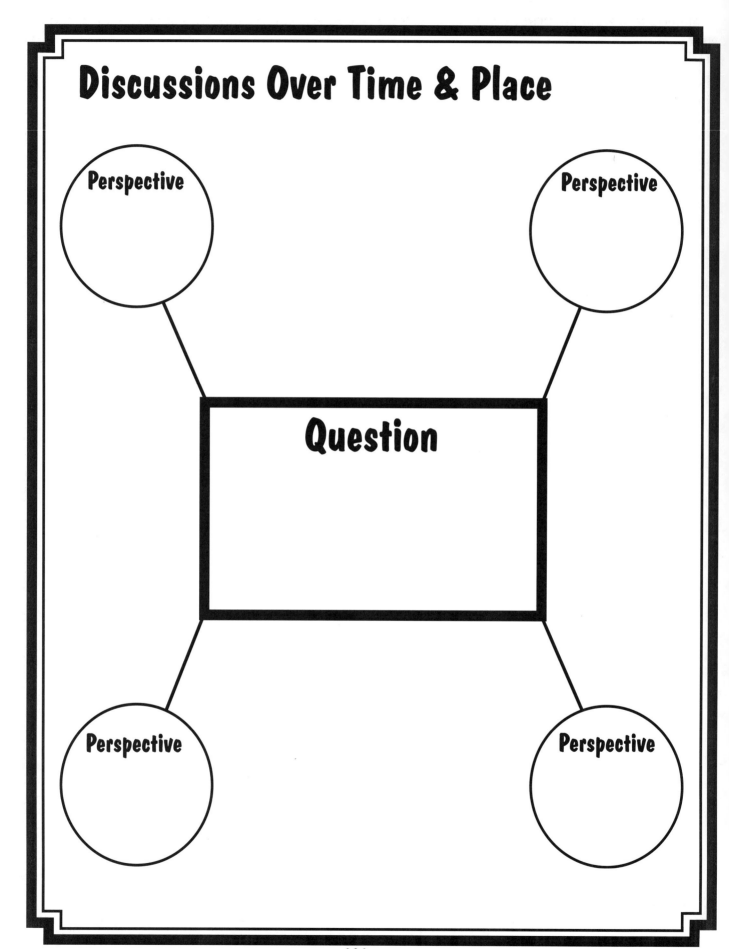

Perspective

Perspective

Question

Perspective

Perspective

Instructional Design Tools

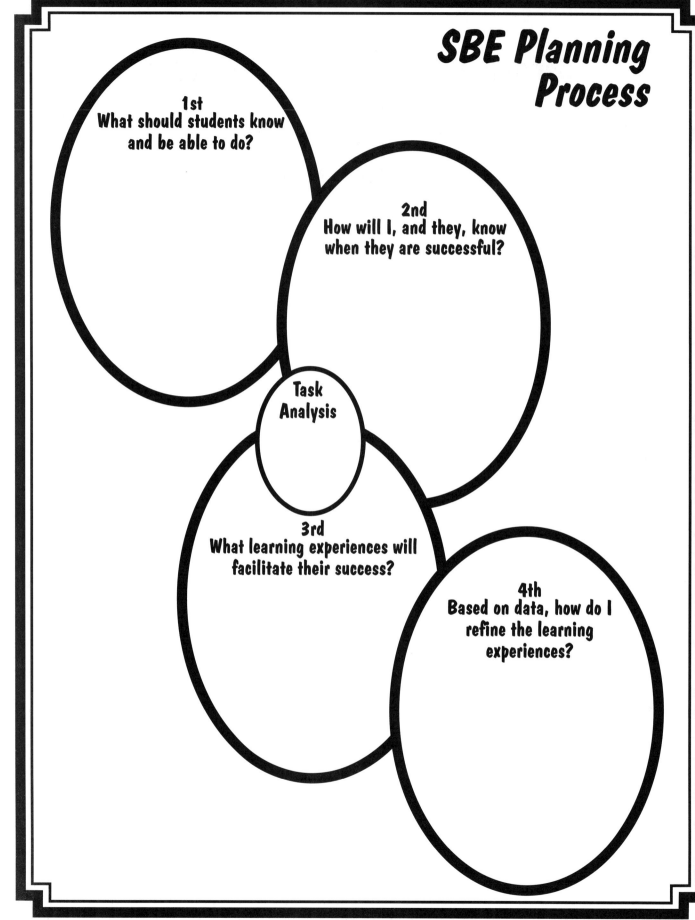

SBE Planning Process

1st
What should students know and be able to do?

2nd
How will I, and they, know when they are successful?

Task Analysis

3rd
What learning experiences will facilitate their success?

4th
Based on data, how do I refine the learning experiences?

Candidates for My Top Ten List
of
Key Concepts/Ideas/Essential Understandings in the Year-Long Study of

_____

1.

2.

3.

4.

5.

6.

7.

8.

9.

10.

Unit Planning Format #1

Unit of Study:

Standards:

Essential Questions/Key Ideas/Concepts:

Assessment Strategies

    Preassessment:

    Formative:

    Summative: (What criteria?)

Possible Learning Experiences/Assignments

Materials and Resources Needed

Unit Planning Format #2

UNIT TITLE:	LEVEL:

STANDARDS/ PROFICIENCIES:	PREVIOUS UNIT(S):
	FOLLOW-UP UNIT(S):
SUMMATIVE ASSESSMENT:	KEY/ESSENTIAL QUESTIONS:

MAP OF THE UNIT: SEQUENCE OF EVENTS/LESSONS	TIME ALLOCATION:

MATERIALS/RESOURCES:	TECHNOLOGY RESOURCES:
VOCABULARY:	**DIFFERENTIATION:**
INSTRUCTIONAL STRATEGIES:	
	FORMATIVE ASSESSMENT STRATEGIES:

Unit Design
Brainstorming Map

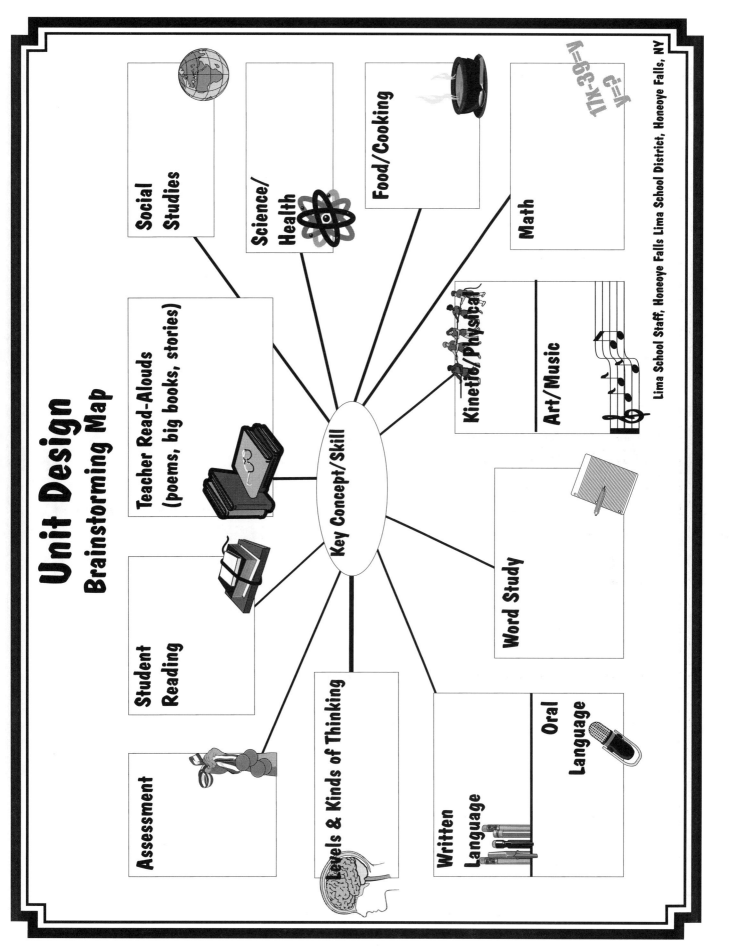

Social Studies

Science/Health

Food/Cooking

Math

Teacher Read-Alouds
(poems, big books, stories)

Student Reading

Assessment

Key Concept/Skill

Kinetic/Physical

Art/Music

Word Study

Levels & Kinds of Thinking

Oral Language

Written Language

17X-39=V
c=f

Lima School Staff, Honeoye Falls Lima School District, Honeoye Falls, NY

Standards Based Instruction Planning/Analysis Matrix

Standard	Assignment #1	Assignment #2	Assignment #3	Assignment #4	Traditional Assessment	Performance Assessment
Indicator #1						
Indicator #2						
Indicator #3						
Indicator #4						
Indicator #5						
Indicator #6						
Indicator #7						
Indicator #8						

Use this matrix to analyze current units or to plan future units. Cross reference each component of the unit with subsets of the standards to ensure a high correlation. Make necessary adjustments before, during, and after instruction.

TOP TEN QUESTIONS
to ask myself as I design lessons

1st Step

1. What should **students know and be able to do** with what they know as a result of this lesson? How are these objectives related to national, state, and/or district **standards**? How are these objectives related to the **big ideas/key concepts** of the course?

2nd Step

2. How will **students demonstrate what they know and what they can do** with what they know? What multiple forms of assessment including **self-assessment** can I use? What will be the **assessment criteria** and what form will it take? See pages 140 through 166.

TOP TEN QUESTIONS
to ask myself as I design lessons

3rd Step: Questions 3 - 10 address the 3rd Step.

3. How will I find out what **students already know (preassessment),** and how will I help them access what they know and have experienced both inside and outside the classroom? How will **I help them** not only **build on prior experiences,** but **deal with misconceptions** and **reframe their thinking** when appropriate? See pages 66 through 106 and 141.

4. How will new knowledge, concepts, skills be introduced? Given the diversity of my students and my **task analysis**, what are **my best options for sources and presentation modes** of new material? See pages 109 through 134.

TOP TEN QUESTIONS
to ask myself as I design lessons

5. How will **I facilitate student processing (meaning making)** of new information or processes? What are the key questions, activities, and assignments (in class or homework)? See pages 52 through 60, pages 68 through 106, and pages 147 through 149.

6. How will **I check for student understanding** during the lesson? See pages 142 through 146.

7. What do I need to do to **differentiate instruction** so the learning experiences are productive for all students? See Chapter VII "Differentiation of Instruction" in *Instruction for All Students.*

TOP TEN QUESTIONS
to ask myself as I design lessons

8. How will I **"Frame the Learning"** so that **students know the objectives**, the **rationale** for the objectives and activities, the directions and procedures, as well as the **assessment criteria** at the beginning of the learning process? See pages 48 through 52 and pages 179 through 180.

9. How will I build in opportunities for students to make **real world connections** and to learn and use the **varied and complex thinking skills** they need to succeed in the classroom and the world beyond? See pages 54 through 60.

10. What adjustments need to be made in the **learning environment** so that we can work and learn efficiently in a positive and productive classroom setting? How is **data** being used to make these decisions? See pages 9 through 42 and pages 224 through 250.

TOP TEN QUESTIONS
to ask myself as I design lessons

Materials to be Gathered or Prepared

Timeline/Sequence for Lesson

Task Analysis

Knowledge   **Skills**

Knowledge   **Skills**

Making Connections

How might I find out what students already know about what we are about to read/study?

How might I help them access what they know and have experience with both inside and outside the classroom that is related to what we are about to read/study?

To Past
Experiences

To Future
Experiences

How might I help them not only build on prior experiences, but reframe their thinking when appropriate?

What are the "beyond the classroom" applications/implications of what we are about to read/study? How might I incorporate them into the learning experience?

Between
Learning Experiences
in the Present

Active Learning Structures	How I Might Use This Strategy	Why It Might Be Useful Here!

Active Learning Structures	How I Might Use This Strategy	Why It Might Be Useful Here!

Homework Planning Sheet

As you plan a unit of study, use the homework categories below to thoughtfully design homework that will help your students move toward mastery of the standards on which the unit is based and will also give you good formative assessment data.

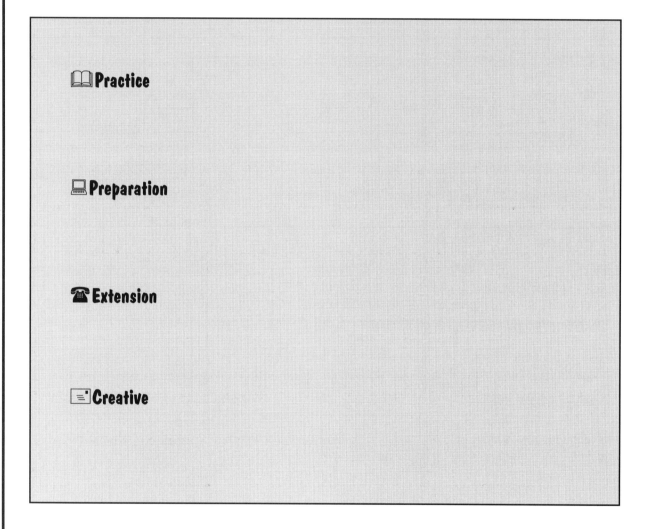

📖 Practice

💻 Preparation

☎ Extension

✉ Creative

What language could you use to communicate the homework assignments in a way that students know what to do, know why they are doing it, and know when they are successful?

Building Your Own RAFT

Role _____
Audience _____
Form (product) _____
Time _____

Role _____
Audience _____
Form (product) _____
Time _____

Role _____
Audience _____
Form (product) _____
Time _____

Worksheet for Creating a Rubric

Standards to be Addressed

Description of the Task:

	Does not Meet Criteria	Meets Criteria	Exceeds Criteria
Skill/Component: ■ ■ ■			
Skill/Component: ■ ■ ■			
Skill/Component: ■ ■ ■			

Getting Started with
Differentiation

Differentiation of instruction does not mean that you individualize instruction or provide something "different" from the normal lesson for a few struggling or advanced students. It means that you think proactively, from the beginning, and that the "normal" lesson includes more than one avenue for success. It means that you think about the diversity of your learners when you are planning and don't ever again fall into the trap of thinking that "One size fits all."

1.   What do you expect your students to know and be able to do when they study
        _____?

2.   What assessment opportunities might you give students to demonstrate what they have learned about the above concept?

3.   Given the task analysis, what is the information and the learning processes with which all students should work? List a few instructional strategies and practice and/or processing activities that would promote learning those items.

4.   What might you do to extend and expand the thinking of students ready to and/or interested in going beyond what you've planned? Include both inside and outside of class possibilities.

5.   What do you know about your struggling learners that you need to address up front? What about your ESL students? Your special education students? List specific examples of instruction strategies, adaptations, and support systems that would be helpful to several of them.

6.   What might you do to reteach or help students who are having difficulties in understanding this concept? Include both inside and outside of class possibilities.

Organizational Systems Tools

Procedure Potpourri

Planning procedures and constantly evaluating their effectiveness is crucial in creating a productive learning environment. Read through the regularly occurring events listed below. List possible procedures you might use. After generating a list of possibilities, evaluate each possibility in terms of the time and energy each would cost you. If the record keeping, implementation, or enforcement of any of them would be too time or energy consuming, consider other possibilities. If what you try does not work, try something else. You may want to check with other teachers who teach the same grade or subject. Remember, you are the professional decision maker and only have to consider their suggestions. What works for one person may not work for another.

Entering the classroom

Beginning the school day or the class period

Taking attendance

Returning from absences

Dealing with tardies

Procedure Potpourri continued...

Distributing materials

Collecting materials

Dealing with broken or missing supplies, restroom visits, drinks, etc.

Asking for and receiving help

Making transitions

What to do when work is finished

Leaving the classroom

Procedure Potpourri...add your own ideas!

Procedure for...

Procedure for...

Procedure for...

Procedure for...

Procedure for...

Procedure for...

Procedure for...

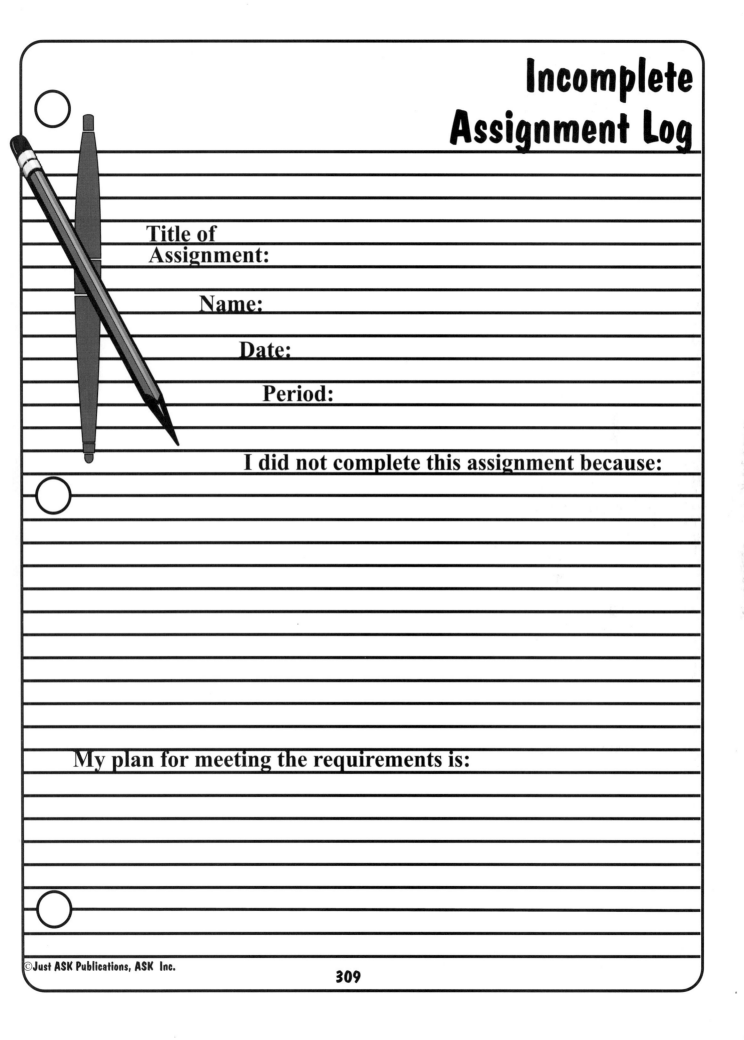

Incomplete Assignment Log

Title of
Assignment:

Name:

Date:

Period:

I did not complete this assignment because:

My plan for meeting the requirements is:

Daily Log for _____

Name of Class _____

Name of Scribe _____

Standards and Essential Understandings: _____

_____

_____

Summary of Activities (include page references and handouts):

_____

_____

_____

_____

_____

_____

_____

Papers Collected: _____

_____

Work Assigned: _____ **Due Dates:** _____

_____

_____

_____

Questions Asked/Discussed: _____

_____

_____

_____

_____

_____

_____

_____

Reminders Given: _____

_____

_____

_____

Other Important Information: _____

_____

_____

Error Analysis Chart

This error analysis chart is maintained by students so they can become aware of the patterns of errors they are making. This chart is easily adaptable to science, writing, spelling, and the study of foreign languages. Use the variables identified in the task analysis as the variables for students to consider on their error analysis charts.

List types of errors above the columns in the graph.

Date	Assignment/ Assessment												

Directions:

For each assignment or assessment completed, write the name and date of the assignment or assessment on the lines to the left of the grid. Identify the type of errors made and check the appropriate boxes. At the end of each unit, identify the pattern of errors.

Source unknown

Small Group Work Observation Form

Student Name	A	B	C	D	Data

In the areas designated A, B, C, and D insert the specific behaviors for which you are observing on a given day. You may choose to observe for only one or two at a time.

If you and your group were

_____,
(Name social or communication skill.)

an observer would...

See	Hear

Ask A Question

Keep Group on Task

Encourage

Build on an Idea

Summarize

Integrate Ideas

Paraphrase

Offer Alternative Perspective

Give an Idea

Use Names

Where Do I Begin?

Which of these tools can I use? What other tools and forms do I need to create?
What might I be able to find on the internet?

XI

Resources & References

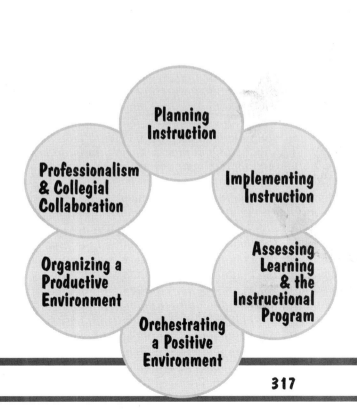

Planning Instruction

Professionalism & Collegial Collaboration

Implementing Instruction

Organizing a Productive Environment

Assessing Learning & the Instructional Program

Orchestrating a Positive Environment

References & Resources

Abaromitis, B. S. "Bringing Lives to Life: Biographies in Reading and the Content Areas." **Reading Today.** June/July, 1994.

Albert, Linda. **Cooperative Discipline**. Circle Pines, Minnesota: American Guidance Services, 1989.

Allen, Janet. **Words, Words, Words: Teaching Vocabulary in Grades 4 - 12.** Portland Maine: Stenhouse Publishers, 1999.

Antunez, Beth. "Implementing Reading First with English Language Learners." **Directions in Language and Education.** National Clearinghouse for English Language Acquisition and Language Instruction Educational Programs. Spring 2002.

Arth, Alfred A. and M. Olsen. "How to Assign Homework." **Middle School Journal**. February, 1980, pp. 4-15.

Bailis, Pamela and Madeline Hunter. "Do Your Words Get Them to Think?" **Learning 85.** August, 1985, p. 43.

Ball, E. W. and B. A. Blachman. "Does Phoneme Awareness Training in Kindergarten Make a Difference in Early Word Recognition and Developmental Spelling?" **Reading Research Quarterly.** 26(1), 1991, pp. 49-66.

Baker, Linda and Brown. A. "Metacognition, Reading and Science Education." in C. M. Santa and D. E. Alvermann (Eds.) **Science Learning: Processes and Applications.** Newark, DE: International Reading Association, 1991.

Beers, Kylene and Barbara G. Samuels. **Into Focus: Understanding and Creating Middle School Readers.** Norwood, MA: Christopher-Gordon Publishers, Inc., 1998.

Benjamin, Amy. **Writing in the Content Areas.** Larchmont, NY: Eye on Education, 1999.

Bennett, Barrie, Carol Rolheiser-Bennett and Laurie Stevahn. **Cooperative Learning: Where Heart Meets Mind**. Toronto, Ontario: Professional Development Associates, 1991.

Black, Susan. "The Truth About Homework." **The American School Board Journal**. October, 1996, pp. 48-51.

Blachowicz, C. L. Z. "Making Connections: Alternatives to the Vocabulary Notebook." **Journal of Reading.** 29, April 1986, pp. 643-49.

Bolton, Robert. **People Skills**. New York: Simon & Schuster, 1979.

References & Resources continued...

Bower, Bert, Jim Lobdell, and Lee Swenson (Teachers' Curriculum Institute). **History Alive!** Menlo Park: Addison-Wesley Publishing Company, 1994.

Brain and Learning, The: Facilitator's Guide. Alexandria, VA: Association for Supervision and Curriculum Development, 1998.

Brock, Barbara L. and Marilyn L. Grady. **From First-Year to First-Rate.** Thousand Oaks, CA: Corwin Press, 1998.

Brophy, Jere. "Occasional Paper #101." **On Motivating Students.** East Lansing, MI: Institute for Research on Teaching, MSU, October, 1986.

-----------------"On Praising Effectively." **The Elementary School Journal.** May 1981, pp. 269-278.

Burke, Kay. **What To Do With The Kid Who... .** Palatine, IL: Skylight Publishing, Inc., 2000.

Carey, Lou M. **Measuring and Evaluating School Learning.** Boston, MA: Allyn and Bacon, Inc., 1988.

Clarke, John H. "Using Visual Organizers to Focus on Thinking." **Journal of Reading.** vol 34, no 7, April, 1991, pp. 526-534.

Classroom Management Training Program: Positive Discipline Participant's Manual. Fredric H. Jones and Associates, Inc., 1983.

Coloroso, Barbara. **Kids are Worth It!** New York: William Morrow and Company, Inc., 1994.

Connors, Neil A. **Homework.** Columbus, OH: National Middle School Association, 1991.

Cooper, Harris. "Synthesis of Research on Homework." **Educational Leadership.** November 1991, pp. 85-91.

Cooper, J. D. **Literacy: Helping Children Construct Meaning.** Boston, MA: Houghton Mifflin Company, 1993.

Costa, Arthur L. Editor. **Developing Minds.** Alexandria, VA: Association for Supervision and Curriculum Development, 1985.

Cronin, Hines, Richard Sinatra and William F. Barkley. "Combining Writing with Text Organization in Content Instruction." **NASSP Bulletin.** vol 76, no 542, March, 1992.

References & Resources continued...

Cruckshank, Donald R. Deborah L. Bainer and Kim K. Metcalf. **The Act of Teaching.** New York: McGraw-Hill, Inc., 1995.

Cummings, Carol. **Winning Strategies for Classroom Management.** Alexandria, VA: ASCD, 2000.

Cunningham, J. W. and Lisa K. Wall. "Teaching Good Readers to Comprehend Better." **Journal of Reading.** March 1994, pp. 481-486.

Curwin, Richard L. and Allen N. Mendler. **Discipline with Dignity.** Alexandria, VA: ASCD. 1998.

----------------------. **Discipline with Dignity : Participant's Resource Handbook.** National Education Service.

Daniels, Harvey. **Literature Circles: Voice and Choice in the Student-Centered Classroom.** York, Maine: Stenhouse Publishers, 2002.

Davey, Beth. "Think Aloud - Modeling the Cognitive Processes of Reading Comprehension." **Journal of Reading.** October, 1983, pp. 44-47.

Deschenes, Cathy, David G. Ebeling and Jeffery Sprague. **Adapting Curriculum and Instruction in Inclusive Classrooms: A Teacher's Desk Reference.** Bloomington, IN: Blooming Publications and Seminars, 1993.

Dodd, Anne Wescott. "Engaging Students: What I Learned Along the Way." **Educational Leadership.** September 1995, pp. 65-67.

Dreikurs, Rudolf, Bernice Bronia Grunwald and Floy Childers Pepper. **Maintaining Sanity in the Classroom.** New York: Harper and Row, 1982.

Educators in Connecticut's Pomeraug Regional School District 15. **Performance-Based Learning and Assessment.** Alexandria, Virginia: ASCD, 1996.

Edwards, Phyllis R. "Using Dialectical Journals to Teach Thinking Skills." **Journal of Reading.** vol 35, no 4, December, 1991, pp. 312-314.

Echevarria, Jana and Deborah J. Short. "Using Multiple Perspectives in Observations of Diverse Classrooms: The Sheltered Instruction Observation Protocol (SIOP)." Center for Research on Education, Diversity and Excellence. 2002.

Faber Adele and Elaine Mazlish. **How to Talk So Kids Will Listen and Listen So Kids Will Talk.** New York, NY: Avon, 1980.

References & Resources continued...

-------------------- **Teaching Skillful Thinking: A Staff Development Program for Educators**. Alexandria, VA: ASCD.

Farr, Roger. "Teaching Good Habits with Think-Alongs." **Educational Leadership**. November, 1989, p. 94.

Fogarty, Robin. **Designs for Cooperative Interactions**. Palatine, IL: Skylight Publishing, Inc., 1990.

Forte, Imogene and Sandra Schurr. **The Definitive Middle School Guide**. Nashville, TN: Incentive Publications, Inc., 1993.

Fulghum, Robert. **All I Really Need to Know I Learned in Kindergarten**. New York: Random House, 1993.

Gilbert, Judy, Editor, with the Northern Colorado BOCES SBE Design Team. **Facilitator's Guide and Workbook: Common Ground in the Standards-Based Education Classroom.** Longmont, Colorado, 1997.

Glasser, William. **Control Theory in the Classroom.** New York: Harper and Row, 1986.

Good, Thomas L. and Jere E. Brophy. **Looking in Classrooms.** New York: Harper and Row, 1987.

Gronlund, Norman E. **Measurement and Evaluation in Teaching.** New York: MacMillan Publishing Company, 1985.

Grossmen, Bonnie and Doug Camine. "Translating Research on Text Structure into Classroom Practice." **Teaching Exceptional Children.** vol 24, Summer, 1992, pp. 48-53.

Gunter, Mary Alice, Thomas H. Estes and Jan Schwab. **Instruction: A Models Approach.** Boston, MA: Allyn and Bacon, 1995.

Harmin, Merrill. **Inspiring Active Learning.** Alexandria, VA: ASCD, 1994.

Hart, Leslie A. "Don't Teach Them, Help Them Learn." **Learning.** March, 1981, pp. 38-40.

Heller, M. "How Do You Know What You Know? Metacognitive Modeling in the Content Areas." **Journal of Reading.** 29, 1986.

Hierstien, Judy. **Interactive Bulletin Boards**. Torrance, CA: Frank Schaffer Publications, Inc., 1993.

References & Resources continued...

Hightshue, Deborah, Dott Ryan, Sally McKenna, Joe Tower and Brenda Brumley. "Writing in Junior and Senior High Schools." **The Kappan.** June, 1988, pp. 725-728.

Hyerle, David. **Visual Tools for Constructing Knowledge**. Alexandria, VA: ASCD, 1996.

Hunter, Madeline. **Mastery Teaching.** El Segundo, CA: TIP Publications, 1982.

"Instructional Staff Development Plan for Diversity." **Seminar Handouts: Day Four - Special Education.** Fairfax County Public Schools, Department of Student Services and Special Education, 1995.

Jackson, Michael C. and Norman D. Anderson. "ROY G. BIV Never Forgets." **The Science Teacher.** The National Science Teachers Association, 1988.

Jacobsen, David, Paul Eggen and Donald Kauchak. **Methods for Teaching: A Skills Approach.** Columbus, OH: Merrill Publishing Company, 1989.

James, Jennifer. **Thinking in the Future Tense.** New York: Simon & Schuster, 1996.

Jensen, Eric. **Teaching with the Brain in Mind.** Alexandria, VA: ASCD, 1998.

Johnson, David R. **Every Minute Counts: Making Your Math Class Work.** Palo Alto, CA: Dale Seymour Publications, 1982.

---------------- **Making Minutes Count Even More: A Sequel for Every Minute Counts.** Palo Alto, CA: Dale Seymour Publications, 1986.

Johnson, David W. and Roger T. Johnson. **Leading the Cooperative School.** Edina, MN: Interaction Book Comany, 1989.

Jones, Beau Fly, Annemarie Sullivan Palinesar, Donna Sederburg Ogle, and Eileen Gylnn Carr. **Strategic Teaching and Learning: Cognitive Instruction in the Content Areas.** Alexandria, VA: ASCD, 1987.

Jones, Fred. **Tools for Teaching.** Santa Cruz, CA: Fredric H. Jones & Associates, Inc., 2000.

Joyce, Bruce and Marsha Weil. **Models of Teaching.** Boston: Allyn and Bacon, 1996.

Kagan, Spencer. **Cooperative Learning.** San Clemente, CA: Kagan Cooperative Learning, 1994.

References & Resources continued...

Kang, Hee-Won. "Helping Second Language Readers Learn from Content Area Text Through Collaboration and Support." **Journal of Reading**. May 1994, pp. 646-652.

Karns, Michelle. **How to Create Positive Relationships with Students.** Champaign, IL: Research Press, 1994.

Keene, Ellin Oliver and Susan Zimmermann. **Mosaic of Thought.** Portsmouth, NH: Heinemann, 1997.

Kletzein, Sharon Benge and Lynda Baloche. "The Shifting Muffled Sound of the Pick: Facilitating Student-to-Student Discussions." **Journal of Reading**. vol 37, no 7, April, 1994, pp. 540-544.

Kohn, Alfie. **Beyond Discipline.** Alexandria, VA: ASCD, 1996.

Kounin, Jacob. **Discipline and Group Management in the Classroom**. New York: Holt, Rinehart and Winston. 1970.

Lapp, Diane, James Flood and Nancy Farnan. **Content Area Reading and Learning Instructional Strategies.** Boston, MA: Allyn and Bacon, 1996.

Lee, J.F. and K.W. Pruitt. "Homework Assignments: Classroom Games or Teaching Tools." **Clearing House.** vol 53, 1979, pp. 31-35.

Larson, Celia O. and Donald F. Dansereau. "Cooperative Learning in Dyads." **Journal of Reading.** vol 29, March 1986, pp. 516-520.

Lundberg, I., J. Frost and O. Peterson. "Effects of An Extensive Program for Stimulating Phonological Awareness in Preschool Children." **Reading Research Quarterly,** 23, 1988, pp. 263-284.

Lozauskas, Dorothy and John Barell. "Reflective Reading." **The Science Teacher.** vol 59, no 8, November, 1992, pp. 42-45.

"Managing Resources for Learning." **Student Manual for X150.** Bloomington, IN: Student Academic Center, Indiana University, 1994.

Manzo Anthony V. "The ReQuest Procedure." **The Journal of Reading.** no. 13, 1969, pp.123-126.

Manzo, Anthony V. and Ula Manzo. **Content Area Literacy.** Upper Saddle River, NJ: Merrill, 1997.

References & Resources continued...

Marzano, Robert J. "Fostering Thinking Across the Curriculum Through Knowledge Restructuring." **Journal of Reading.** vol 34, no 7, April, 1991, pp. 518-525.

Marzano, Robert J., Debra J. Pickering and Jane E. Pollock. **Classroom Strategies That Work.** Alexandria, VA: ASCD, 2001.

Masztal, Nancy B. "Cybernetic Sessions: A High Involvement Teaching Technique." **Reading, Research and Instruction.** vol 25, Winter, 1986, pp. 131-138.

Mathison, Carla. "Activating Student Interest in Content Area Reading." **Journal of Reading**. December, 1989, pp. 170-176.

McKenzie, Gary R. "Data Charts: A Crutch for Helping Pupils Organize Reports." **Language Arts**. vol 56, no 7, October, 1979, pp. 784-788.

McNergney, Robert B. **Assisting the Beginning Teacher.** Richmond, Virginia: Virginia Department of Education, 1985.

Morison, Kay and Suzanne Brady. **Homework: Bridging the Gap.** Redmond, WA: Goodfellow Press, 1994.

Mendler, Allen N. **Power Struggles.** Rochester, NY: Discipline Associates, 1997.

Metzger, Margaret. "Maintaining a Life." **Phi Delta Kappan.** January 1996, pp. 346-351.

Murnane, Richard, J. and Frank Levy. **Teaching the New Basic Skills**. New York: Martin Kessler Books, 1996.

Nelson, Jane, Lunn Lott and H. Stephen Glen. **Positive Discipline in the Classroom.** Roseville, California: Prima Publishing, 2000.

Novak, Joseph. "Clarify with Concept Maps." **The Science Teacher.** October, 1991, pp. 45-49.

Ohanian, Susan. "There's Only One True Technique for Good Discipline." **Learning.** August, 1982, pp. 16-19.

Palinesar, A.S. and A.L. Brown. "Reciprocal Teaching of Comprehension-Fostering and Comprehension-Monitoring Activities." **Cognition and Instruction.** no 2, 1984, pp. 117-175.

References & Resources continued...

Peresich, Mark Lee, James David Meadows and Richard Sinatra. "Content Area Cognitive Mapping for Reading and Writing Proficiency." **Journal of Reading.** March, 1990, pp. 424-432.

Pigford, Aretha B. "It's What Happens After the Teacher Stops Talking That Counts." **Principal.** May, 1989, pp. 38-40.

Rakes, Thomas A. and Lana McWilliams. "Assessing Reading Skills in the Content Areas." **Reading in the Content Areas: Improving Classroom Instruction.** Dubuque, IA: Kendall/Hunt, 1985.

Raphael, Taffy E. "Teaching Learners About Sources of Information for Answering Comprehension Questions." **Journal of Reading.** vol 27, no 4, January, 1984, pp. 303-310.

Readence, J.E., T.W. Bean and R.S. Baldwin. **Content Area Reading: An Integrated Approach.** Dubuque, IA: Kendall/Hunt, 1995.

Reading Across the Curriculum Resource Guide. Office of High School Instruction, Fairfax County Public Schools, Fairfax, VA. February 1999.

Rief, Sandra F. **How to Reach and Teach ADD/ADHD Children.** West Nyack, NY: The Center for Applied Research in Education, 1993.

Rief, Sandra F. and Julie A. Heimburge. **How to Reach and Teach All Students in the Inclusive Classroom.** West Nyack, NY: The Center for Applied Research in Education, 1996.

Rodriguez, Rely, Editor. **Instructional Strategies for All Students. A Compendium of Instructional Strategies for High School Teachers.** Fairfax, VA: Fairfax County Public Schools, 1995.

Rosenshine, Barak and R. Stevens. "Teaching Functions." **Handbook of Research on Teaching.** New York: Macmillan, pp. 376- 391.

Rosenshine, Barak and Carla Meister. "The Use of Scaffolds for Teaching Higher-Level Cognitive Strategies." **Educational Leadership.** vol 49, no 7, April, 1992, pp. 26-33.

Rutherford, Paula. **Instruction for All Students.** Alexandria, VA: Just ASK Publications, 2002.

References & Resources continued...

Saphier, Jon and Bob Gower. **The Skillful Teacher.** Carlisle, MA: Research for Better Teaching, 1997.

Saphier, Jon and Mary Ann Haley. **Activators.** Carlisle, MA: Research for Better Teaching, 1993.

-------------- **Summarizers.** Carlisle, MA: Research for Better Teaching, 1993.

Saunders, Hal. **When Are We Ever Gonna Have to Use This?** Palo Alto, CA: Dale Seymour Publications, 1991.

Schurr, Sandra L. **Dynamite in the Classroom**. Columbus, OH: National Middle School Association, 1989.

Shaughnessy, John G. and Maureen Coughlin. "Dealing with Disruptive Behavior in High School Classrooms." **The High School Magazine.** June/July 1997, pp. 44-47.

Smith, R. and V. Dauer. "A Comprehension Monitoring Strategy for Content Reading Materials." **Journal of Reading.** November, 1984.

Silberman, Mel. **101 Ways to Make Training Active.** San Francisco, CA: Jossey-Bass, 1995.

Stevenson, Harold W. and James W. Stigler. **The Learning Gap**. New York: Summit Books, 1992.

Strategic Reading Project. Developed by North Central Regional Educational Laboratory and piloted in Chicago Public Schools. Palatine, IL: IRI/Skylight Publishing.

Taba, Hilda. **Teacher's Handbook for Elementary Social Studies: An Inductive Approach.** Reading, MA: Addison Wesley Publishing Company, 1971.

Tierney, Robert J. and James W. Cunningham. "Research on Teaching Reading Comprehension." **Handbook of Reading Research.** 1984, pp. 609-641.

Tierney, Robert J., John E. Readence and Ernest K. Dishner. **Reading Strategies and Practices.** Boston, MA: Allyn and Bacon, 1995.

Tomlinson, Carol Ann. **How to Differentiate Instruction in Mixed-Ability Classrooms.** Alexandria, VA: ASCD, 1996.

U.S. Congress. **No Child Left Behind Act** (P.L. 107-110), 2001.

References & Resources continued...

Vacca, Richard T. and JoAnne L. Vacca. **Content Area Reading**. New York, NY: Longman, 1999.

Verble, Margaret. "How to Encourage Self-Discipline." **Learning 85**. August, 1985, pp. 40-41.

Villanni, Susan. **Mentoring Programs for New Teachers.** Thousand Oaks, CA: Corwin Press, Inc., 2002.

Wassermann, Selma. **Asking the Right Question: The Essence of Teaching.** Bloomington, IN: Phi Delta Kappa Educational Foundation, 1992.

Weiner, Bernard. **Human Motivations.** New York: Holt, Rinehart and Winston, 1970.

Wiggins, Grant and Jay McTighe. **Understanding By Design.** Alexandria, VA: ASCD, 1998.

Winebrenner, Susan. **Teaching Gifted Kids in the Regular Classroom.** Minneapolis, MN: Free Spirit, 1992.

Wong, Harry K. and Rosemary Tripi Wong. **The First Days of School.** Sunnyvale, CA: Harry Wong Publications, 1998.

Wood, Judy W. **Adapting Instruction for Mainstreamed and At-Risk Students.** Columbus, OH: Merrill, 1992.

Wood, Judy W. and John A. Wooley. "Adapting Textbooks." **The Clearing House.** March, 1986, pp. 332-335.

Wood, Karen D. "Fostering Cooperative Learning in Middle and Secondary Level Classrooms." **Journal of Reading.** October, 1987, pp. 10-18.

Wyatt, Flora. "Rethinking the Research Project Through Cooperative Learning." **Middle School Journal.** September, 1988, pp. 6-7.

Zemelman, Steven, Harvey Daniels and Arthur Hyde. **Best Practice: New Standards for Teaching and Learning in America's Schools.** Portsmouth, NH: Heinemann, 1998.

Just ASK Publications presents...

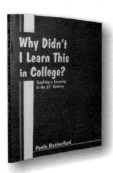

Just ASK Publications Order Form

Name _____

Title _____

School/District _____

Address _____

City _____ State _____ ZIP _____

E-mail _____

Telephone _____

Fax _____

Make checks or purchase orders payable to Just ASK Publication

Mail or FAX to:

Just ASK Publications
2214 King Street
Alexandria, VA 22301

FAX: 703-535-8502

Item	Price*	Qty.	Amount
Instruction for All Students by Paula Rutherford	$29.95	_____	_____
Why Didn't I Learn This in College? by Paula Rutherford	$29.95	_____	_____
21ⁿ Century Mentor's Handbook by Paula Rutherford	$34.95	_____	_____
Leading the Learning by Paula Rutherford (Bound version)	$44.95	_____	_____
Leading the Learning by Paula Rutherford (3-ring binder)	$59.95	_____	_____
ASK Charts and Overheads CD	$500.00	_____	_____
Overheads for *Instruction for All Students*	$250.00	_____	_____
Overheads for *Why Didn't I Learn This in College?*	$250.00	_____	_____
Results-Based Professional Development Models	$70.00	_____	_____
Operator's Guide for the Standards-Based Classroom	$45.00	_____	_____
Teaching Matters	$15.00	_____	_____
Points to Ponder Video: Volume One	$19.95	_____	_____
Points to Ponder Video: Volume Two	$19.95	_____	_____
Success Factors in a Standards-Based Classroom Video	$75.00	_____	_____

SUBTOTAL _____

Please include 15% shipping and handling on orders under 10 units. Over 10 is 10% (outside U.S. is additional) _____

S&H is included in the price of overheads and chart CD   **TOTAL** _____

*Contact Just ASK Publications at 800-940-5434 for quantity discounts.

Payment Method

☐ Check or purchase order payable to Just ASK Publications.

☐ Visa, AMEX, MasterCard #_____Expiration Date _____

Name as it appears on the card _____

☐ Check here to receive information about ASK Group Consulting services and workshops.